A GRAMMAR OF
JUSTICE

A GRAMMAR OF
JUSTICE

THE LEGACY OF IGNACIO ELLACURÍA

EDITED BY

J. MATTHEW ASHLEY, KEVIN F. BURKE, SJ, AND
RODOLFO CARDENAL, SJ

ORBIS BOOKS

Maryknoll, New York 10545

ORBIS BOOKS
Maryknoll, New York 10545

Fathers and Brothers
MARYKNOLL™

Founded in 1970, Orbis Books endeavors to publish works that enlighten the mind, nourish the spirit, and challenge the conscience. The publishing arm of the Maryknoll Fathers and Brothers, Orbis seeks to explore the global dimensions of the Christian faith and mission, to invite dialogue with diverse cultures and religious traditions, and to serve the cause of reconciliation and peace. The books published reflect the views of their authors and do not represent the official position of the Maryknoll Society. To learn more about Maryknoll and Orbis Books, please visit our website at www .maryknollsociety.org.

Publication of this book is made possible in part by support from the Institute for Scholarship in the Liberal Arts, College of Arts and Letters, University of Notre Dame.

Manufactured in the United States of America.

Manuscript editing and typesetting by Joan Weber Laflamme.

Library of Congress Cataloging-in-Publication Data

A grammar of justice : the legacy of Ignacio Ellacuría / edited by J. Matthew Ashley, Kevin F. Burke, S.J., and Rodolfo Cardenal, S.J.
    pages cm
    Includes bibliographical references and index.
    ISBN 978-1-62698-086-0 (pbk.)
    1. Ellacuría, Ignacio. 2. Christianity and justice—Catholic Church. 3. Liberation theology. I. Ashley, James Matthew, 1958– editor.
BX4705.E46G73 2014
230'2092—dc23

                                                                    2014017356

Contents

Introduction

Memory, Martyrdom, Hope

The Gift of Ignacio Ellacuría

KEVIN F. BURKE, SJ

In this quite trivialized and gray world, without utopias or dreams, it is important to meet persons who communicate light and inspiration by their manner of being. This enables us to be human and Christian. These persons must be sought out like the precious pearl and thanks should be given when they are found.[1]

On April 9, 1977, a Jesuit priest living in exile wrote a letter to his local bishop to reflect with him on the current state of the diocese, including the recent dramatic assassination of one of the priests from the countryside. Significantly, like the priest about whom the letter was written, both the bishop who received it and the priest who wrote it eventually became martyrs. Viewed in this light, these events seem more like something from the pages of the New Testament or the *Acta Martyrum* than an episode from our own day. But the martyrdoms of Rutilio Grande, SJ, Monseñor Oscar Romero, and Ignacio Ellacuría, SJ, belong to the history of the church of our day.[2] The story ever ancient, ever far away, is also close at hand and new. And like many interpretations of martyrdom written down through the centuries

---

[1] Jon Sobrino, "Ignacio Ellacuría, the Human Being and the Christian: 'Taking the Crucified People Down from the Cross,'" in *Love that Produces Hope: The Thought of Ignacio Ellacuría*, ed. Kevin F. Burke and Robert Lassalle Klein (Collegeville, MN: Liturgical Press, 2006) 3.

[2] Rutilio Grande and his two companions were assassinated by a death squad while traveling to celebrate an evening mass on March 12, 1977. Archbishop Romero was shot while celebrating mass three years later, on March 24, 1980. Ignacio Ellacuría, five other Jesuit priests, and two women colleagues were murdered in the middle of the night outside the Jesuit residence on the campus of the University of Central America (UCA) on November 16, 1989.

this letter is as theologically bold as it is evangelically passionate.[3] People like these martyrs "communicate light and inspiration by their manner of being." They teach us, in this world at times so inhospitable and inhumane, how to be Christian and how to live as human beings.[4]

All of this helps us remember that a dramatic story of light and darkness, of passion and hope, of brute force and committed love lies between every line and beneath every scholarly interpretation found in this book. The letter of Ignacio Ellacuría also lends color to the otherwise pedantic recollection that the original meaning of the Greek noun for *martyr* translates into English as "witness." The original secular currency of the term sprang from a legal context—the martyr as "one who gives witness" in, for example, a court of law. Meanwhile, in the New Testament and later Christian usage, *martyr* came primarily to signify "one who suffers persecution and death for his or her faith." But even in this later usage the root meaning of the word was never lost. Consequently, the moment of martyrdom is less the actual moment of spilled blood—Rutilio on the road, Monseñor at the altar, Ellacuría in his bedclothes lying face down in the grass—than those moments of decision when a word needed to be spoken, an act of witness placed. In those moments, often hidden, always decisive, the martyr forges her or his testimony. And the monuments to the martyr's witness, like this letter from Ignacio Ellacuría to Monseñor Romero, touch the heart of a great divine-human narrative.

Years have passed since the events that have come to be known as the UCA massacre, the UCA martyrdoms. Much has been said and written about these events.[5] Their effects continue to unfold. The world has changed, of course, and in many ways El Salvador and Latin America have tried to "move on" from the war years. But something deep in the human heart

---

[3] Both the original letter and a profound theological reflection on the meaning of this letter written by Jon Sobrino, SJ, can be found in this present volume; see "Letter from Ignacio Ellacuría to Monseñor Oscar Romero," and Jon Sobrino, SJ, "Monseñor Romero's Impact on Ignacio Ellacuría."

[4] Sobrino, "Ignacio Ellacuría, the Human Being and the Christian."

[5] Perhaps the most moving biography/theological interpretation of the life of Ignacio Ellacuría is the one cited in the epigraph above: Sobrino, "Ignacio Ellacuría, the Human Being and the Christian," 1–67. For a partial biography of Ellacuría's life and an informative, balanced account of the events surrounding the UCA massacre, see Teresa Whitfield, *Paying the Price: Ignacio Ellacuría and the Murdered Jesuits of El Salvador* (Philadelphia: Temple University Press, 1994), esp. 41–45, 57–60, 203–29. An exhaustive study of the UCA massacre and the attempt to cover it up can be found in Martha Doggett, *Death Foretold: The Jesuit Murders in El Salvador* (Washington, DC: Georgetown University Press, 1993). For official documentation, see the United Nations, "From Madness to Hope: The Twelve-Year War in El Salvador," *Report of the Commission on the Truth for El Salvador*, April 1, 1993.

refuses to forget the martyrs, and remembrance serves as a protest against the repressive violence and against the whitewashing of the effects of that violence. At the same time, remembrance is an exercise in grieving—which is also a form of loving suffused with hope and deep faith. The act of remembering the martyrs is not an exercise in masochism. This is not suffering for suffering's sake. Rather, such remembrance undergirds the option to engage a suffering world in order to overcome its suffering.

This remembrance does more. Martyrs like these and many others, named and canonized, help us to focus on those who are not named, whose lives are unknown, whose acts of witness will never be canonized, yet who, in the mysterious logic of the gospel, are held in the very center of God's gaze. Ignacio Ellacuría scandalously named them "the crucified people." Remembering the martyrs awakens us to crucified people, impels us to make an option for them, and enables us to build a different future for our world with them. The paradox implicit here should not be missed: in the remembrance of the martyrs we are not only or even primarily remembering the past; rather, we are remembering the future for which the martyr lived and died. As such, the enacted *memory* of the martyrs mirrors the twofold original meaning of *martyrdom* that links testimony to suffering and suffering to *hope*. Remembrance expresses faith in the God of life who triumphs over death. Remembrance fuels protest against the injustices of our history and moves us to remake history, to replace what Denise Levertov calls the "imagination of war" with an "imagination of peace," to find words for a future that

> can't be imagined before it is made,
> can't be known except
> in the words of its making,
> grammar of justice,
> syntax of mutual aid.[6]

The ways we remember our martyrs are many and varied. The UCA martyrs are a case in point. Their impact has been felt far abroad, throughout the world where their story is recalled, and profoundly in the country of El Salvador and in other parts of Latin America, everywhere, above all, where poor people gather to give one another succor, courage, help, and sometimes simply companionship. The martyrs are remembered in the homes and churches of El Salvador's poor with photographs and crosses,

---

[6] Denise Levertov, "Making Peace," *Breathing the Water* (New York: New Directions, 1987) 40.

murals and prayers, and significantly, those intimate stories told by the poor
themselves of how the martyrs have come to their aid.

The remembrance also embraces those who, while not among the poor,
are people who have had their hearts broken by the poor, to paraphrase a
favorite saying of Dean Brackley, a New York Jesuit who came to El Salvador
after the UCA massacre to help take up the cross by carrying on the work.
At the UCA itself, and at many Jesuit schools around the world—and not
only Jesuit schools—students, teachers, Jesuits, and friends join with the
poor to find ways to celebrate the UCA martyrs. They come every November—from London, Seoul, Omaha, Lima, Delhi, Barcelona, and many other
places—to march twenty thousand strong with students and *campesinos*
in the candlelight procession at the UCA. They travel in buses from high
schools and colleges spread across the United States to learn about the faith
that does justice at the annual Ignatian Family Teach-in sponsored by the
Ignatian Solidarity Network. They bend down to read the names scrawled on
the insubstantial crosses permanently in place near the doors of the mission
church at Santa Clara University, or sit quietly in the beautiful, student-
erected prayer garden at Regis University, or attend the annual "martyr's
lecture" at Loyola University in Chicago. And consciously or not, they are
drawn into the drama of remembrance.

However, the genuine memory of the martyrs is not a kind of romantic
nostalgia. Rather, it retains a dangerous double edge, both as an act of faith
in the God of life and as a protest in faith against the reign of death that
dominates our world. It is helpful, in this context, to remember two stories.
The first involves a small but significant detail in the narrative of the UCA
massacre. Lucía Cerna lived behind the Jesuit community where the massacre occurred and she witnessed the final words of Ignacio Martín-Baró,
the last of Jesuits executed outside.

> Padre Nacho was yelling—really, really yelling—on the path behind
> the house where we were. The shooting did not stop. It was serious.
> My blood went cold, like ice. . . . Then Padre Nacho yelled they are
> all *carroña* [scum] and "this is an injustice!" . . . After his words there
> was only quiet, very deep quiet.[7]

A martyr's final words and final act of witness: an act of protest. "This is an
injustice!" Those who would spiritualize the martyrs and sanitize martyrdom might be scandalized. This does not fit the pious image presented in
so many hagiographies. But then, neither do the words attributed to Jesus

---

[7] Lucía Cerna and Mary Jo Ignoffo, *La Verdad: A Witness to the Salvadoran Martyrs*
(Maryknoll, NY: Orbis Books, 2014), 83.

and uttered in protest from the cross, words spoken not to his murderers but to his Father in Heaven: "My God, my God, why have you abandoned me" (Mk 15:34).

The second story comes from the state of Chalatenango in El Salvador, where among the many tiny resettlement communities, home to those refugees who fled to Honduras and elsewhere during the most savage years of the Civil War, there is one that took for itself the name "Comunidad Ignacio Ellacuría." It can be difficult from a distance to notice that the very act of creating a resettlement community is an act of protest and can provoke reprisal.

> The government [of El Salvador] wanted to annihilate these communities of re-population for reasons that went beyond their physical presence. In Comunidad Ellacuría, as in the other villages, there was an irrepressible spirit of resistance that sustained hope. . . . The kind of resistance demonstrated by reclamation of the land and the construction of new social and economic structures on a small scale was a threat to the prevailing order. The fact that the communities took on the names of martyrs such as Ignacio Ellacuría testified to their belief that the spirit of those murdered in the struggle for justice was resurrected in the poor. And it is precisely this kind of hope that repressive powers cannot abide.[8]

Less than three months after the UCA massacre, on February 10, 1990, the Salvadoran army attacked this village from helicopters. Today there is a tiny house-museum in the village—a monument at the intersection of ordinary rural life and the indiscriminate fury of bombs—where three children in a family of four died with their father and today lie buried beneath the dirt floor. Their aging mother, Maria Miranda, partially blinded by that same bomb, prays in the local church each Sunday. One can find her after mass standing near the large, colorful Salvadoran cross in the front of the church.

> It was unlike any cross I had ever seen: it was not empty nor did it bear the image of the crucified Jesus. The Salvadorans placed on the cross dozens of photographs of the mangled bloody bodies of the small children killed during the recent strafing of the village. . . . The large cross stood in silent rebuke to the madness of war and to the artillery shells, made in the United States, which had been carefully collected and placed at its base. As in most wars, it is the children who suffer the most and who pay the highest price.[9]

---

[8] Linda Crockett, *The Deepest Wound: How a Journey to El Salvador Led to Healing from Mother-Daughter Incest* (Lincoln, NE: Writer's Showcase, 2001), 85–86.

[9] Ibid., 87.

The cross bears pictures of Monseñor Romero and the UCA Jesuits, of Elba and Celina, and photographs of Maria Miranda's children. It links the protest of remembrance to the celebration of hope. It renders—in an inconspicuous local vignette—the profound and endless narrative that weaves all through our human history. It is Maria Miranda's hopes and the future of her village that Ignacio Ellacuría and the UCA martyrs died for. It is her story that they recall for us.

The witnesses—the martyrs—form a great chain, stretched across continents and through time. The chain links people living today in the villages of Chalatenango and Morazan to the crucified peoples of Rio Sampul and El Mozote of yesterday. It connects those who enter the candlelight procession around the UCA campus every November to the thirty thousand names on the memorial wall, the Monument to Memory and Truth, in a large park in downtown San Salvador. It includes not only Rutilio Grande, but also Jon Cortina, a Jesuit who labored during and after the Salvadoran Civil War to heal the wounds of violence, who founded Asociación Pro-Búsqueda de Niñas y Niños Deseparecidos to reconnect children often missing for years with surviving members of their families. It includes not only the American missionary women martyrs—Ita Ford, Maura Clarke, Dorothy Kazel, and Jean Donovan—but also Sister Ann Manganero, a medical doctor who ran the only medical clinic in Chalatenango during the war years and whose large mural, alongside that of Monseñor Romero, graces the wall of the Clínica Ana Manganero in Guarjila a few miles from Comunidad Ignacio Ellacuría.

Above all, the reality of martyrdom both as prayer and as protest threads not only through the witness of those who died but also the ongoing witness of those who continue to live. In this light one of the great "living martyrs" of El Salvador is the Jesuit theologian, writer, and teacher Jon Sobrino. Tireless in the labor of remembering the stories of the martyrs, profound in his ability to interpret those narratives not only as dramatic historical-ethical lessons but as theologal moments of revelation, his living witness has kept the martyrs alive. His latest contribution in that long service will be found in the pages of this book, and it exemplifies the intrinsic, sacramental link among remembrance, martyrdom, and hope.[10]

---

[10] Two other contributors to this book likewise merit attention: Rodolfo Cardenal, SJ, a member of the UCA community who, like Jon Sobrino, escaped the massacre, has sustained for twenty-five years, first at the UCA San Salvador and now the UCA Managua, the labors of his martyred brothers. And from Germany, Ellacuría's student, Martin Maier, SJ, one of those living at the nearby formation community where Elba was the cook at the time of the massacre, has exercised his lifelong Jesuit ministry remembering his teachers, his brothers, and passionately keeping their witness alive.

Finally, then, this book itself attempts to be but one more small act of remembrance. Written in dialogue with the philosophical and theological vision of Ignacio Ellacuría, it seeks to continue and expand his profound theoretical praxis. The authors of these chapters previously have written dissertations, books, and scholarly articles on Ignacio Ellacuría. They teach classes and deliver public lectures that reflect their debt to his towering vision. And in recent years they joined together to form a colloquium on his thought. This book emerged from the most recent gathering of the colloquium, in San Salvador, in 2013. At the same meeting the title for this collection emerged, alluding, of course, to John Henry Newman's classic work "An Essay on a Grammar of Assent to God."

The thematic similarities that link Newman and Ellacuría transcend the obvious differences of their eras, cultures, and biographies. Beyond their brilliance and breadth of intellectual interests and accomplishments, both focused on history, both reflected theologically on how human beings come to encounter God, and both addressed the nature of the university. These and other connections appear overtly and implicitly at various points in the chapters that follow. For the moment, however, I wish to dwell briefly on the fundamental question of faith, perhaps the most important theme that links them.

As Newman sought to overcome the interminable rationalism-fideism conflicts of the nineteenth century by outlining a "grammar" of assent, so Ellacuría, facing the challenges of a dawning postmodern, postcolonial age, hit upon the practical hermeneutics involved in the encounter with the God of Jesus. In this regard the "grammar of justice" that can be discerned running all through his writings (as well as his praxis) functions not only or even primarily as a social ethic, although it is that, too. Rather, above all, *A Grammar of Justice* points to Ellacuría fundamental *theologal* spirituality, his extraordinary Ignatian-inspired contribution to a grammar of discipleship in a world that "does not need words, but lives which cannot be explained except through faith and love for Christ poor."[11]

The reflections that follow do not fall neatly into one or other disciplinary category, something that is also true of Ellacuría's own writings. Nevertheless, certain accents and affinities emerge that allow us to group these chapters into four parts. Part I begins with the sources of Ellacuría's "grammar" as he himself articulated them, along with the reflections of his friend Jon Sobrino and the theologian most credited with the emergence of liberation theology, Gustavo Gutiérrez. Part II pays particular attention to the dynamics of Ellacuría's significant contributions to theological

---

[11] Pedro Arrupe, "Final Address of Father General to the Congregation of Procurators," *The Spiritual Legacy of Pedro Arrupe, SJ* (Rome: Jesuit Curia, 1985), 38.

method—the grammar, if you will, of fundamental theology. In Part III two of the main audiences and foci of Ellacuría's work—the university and the church—come to the fore. Finally, Part IV turns to the "public" of civil society and addresses the social-ethical quest for justice in an unjust world. In all of these chapters we are pleased to showcase the work of younger scholars as well as that of scholars who have been studying Ellacuría's thought for several decades. Above all, it is a joy to introduce a group of scholars who are not only collaborators but friends. Friendship has helped us discover the many facets of the gift—the precious pearl—of the human being and the Christian, Ignacio Ellacuría.

✳✳✳

The production of this book resulted from the efforts and friendship of many people. Among them we wish especially to single out all of our contributors, our translators, Raúl Zegarra, Teresa Malave, VDMF, and Lil Milagro Henriquez-Cornejo, and all those who have attended the two gatherings of the International Colloquium on the Thought of Ignacio Ellacuría, above all, our friends Jon Sobrino, SJ, and the late Dean Brackley, SJ. Particular thanks go to Martin Maier, SJ, an original co-founder of the colloquium and the tireless champion of this collection. In addition, we wish to thank our UCA colleagues and friends, Professors Marta Zechmeister and Sonia Suyapa Pérez Escapini, who hosted our gathering in San Salvador in 2013, along with our co-editor and friend, Rodolfo Cardenal.

Special thanks go to various funders of our colloquium gatherings, including the Jesuit School of Theology of Santa Clara University, the Jesuit Community of JST, the Lilly Endowment, the University of Notre Dame, and the German Province of the Society of Jesus. Publication of this book was partially funded by a generous grant from the Institute for Scholarship in the Liberal Arts of the University of Notre Dame and a similarly generous Hackworth Fellowship from the Markkula Center for Applied Ethics at Santa Clara University. In addition, this book would not have been possible without the extraordinary talent and energy of our editor and publisher, Robert Ellsberg, and his colleagues at Orbis Books.

Finally, we dedicate this book to the memory of our friend, Dean Brackley, SJ, who showed us how to live this grammar of justice.

PART I

THE PROPHETIC, LIBERATING PRAXIS OF FAITH

Primary Source for a Grammar of Justice

I

Letter from Ignacio Ellacuría to Monseñor Oscar Romero

During the winter months Ignacio Ellacuría often went back to Spain to work in Madrid with his former teacher and mentor Xavier Zubiri. In 1977 the Salvadoran government blocked his return to San Salvador. He only was able to return, covertly, in 1978, at no small risk to his life. Thus, he was in involuntary exile when Rutilio Grande, SJ, and two companions were assassinated by a Salvadoran death squad on their way to celebrate a Saturday evening mass on March 12, 1977, just three weeks after Monseñor Romero had become archbishop of San Salvador on February 22, 1977. News of the assassination was communicated to the worldwide Society of Jesus by the Superior General of the Jesuits, Father Pedro Arrupe, SJ.

The subsequent events are well known. Monseñor Romero immediately interpreted the murder of Father Grande and his companions as an act of persecution against the church. He wrote to the president of the country and demanded a full investigation. Most widely known (and controversial at the time), he decided to have only a single mass in the archdiocese the following Sunday and to close all the Catholic schools for several days. Despite strong objections from the papal nuncio and several of the more conservative bishops, the one mass was held on March 20, 1977, at the Cathedral of San Salvador. Archbishop Romero presided with nearly all the priests of the archdiocese and affiliated religious congregations concelebrating. The cathedral was packed, and a congregation of more than 100,000 people participated from the plaza outside the cathedral, with many more listening on the radio. At the time this mass was the largest public gathering of any kind in the history of El Salvador.

Ellacuría was deeply impressed by the events. Above all, he was moved and surprised by Romero's response in the face of fierce internal and external opposition. In that context he wrote this letter to Monseñor Romero. It was the beginning of a close and formative relationship, as Jon Sobrino discusses at length in his chapter, "Monseñor Romero's Impact on Ignacio Ellacuría" herein.

THIS IS THE FIRST PUBLICATION OF THIS LETTER IN ENGLISH.—EDS.

3

April 9, 1977
Mons. Oscar Romero
San Salvador

Dear Monseñor:

I have been following very closely and with abundant information the blessed events—death and resurrection—that have taken place especially during the month of March in El Salvador, and very particularly in the archdiocese. So I have learned of your interventions as archbishop of San Salvador. God has willed to place you at the very beginning of your ministry in an extremely difficult dilemma, yet an extremely Christian one, because if in it transgression has been superabundant, grace has been even more superabundant. I have to say, from my humble status as a Christian and a priest of your archdiocese, that I feel proud of your performance as a pastor. From this far-off exile I want to let you know of my admiration and my respect, because I have seen the finger of God in your action. I cannot deny that the way you have behaved has exceeded all my expectations, and this has caused in me a profound joy that I want to share with you on this glorious Holy Saturday.

Permit me, given my status as a scholar of theology, to share with you a little of what motivates my pride, admiration, and respect. I believe that, because of the martyrdom of Padre Grande and of all the other Christians, El Salvador ought to have a uniquely exemplary character for the entire Church of Latin America. I do not know of any other place where the priests and their pastors have been able to live up to such heights.

The first aspect that impressed me is your evangelical spirit. I understood this from the first moment through Father Arrupe's communication. Many are the pastors who boast of the spirit of the gospel, but who, when put to the test of fire—and we have seen this in El Salvador itself—show that there is no such spirit. You immediately perceived the clear meaning of Father Grande's death, the meaning of religious persecution, and backed up this meaning with all your energy. This shows your sincere faith and Christian discernment. It shows also your courage and your evangelical prudence in contrast to clear cowardice and worldly prudence. It is very difficult that in cases like this the gospel is put on the side of the National Association of Private Enterprise (ANEP) or of the government; you saw this clearly and, with independence and steadfastness, you drew your conclusions and made your decisions.

This brings me to see a second aspect: a clear Christian discernment. You, who are familiar with the *Exercises of Saint Ignatius,* know how difficult it is to discern and make decisions following the spirit of Christ and not the spirit of the world, which can present itself *sub angelo lucis,* as an angel of light. You were able to listen to everyone but ended up deciding for that which seemed most risky to prudent eyes. When it came to the single mass, to the cancellation of all activities in the schools, to your keeping clear distance from every official act, and so on, you discovered how to discern where the will of God was and how to follow the example and the spirit of Jesus of Nazareth. This has given me great hopes that your ministry, which must be very difficult, can continue being fully Christian in a time in Latin America when the true life of the church appears so difficult, where more than ever it is called to be a life of testimony and of martyrdom.

I see the third aspect as a conclusion from the earlier ones and their confirmation. On this occasion you have built a church, and you have built unity in the church. You know how difficult it is to do these two things in El Salvador today. But the mass in the cathedral and the almost complete and unanimous participation of the clergy, of religious, and of so many people of God show that on this occasion you succeeded. You could not have started off on a better foot to build a church and to build unity in the church in the archdiocese. It will not have escaped you that this is hard to do. And you succeeded. And you were able to do it not by taking the paths of flattery or cunning, but by the gospel path: being faithful to it and being courageous on it. I think that while you continue in this vein and have as your primary criterion the spirit of Christ, lived in a martyrial way, the best part of the church in El Salvador will be with you, and those who need to pull away will do so. In this hour of trial we can see who are the faithful sons of the church, which continues the life and mission of Jesus, and who are the ones who want to use the church. It seems to me that in this we have an example in the closing years of Father Grande's life, far removed from the extremisms of the Left, but much more distant from the oppression and from the blandishments of unjust wealth, as Saint Luke says.

Finally, I believe that this sorrowful and joyful occasion will have given you the opportunity to reencounter the true Society of Jesus, which people with vested interests have wanted to keep you away from. From what I have been able to hear and read, you have given yourself to the Society and the Society has given itself to you. You will have seen that the Society in El Salvador wants to be faithful to Christ and to the church, and it wants to do so no matter what the consequences. This is not always easy, and there are sometimes mistakes. The Society lives its vocation on the frontier, in the limit-situation where dangers of all kinds are greater. On this terrain it is not easy always to get it right either in ideas or in actions. But I think that there is sufficient spirit in the Society to recognize its errors and never relent in its efforts. You must have realized in this difficult hour how many men there are in the Society who are truly spiritual and truly capable of serving Christ and the Church of El Salvador.

I ask God that all these things continue for the good of all. It has been nothing more than a beginning, but it has been an extraordinary beginning. The Lord has provided you with an extraordinarily Christian start to your new ministry. I pray that he grants you to go forward in the midst of such exceptional difficulties. If you continue to maintain the unity among your priests through your maximum fidelity to the gospel of Jesus, everything will be possible.

This is what this member of your archdiocese desires with all his heart—one who now is far away completely against his will—I believe, for announcing the gospel. Let me reiterate my admiration and my gratitude for your first steps as archbishop of San Salvador—steps that I know well in all their complexity.

Sincerely in Christ,

Ignacio Ellacuría

—TRANSLATED BY KEVIN F. BURKE, SJ, AND J. MATTHEW ASHLEY

2

Utopia and Propheticism from Latin America

A Concrete Essay in Historical Soteriology

IGNACIO ELLACURÍA, SJ

Editors' Introduction

In 1989, when Ignacio Ellacuría wrote "Utopía y profetismo desde América Latina: un ensayo concreto de soteriología histórica,"[1] he was fifty-eight years old and had served as president of the University of Central America (UCA) for nearly a decade. El Salvador was finally lurching toward a negotiated settlement of its protracted civil war, an outcome to which Ellacuría dedicated enormous energy and in which the UCA played a major role. The completion of that tenuous process was still several years off, however, and unbeknown to Ellacuría, he and his companions would be murdered within just a few months. This would be his final major essay.

As much as Ellacuría immersed himself in the concrete historical realities around him, he also always remained a systematic thinker with a keen eye

---

[1] Ignacio Ellacuría, "Utopía y profetismo desde América Latina: un ensayo concreto de soteriología histórica," in *Revista Latinoamericana de Teología* 17 (1989) 141–84. See also, I. Ellacuría et al., *Utopía y Profetismo* (Madrid: Centro Evangelio y Liberación, 1989), 81–101; *Christus* 632 (1990): 49–55; *Ignacio Ellacuría: Teólogo mártir por la liberación del pueblo* (Madrid: Editorial Nueva Utopía, 1990), 103–29; *Escritos Teológicos*, vol. 2 (San Salvador: UCA Editores, 2000), 233–93; also published as "Utopía y profetismo" in *Mysterium Liberationis: Conceptos Fundamentales de la Teología de la Liberación*, vol. 1 (Madrid: Editorial Trotta, 1990), 393–442; "Utopia and Prophecy in Latin America," in *Towards a Society That Serves Its People: The Intellectual Contribution of El Salvador's Murdered Jesuits*, ed. J. Hassett and H. Lacey, trans. James R. Brockman, 44–88 (Washington, DC: Georgetown University Press, 1991); see also "Utopia and Prophecy," in *Mysterium Liberationis: Fundamental Concepts of Liberation Theology*, ed. Ignacio Ellacuría and Jon Sobrino, 289–328 (Maryknoll, NY: Orbis Books, 1993).

on the far horizon. In this essay he draws upon his rigorous philosophical vision and passionate theological faith commitments to enunciate a comprehensive theological-ethical statement addressed to both civil society and the churches. He draws an explicit connection between the concrete historical sufferings of the Salvadoran population and the economic, political, cultural, and religious structures that cause those sufferings. At the same time, as one buoyed by theological hope and not mired in fatalism, he also elaborates both the possibility and the necessity to launch history in a different, humanizing direction. The same globalized historical structures that continue to produce victims hold the key to the necessary and possible liberation of history. For this reason Ellacuría sought to stir the consciences of those who drive those structures and to build an argument for a concerted effort to dare a new approach to history.

Throughout this "concrete essay in historical soteriology," Ellacuría makes use of a technical vocabulary that is difficult but rewarding. In order to capture his precision, we have chosen to revise the translation by James Brockman that appeared for the first time in 1991 in *Toward a Society That Serves Its People* and reappeared in 1993 in *Mysterium Liberationis*. Most important, we translate Ellacuría's term of art *profetismo* (which is related to but distinct from *profecía* and *lo profético*) as "propheticism"; we retain "prophecy" to translate *profecía*. *Propheticism* implies something beyond the discrete word or act of prophecy; it refers to an integrated and integrating vision, a structuring principle, a way of life. Similarly, we have restored Ellacuría's rather spare four-part division of the essay around four thesis statements. These and other changes are meant to make this translation reflective of the original Spanish and consistent with the new translations found in *Ignacio Ellacuría: Essays on History, Liberation, and Salvation*, the volume of Ellacuría's writings that appeared in 2013 in English.[2]

Text

Utopia and propheticism, if presented separately, tend to lose their historical effectiveness and become idealistic escapism; and so, instead of becoming forces for renewal and for liberation, they are at best reduced to functioning as a subjective solace for individual persons or for whole peoples.

That is not the case in the classic manifestations of propheticism and of the great utopian concerns. It is not so in the Bible of course, but neither is it so in other significant events of the history of salvation. However, a real danger must be acknowledged. It repeatedly happens that utopia and

---

[2] *Ignacio Ellacuría: Essays on History, Liberation, and Salvation*, ed. Michael E. Lee (Maryknoll, NY: Orbis Books, 2013).

propheticism are separated and both utopia and prophecy are disincarnated, whether by subjectivist reductionism or transcendentalist reductionism. They are read in a timeless key of eternity even though Christian eternity has been inexorably linked to temporality ever since the Word became history.

To achieve an adequate conjunction of utopia and prophecy, however, it is necessary to situate oneself in the proper historical place. Every conjunction of these two human and historical dimensions, if it is to be realistic and fruitful, must be situated in precise geo-socio-temporal coordinates. Otherwise the unavoidable thrust of the principle of reality disappears, and without that both utopia and prophecy are a mental game, more formal than real. But some historical places are more favorable to the emergence of prophetic utopians and of utopian prophets. It is said that in cultures that have grown old there is no longer a place for propheticism and utopia, but only for pragmatism and selfishness, for the countable verification of results, for the scientific calculation of input and output—or, at best, for institutionalizing, legalizing, and ritualizing the spirit that renews all things. Whether this situation is inevitable or not, there are nonetheless still places where hope is not simply the cynical adding up of infinitesimal calculations; they are places to hope [*esperar*] and "to give hope" [*esperanzar*] against all the dogmatic verdicts that shut the door on the future of the project [*proyecto*] and the struggle.

One of these places is Latin America. At least, this is a preliminary supposition that I shall return to. For the moment, I can point to facts such as revolutionary movements and liberation theology. In the case of Latin America not only can the theoretical relationship between utopia and prophecy be better historicized, but the general outlines of a utopian future of universal scope can also be marked out through a concrete exercise of historical propheticism.

To think that utopia in its own intrinsic formality is something outside of every historical place and time supposes an emphasis on a single characteristic of utopia to the neglect of its real nature as it is found in the thought of those who have been true utopians in one form or another. There is no escape from the historicity of place and time, although neither is it inevitable to remain locked into the limits of a certain place and a certain time. Neither can it be said that the best way to universalize prophecy and utopianism is to try and abolish or escape every limit that might condition them. In themselves, prophecy and utopia are dialectical. Prophecy is past, present, and future, although above all it is the present facing the future and the future facing the present. Utopia is history and meta-history, but above all meta-history, although springing from history and inexorably referring to history, whether by way of escape or by way of realization. Hence our need to place our feet firmly on a fixed earth in order not to lose strength as Antaeus did when he was lifted off the ground.[3]

That is what I propose to do here by setting forth propheticism as method and utopia as horizon from the historical context of Latin America. I undertake all this from an explicitly Christian perspective in regard both to prophecy and to utopia.

1. The Christian utopia can only be constructed from propheticism, and the Christian propheticism must take into account the necessity and the characteristics of the Christian utopia.

The historical concretion of Christian utopia is not settled in advance and even less *a priori,* and only the concrete, Christian utopia will function to historicize the reign of God. This global affirmation includes a whole set of affirmations, which I am not going to anticipate here, since my development will explain their meaning and justification. Such affirmations are (a) there is a general and undefined Christian utopia; (b) this general utopia must be concretized in historico-social terms; (c) this utopia is in relationship with the reign of God; (d) the reign of God must be historicized; and (e) the reign of God is rendered operational through the setting in motion of a concrete utopia.

Certainly, Christian utopia, born of revelation, tradition, and even the magisterium, has certain characteristics without which it cannot be called Christian. For example, a utopia that means to be Christian cannot set aside the propheticism of the Old Testament (prophetic and non-prophetic books), the Sermon on the Mount, the Last Supper discourse, the Book of Revelation, the primitive community, the fathers of the church, the great saints, or certain conciliar and papal documents, to cite some sources by way of example. But the importance of these or other characteristics, their joining together to form a whole, their historical realization in each time and place, is not only an evolving problem but an open-ended one. Solutions to the problem must be attained by means of an option that, when all is said and done, is an option by God's people, whose organic character has priority over the hierarchical (Rom 12:4–8; 1 Cor 12:4–31), and in whom there is room for many charisms, functions, and activities, some more pertinent than others in defining the observable historical characteristics of the Christian utopia.

---

[3] Antaeus, the son of Poseidon and Gaia in Greek mythology, could not be defeated in a wrestling match as long as he remained in contact with the ground (his mother, the earth). He was finally defeated by Hercules, who lifted him off the ground and crushed him while holding him in the air.—*Eds.*

This utopia can be called general and universal, because it possesses certain minimums that cannot be absent, at least in the intention and in the project, and because it points toward a universal future with an eschatological outcome. This utopia must be precisely concretized if we are to succeed in progressively approximating the reign of God. Up to a certain point Christian utopia and the reign of God can be considered the same, although when one speaks of Christian utopia one accents the utopian character of the reign of God and not its other characteristics. But the concretion of utopia is what historicizes the reign of God, both in the hearts of human beings and in the structures without which that heart cannot live. This is not the time or place to develop the idea, much treated by liberation theology, that a historicizing of the reign of God must be achieved in the personal, in the societal, and in the political. Although liberation theology has done this in its own way, all of the church's tradition has always tried to do this. If one reads, for example, *Gaudium et spes*[4] or the various papal encyclicals on the church's social teaching, one sees there the need to historicize, if not the reign, at least the faith and the Christian message. Whether this be done with greater or lesser prophetic and utopian vigor, the need to do it is still recognized.

The question, then, is how better to achieve that concretion, accepting the fundamental proposition that the general and universal utopia is already proclaimed and promised, so that its concretion not only cannot negate it or supersede it but must live by it, although creatively, because the same Spirit that animated it in its earlier and foundational dynamisms keeps on making new dynamisms possible. The answer to this question points toward Christian propheticism. Propheticism, rightly understood in its complexity, is at the origin of the universal and general utopia; that same propheticism is what is necessary for the concretion of utopia. It is a propheticism that will need the help of other authorities—for example, that of the magisterium—but that cannot be replaced by them. Without propheticism there is no possibility of making a Christian concretion of utopia and, consequently, a historical realization of the reign of God. Without an intense and genuine exercise of Christian propheticism, the concretion of Christian utopia cannot be arrived at theoretically, much less practically. Here, too, the law cannot replace grace, the institution cannot replace life, and established tradition cannot replace the radical newness of the Spirit.

Propheticism is understood here to be the critical contrasting of the proclamation of the fullness of the reign of God with a specific historical situation. Is this contrasting possible? Are not the reign of God and historical realities

---

[4] Second Vatican Council, *Pastoral Constitution on the Church in the Modern World* (1965).

with their worldly projects two radically distinct things moving on different planes? The reply to this objection or question, although complex, is still clear: the fullness of the reign, without identifying itself with any personal or structural project or any specific process, is in necessary relationship with them. One need only see how the Old and New Testaments approach the matter. There can be, as the case may be, greater importance given to the transcendent than to what happens in time, to the interior than to the exterior, to what is intended than to what is actually brought about. But both must be there, at least to some extent. The reign of God is, after all, a transcendent history or a historical transcendence in strict parallel with what the life and person of Jesus is, but in such manner that it is the history that leads to the transcendence, because indeed God's transcendence has become history ever since the beginning of creation.

The fullness of the reign of God, which implies that all of the reign of God and all of the projection of the reign of God be taken into account, must be placed in contrast with a specific historical situation. For example, if the reign proclaims the fullness of life and the rejection of death, and if the historical situation of human beings and of structures is the reign of death and the negation of life, the contrast is evident. The contrasting of a historicized reign makes manifest the limitations (lack of divinization or of grace) and above all the evils (personal, social, and structural sins) of a specific historical situation. This is just how propheticism, which starts with this kind of contrasting—assuming indeed that there is the general vision of the reign previously alluded to which God's revelation has been making known to humanity in various ways—is able to predict the future and to go toward it. In this manner, which could be called dialectical, reaching beyond the limits and the evils of the present, which are historical limits, the desired future is taking shape by way of overcoming [*superación*],[5] a future that is ever more in accord with the exigencies and dynamisms of the reign. At the same time, the announced and hoped-for future—precisely as something that overcomes the present—helps to overcome those limits and those evils.

When propheticism is conceived thus, it is seen how necessary it is in order that utopia not become an abstract evasion of historical commitment.

---

[5] *Superación* is translated here and throughout as "overcoming." Although other terms such as "surpassing" or "superseding" could be used, they lack the implications of opting and struggling central to Ellacuría's liberation perspective. *Superación* is an important term taken from Zubiri's understanding of the dynamic structure of reality. Ellacuría draws it into his philosophy as a process operative in historical reality that almost necessarily involves conflict (though not necessarily violence). This, in turn, has important implications for the thesis he develops here: a key moment in the prophetic-utopian project involves the overcoming [*superación*] of "the limits and evils of the (historical) present."—*Trans.*

"*Religious* misery is, on the one hand, the *expression* of real misery and, on the other, the *protest* against real misery. Religion is the sigh of the oppressed creature, the heart of a heartless world, just as it is the spirit of a situation without spirit."[6] But, if this is so, it does not have to become the opium of the people, as the same text of Marx goes on to call it. If it is more a protest than a mere expression, if it is more a struggle than a mere comfort, if it does not remain a mere sigh, if the protest and contrast become historical utopia that negates the present and impels into the future, if, in short, prophetic action is initiated, then history is made by way of repudiating and overcoming and not by way of evading. Thanks to propheticism, utopia does not fail to be efficacious in history, even though it is not fully realizable in history, as is the case with Christian utopia. If it were not realizable at all, it would run the almost insuperable risk of becoming an evasive opium; but if it must achieve a high degree of realization and is put into close relation to prophetic contradiction, it can be something that animates correct action. A utopia that is not in some way something that animates and even effects historical realizations is not a Christian utopia. It is not even an ideal vision of the reign; instead, it is an idealistic and ideologized vision of itself. For example, if nothing is done toward turning swords into plowshares but it is only dreamed about evasively, utopia fades away. Instead of fighting against the arms race, it becomes a bucolic expenditure of leisure time. This is not the intention or the reality of utopia and of Christian propheticism.

But if utopia cannot really be Christian utopia without propheticism to inspire it, neither will propheticism be really Christian without the animation of utopia. Christian propheticism lives by Christian utopia, which, as utopia, lives more and is nourished by the intercession that the Spirit makes throughout history. But, as Christian, utopia lives more by the proclamation and the promise that are explicitly and implicitly expressed in the revelation already given. A propheticism that did not take into account the proclamation and the promise already given would be ill-prepared to contradict evil. Above all, it would be completely unprepared to put together a historical design of something that would try to respond to the concrete demands of the reign of God, such as it has been proclaimed from of old, but especially by the historical Jesus.

Priority in the fullness of Christian action is to be attributed to the revelation and the promise of Jesus, even in the destructive phase of prophecy. This is even more valid when what is sought is to realize God's will or designs, for the discernment of which both the Spirit of Christ and the historical outlines of Jesus of Nazareth's movement through history are

---

[6] Karl Marx, "A Contribution to the Critique of Hegel's Philosophy of Right," first published in *Deutsch-Französische Jahrbücher* (Paris: February 7–10, 1844).

indispensable. It almost seems tautological and unnecessary to say that the Christian character of utopia cannot be given in fullness except from Christian faith explicitly accepted and lived, although without ignoring either that the Spirit can make use of Christians who are not formally such—and even of anti-Christians, as in the case of Caiaphas—to announce and realize some fundamental features of the Christian utopia.

It happens, however, that what is given must be actualized, in Zubiri's meaning of the term.[7] *Actualizarse* does not primarily mean "to bring something up to date," at least in the sense that this expression could have of "being fashionable." To actualize means, rather, to give present reality to what is formally a historical possibility; you can take it or leave it, read it this way or that, as you choose. What must be actualized, then, is what is given, but the reading and interpretation of what is given, the option for one part or other of what is given, depend on a historical present and on historical subjects. The historical actualization of the already given utopia arises especially from the intercession (signs of the times) that is being given through the Spirit in history. But the signs are historical, even though what is signified by them transcends the merely historical. The Spirit once again has priority for that transcendence, but in inseparable relationship with historical concretions. This is valid for the interpretation and even more so for the realization.

Indeed, utopia has a certain character of an ultimately unrealizable ideal, but at the same time it has the character of something asymptotically realizable in a permanent process of approximation, and therefore, it implies theoretical and practical mediations taken more from the categorial dimension of history.[8] It is, of course, a Christian utopia that is under discussion, and thus it maintains very explicitly the transcendent dimension of the reign. But even this dimension cannot be formulated apart from what is categorial, even in the most strictly evangelical formulations. It is not only or primarily a language problem—the reign as a banquet, as a vineyard, and so forth—but of something deeper, of the unavoidable need to make the reign's transcendence historical. This is easy to see in the moral recommendations related to everyday life [*vida cotidiana*], but it also refers to political and social objectifications—cases about soldiers, about authorities, about laws, about social customs, and so on. Such cases occur not only in all of the Old Testament but also in the New Testament.

---

[7] Xavier Zubiri (1898–1983), a Spanish philosopher, was Ellacuría's teacher. His influence on Ellacuría's thought is significant. For a brief overview and bibliography of his work, see *The Encyclopedia of Philosophy* (1967), 8:282–83.—*Eds.*

[8] Ellacuría's Spanish reads *categorial de la historia* throughout this article, not the more familiar *categorico.*—*Trans.*

And so, we must insist without exception that the Spirit's "challenge" in history is needed in order to hit upon the transcendent character of the categorial and to categorize the transcendent interpretively and practically. It is by means of the true and the false, the good and the bad, the just and the unjust, and so forth, valued without exception from what faith is (both as gift received and as daily practice) that the transcendence of the historical is grasped and, in turn, something that is unitarily historical and supra-historical is projected and realized transcendently. What propheticism gathers and expresses is the historico-transcendent challenge of the Spirit that makes present the utopia already offered and contrasts it with the signs of the times. Thus propheticism and utopia, history and transcendence, nourish each other. Both are historical and both are transcendent, but neither becomes what it is meant to become except in relation to the other.

2. Latin America is today a privileged place for propheticism and utopia, although so far the actualization of its prophetic and utopian potentiality is far from being satisfactory.

It is not a willful or arbitrary affirmation to designate Latin America at the present time as a privileged place of utopia and propheticism, because its own reality and some of its achievements demonstrate it.

As *reality*, Latin America is a continent with particular characteristics like those attributed to the Servant of Yahweh.[9] This condition makes it like other regions of the world, almost the greater part of the world's regions. It is a region ill-treated ever since the armed conquest effected by Spanish Christendom. Without losing its human heart, it nonetheless has its face disfigured, almost unrecognizable as human except in its pain and tragedy (Is 52:2–12); it has, besides, almost lost its own identity as a people (Hos 1:6–9; 1 Pt 2:10). But that identity, which in great part shapes it as an objective reality, contains a very active protest-conscience [*conciencia*][10] and, more specifically, a very vibrant Christian liberation-conscience. All this places it in an excellent position to exercise a strong theoretical and practical propheticism. This is confirmed by its great and significant achievement in

---

[9] Ellacuría alludes to the Songs of the Servant of Yahweh in Second Isaiah, a theme that he explores in depth in his earlier essay "The Crucified People." See Ignacio Ellacuría, "The Crucified People: An Essay in Historical Soteriology," in *Ignacio Ellacuría: Essays on History, Liberation, and Salvation*, ed. Michael E. Lee (Maryknoll, NY: Orbis Books, 2013), 195–224.—*Eds.*

[10] The term *conciencia* can be translated as both "conscience" and "consciousness/awareness." Both meanings apply simultaneously, but in this paragraph the theme of conscience must not be submerged.

this regard with its recent martyrs and prophets, who have arisen everywhere in every stratum of the people and of the church. Latin America is a region where great potentiality and wealth of resources contrast with the state of destitution, injustice, oppression, and exploitation imposed upon a great part of the people. This provides an objective basis for the contrast of utopia, found in its rich potentiality, with propheticism, already present in the negation of utopia by the everyday reality. The ceaseless revolutionary movements in the political arena and the Christian movements in the religious arena are distinct ways that a powerful collective utopian—and prophetic—conscience has reflected and apprehended the objective reality.

As *realization*, Latin America struggles both outside and inside the church in a powerful attempt to break its chains and build a different sort of future, not only for itself but for all humanity. The conditions suffered in its own flesh, along with its effective protest, constitute trustworthy evidence that convicts the historical world order—and not only the international economic-political order—and by negation, announces a different order. The real truth of the present-day historical arrangement is cruelly reflected, not only or principally in the fringes of destitution and, especially, of degradation in the wealthy countries, but in the reality of the Third World, consciously expressed in Latin America's many-sided protest.

That truth demonstrates the impossibility of reproducing and, especially, of enlarging the present historical order significantly. It demonstrates, even more radically, its undesirability, since this present order cannot be universalized. Rather, it brings with it the perpetuation of an unjust and predatory distribution of the world's resources, and even of each nation's resources, for the benefit of a few nations. The result is that our prophetic and utopian Latin America does not seek to imitate those who today are in the forefront and position themselves on top. Rather, it seeks a different order in the objective and in the subjective, an order that will allow a humane life not only for a few but for the greater part of humanity. The developed world is not at all the desired utopia, even as a way to overcome poverty, much less to overcome injustice. Instead, it is the sign of what should not be and of what should not be done.

This historical movement is reflected inside the church as something qualitatively new. The preferential option for the poor, understood in a radical and effective way in which the poor are those who dynamically take the initiative, can, first of all, transform the church radically, and it can thus become the key to and the engine of what a Christian utopia must be as a liberating historical project. Such a movement is reflected already in the different theoretical and practical forms of liberation theology, which in itself is an effective kind of propheticism for animating a new historical Christian utopia. That is why it is feared both inside and outside the church.

But the privileged place that Latin America is for propheticism and utopia must not lead to the illusion that all of it or all of the Latin American church is presently exercising the prophetic-utopian mission. Latin America as a whole is shaped by the same "sin of the world" that affects the rest of humanity. The "structures of sin" prevail there, and Latin America is not only the passive subject that suffers them but the active subject that produces them. The modes of realizing the capitalist pseudo-utopia and, in far lesser degree, the socialist pseudo-utopia prevail in the makeup of the society and peoples of Latin America. The economic as well as the social, political, and cultural modes of capitalism are reproduced and aggravated in Latin America because it consists of dependent societies, the kind that cannot dodge the effects and waste products of their exploitation, which they have to leave within their own borders instead of sending them elsewhere, as more powerful nations try to do. There are no reforms of capitalism in Latin America, although some attempts at reforms of socialism have begun. Nowhere is the preferential option for the poor lived out, or anything beyond the dynamism of capital and the demands of the international order. Least of all has a way been found for the dominated and oppressed people to be the primary subject of the processes. But it is not right to lay all the blame for all the ills of Latin America on others, because such an exoneration either legitimates or covers up behaviors and actions that are totally blameworthy. The systems, the processes, the leaders, even though dependent, still assume and even take advantage of the evils of their dependence.

Neither is the whole church in Latin America, nor even a large part of it, fulfilling its vocation of utopian propheticism. Scandalous as this is in a situation like that of Latin America—a continent where injustice and faith live side by side—a great many Christians, including religious, priests, bishops, cardinals, and nuncios, not only lack the prophetic charism but contradict it and even set themselves up as adversaries and persecutors of propheticism and as favorers of the structures and forces of domination, so long as these structures and forces do not put their institutional advantages and privileges in jeopardy. Although the elements of the church that play an anti-prophetic and anti-utopian role do not constitute the majority, an a-propheticism and even a distrust of propheticism predominate in the ecclesiastical institution. Propheticism tends to be confused with the misnamed "parallel magisterium." If the preferential option for the poor is taken as the touchstone, a certain nominal respect for it can be seen after long struggles, but the hierarchy has done little to put it into practice. If the criterion is the stance taken toward the liberation theology movement, there has been some formal improvement, but distrust continues, if not more subtle forms of attack.

However, even though there are these negative aspects, it cannot be ignored that, as was said earlier, there has been a flowering of utopia and of propheticism in Latin America, situating its people and in some way its church in a vanguard position for defining what is to be its mission in the present-day world. This cannot be seen from an abstract place, still less from a place incarnated in the structures of the dominant world.

3. The utopic propheticism of Latin America points toward a new form of freedom and humanity mediated by a historical process of liberation.

The very reality of Latin America, especially when seen from the vantage point of Christian faith, constitutes a radical prophetic protest against the international order, both in its North-South confrontation and in its East-West confrontation. It is also a protest against the attitude, behavior, and expectations promoted by those in the cultural vanguards and the models previously proposed as ideals of freedom and humanity.

The clash of interests in the North-South and East-West conflicts makes most countries in the world more and more dependent and systematically impoverished. In particular, it gets them into a process whereby they lose their identity because of the pressure for imitation, which reinforces their dependency and even slavery. This is not to deny that there are in the advanced capitalist and socialist countries valuable theoretical and practical principles that can and should be assumed critically and creatively by other countries. Simply going back to a supposed primitive state is impossible and can lead to multiple forms of dependency. Furthermore, it is impossible to escape the only real history, that of interdependence, in which all peoples must necessarily play a part. But the imperialistic form in which North-South, East-West relations exist must be rejected for the good of the countries that suffer it and for the good of the countries that impose it.

This is an indictment made very clearly by dependency theory and then by liberation theology. It has been understood and expressed prophetically by John Paul II in *Sollicitudo rei socialis,* following Paul VI's *Populorum progressio,* and Vatican II's *Gaudium et spes.* "Each of the two blocs harbors in its own way a tendency toward imperialism, as it is usually called, or toward forms of neocolonialism: an easy temptation to which they frequently succumb, as history, including recent history, teaches" (*Sollicitudo rei socialis,* no. 22).

A phenomenon as dramatic as Latin America's external debt is one of the clearest symptoms, both in its origin and in the way its payment is demanded, of how unjust the relationship is and how deadly the harm done to peoples is, when supposedly the desire is to help them.[11] In general, it can be said that the present type of relationship between the powerful and less powerful is making a few countries or social groups richer, while the majority are made poorer and the gap between them widens and becomes more serious. In the case of foreign debt it can be seen concretely how the originating loans were often made one-sidedly and with the complicity of governments and the upper social classes, yet without any benefit whatever for the mass of the people. But the demand for payment of these debts weighs especially heavily on the common people whom it deprives of the possibility of escape from their poverty through harmonious development. It favors the interests of capital much more than the demands of labor, thus contradicting a basic principle of humanity (the priority of work over capital) and a basic principle of the Christian faith (the priority of the many poor over the few rich). The world thus comes to be ruled by the lack of solidarity, the lack of mercy and concern for others, and so it is configured and conformed by injustice and opposition to the gospel. It shows itself as the patent and verifiable negation of the reign of God proclaimed by Jesus.

In particular, the current situation of Latin America prophetically denounces the intrinsic malice of the capitalist system and the ideological falsehood of the semblance of democracy that accompanies, legitimates, and cloaks it.

It is customary to ask why the voices of Latin American propheticism do not denounce the socialist politico-economic forms of the socialists and tend instead to design utopias of an anti-capitalist type. The factual reason is that propheticism currently devotes itself to present evils and these, for the most part, are due to capitalist forms of domination. The evils of the socialist systems, both in the economic and the political arenas, appear in situations like those in Cuba, Nicaragua, and some revolutionary movements. But, excluding extreme cases like that of the Shining Path [Sendero Luminoso] in Peru, the evils of the socialist systems cannot begin to compare with the dimensions and degrees of the evils of the capitalist system in Latin America. Hence, historical propheticism is directed mainly to rejecting capitalism rather than socialism.

The church, previously more inclined to condemn socialism than capitalism, and readier to see in the latter correctable defects and in the former intrinsic evils springing from its very historical essence, today tends at least to place both systems on an equal footing.

---

[11] Luis de Sebastián, *La deuda externa de América Latina y la banca internacional* (San Salvador: UCA Editores, 1987).

As we know, the tension between East and West is not in itself an opposition between two different levels of development but rather between two concepts of the development of individuals and peoples, both concepts being imperfect and in need of radical correction. . . . The church's social doctrine adopts a critical attitude toward both liberal capitalism and Marxist collectivism.[12]

But local propheticism should be centered, by its very nature, on the negation of what is in fact the cause of the evils that affect any given reality.

In regard to capitalism especially, once it passed through its stage of pitiless exploitation in the Western countries, permitting the first accumulation of wealth, its intrinsic malice has been observed in all its magnitude only beyond the boundaries of the rich countries, which in numerous ways export the evils of capitalism to the exploited periphery. The problem is not just that of the foreign debt or the exploitation of raw materials or the search for third-world sites to dispose of the wastes of all sorts that the more developed countries produce. More than that, it is an almost irresistible pull toward a profound dehumanization as an intrinsic part of the real dynamics of the capitalist system: abusive and/or superficial and alienating ways of seeking one's own security and happiness by means of private accumulation, of consumption, and of entertainment; submission to the laws of the consumer market promoted by advertising—in effect, sheer propaganda—in every kind of activity, including the cultural; and a manifest lack of solidarity in the individual, the family, and the state with regard to other individuals, families, or states.

The fundamental dynamic of selling one's own goods to another at the highest price possible and buying the other's at the lowest price possible, along with the dynamic of imposing one's own cultural norms so as to make others dependent, clearly shows the inhumanity of the system, constructed more on the principle of *homo homini lupus* (the human as a wolf toward other humans) than on the principle of a possible and desirable universal solidarity. Predatory ferocity becomes the fundamental dynamic, and generous solidarity remains reduced to incidentally and superficially treating the wounds of the poor caused by the depredation.

The fact is that of the approximately 400 million inhabitants of Latin America, 170 million now live in poverty. Poverty levels in the Third World are not the same as those in the First World; those in the latter would be levels of affluence in the former. (A family of four with an annual income

---

[12] John Paul II, *Sollicitudo rei socialis*, no. 21.

below $10,000 is classified at the poverty level in the United States.)[13] Of the 170 million in poverty, 61 million live in extreme poverty. To overcome this situation, $280 billion would be needed, equivalent to 40 percent of the gross domestic product of Latin America. But this is so difficult as to be almost impossible, because debt service produces a net export of capital, without counting capital flight, which is estimated to be much greater than all the investment and foreign aid received by the whole region. This reality—fomented both by international capitalism and by the capitalism of each nation and due not to the will of persons but to the structure and dynamics of the system—is an overwhelming historical proof of the evils that capitalism has brought about or has been unable to avoid in Latin America.

On the other hand, the ideologized propaganda about capitalist democracy, as the only and absolute form of political organization, becomes an instrument of cover-up and, at times, an instrument of oppression. Certainly, in the democratic package come values and rights that are very much worth taking into account, especially if they are carried out to their final consequences and real conditions are created for enjoying them. But the ideologized operation of the democratic model seeks not to let the people determine their own political and economic model, but to cover up the imposition of the capitalist system and, especially in the case of Central America, the imposition of United States interests. Democracy is supported only insofar as those interests are presumed to be furthered.

Therefore, more regard is paid to national security by the United States than to the self-determination of peoples, or to international law, or even to respect for fundamental human rights, which are defended derivatively so long as they do not endanger the military and police structures. It is in these military and police structures that confidence is placed for the defense of United States' interests rather than in any democratic structure. Thus it becomes a point of honor to have elections involving awful decisions affecting millions of people and to assure the enjoyment of certain civil rights that can only be actively exercised by the economically privileged, who have sufficient resources, while much less vigor is shown in demanding an end to murders, disappearances, tortures, and such, which even includes undercover operations undertaken by the CIA that involve not only illegal actions but strictly terrorist practices.

But what is most serious is that the offer of humanization and freedom that the rich countries make to the poor countries is not universalizable and consequently is not human, even for those who make it. Kant's keen

---

[13] Ellacuría wrote this essay in 1989. In 2014, the poverty level for a family of four in the United States is $23,850.—*Eds.*

way of putting it could be applied to this problem: "Act only according to that maxim whereby you can, at the same time, will that it should become a universal law."[14] If the behavior and even the ideal of a few cannot become the behavior and the reality of the greater part of humanity, that behavior and that ideal cannot be said to be moral or even human, all the more so if the enjoyment of a few is at the cost of depriving the rest. In our world the practical ideal of Western civilization is not universalizable, not even materially, since there are not enough material resources on earth today to let all countries achieve the same level of production and consumption as that of the countries called wealthy, whose total population is less than 25 percent of humanity.

That universalization is not possible, but neither is it desirable. The lifestyle proposed in and by the mechanics of development does not humanize, it does not fulfill or make happy, as is shown, among other indices, by the growing drug consumption that has become one of the principal problems of the developed world. That lifestyle is motivated by fear and insecurity, by inner emptiness, by the need to dominate so as not to be dominated, by the urge to exhibit what one has because one cannot communicate what one is. It all supposes only a minimum degree of freedom, and it supports that minimum freedom more in externals than internals. It likewise implies a maximum degree of a lack of solidarity with the greater part of human beings and of peoples of the world, especially with those most in need.

And if this type of historical law, which proposes to go on shaping our times, has scarcely anything of what is human and is fundamentally inhuman, it must even more clearly be said to be anti-Christian. The Christian ideal of finding happiness more in giving than in receiving—and still more than in seizing (Acts 20:35)—more in solidarity and community than in confrontation and individualism, more in personal development than in accumulating things, more in the viewpoint of the poor than in that of the rich and powerful, is contradicted and hindered by what is in practice (above and beyond the stated ideal, which is toothless) the real dynamism of the present-day models.

From the reality of Latin America there also comes a prophetic protest against the way the institutional church is structured and behaves. The Latin American church has been too tolerant of the conditions of structural injustice and institutionalized violence that prevail in the region. Above all, until recently, the universal church itself has been blind and mute before the responsibility of the developed countries relating to that injustice.

---

[14] Immanuel Kant, "Handle so, dass die Maxime deines Willens jederzeit zugleich als Prinzip einer allgemeinen Gesetzgebung gelten koenne," *Grounding for the Metaphysics of Morals* [1785], 3rd ed., trans. James W. Ellington from *Grundlegung zur Metaphysik der Sitten* (Indianapolis, IN: Hackett Publishing, 1993), 30.

Certainly since the time of the conquest, examples can be found of propheticism both in the church's rank-and-file and in its hierarchy. But at the same time those willing to overlook wrongdoing have been preponderant, showing greater concern for personal and institutional interests than for the oppressed mass of the people and for the reign of God. In our own days, Medellín and Puebla, despite their great merit and value, have had little real effect on church structures and behavior. The behavior of martyrs—like bishops Romero, Valencia, Angelelli,[15] and others—although it is not completely rare and exceptional and has been accompanied by that of dozens and even hundreds of laypeople, religious, and priests—is very significant and encouraging. But it is far from being the norm, and it is still seen as "dangerous" and not quite normal.

The universal church, always prompt to condemn Marxism, has been more tolerant of the evils of capitalism, even in its most damaging imperialist forms. There are clear advances by Vatican II and by the recent popes in this respect; very estimable also are some positions taken by the bishops of the United States in regard to their government's stance toward the Latin American peoples.[16] But it was practically necessary for *Sollicitudo rei socialis* to appear in order to make things finally clear after the grand impulse given in this respect by the promulgation of *Gaudium et spes*. However, what has been achieved on the doctrinal plane has scarcely progressed to that of pastoral orientation and to producing a more decidedly prophetic attitude. The church that lives in the wealthy countries does not denounce with sufficient vigor the exploitative conduct of these countries toward the rest of the world. It preaches mercy rather than justice, thus leaving aside one of the central themes of historical propheticism. The fear is still of the evils of Soviet imperialism rather than of the evils of US imperialism, and so the present evils generated by the latter are preferred and tolerated over the potential evils that might come from the former.

Neither has the church made a minimally sufficient effort in Latin America to inculturate itself in a situation very different from that of the North Atlantic countries. It is still thought that there is a historical continuum

---

[15] Bishop Oscar Arnulfo Romero, archbishop of San Salvador, El Salvador, was a great defender of the poor and the victims of repression in his country and an enormous personal influence on the life and thought of Ignacio Ellacuría. He was assassinated while celebrating mass on March 24, 1980. Bishop Gerardo Valencia Cano, the bishop of Buenaventura, Columbia, was one of the few progressive Columbian bishops and the only one to sign the Declaration of Golconda (1968). He died suspiciously in a plane crash on January 21, 1972. Bishop Enrique Ángel Angelelli was an Argentinean bishop assassinated on August 4, 1976 because of his commitment to the poor and his outspoken involvement on social issues during the so-called Dirty War—*Eds.*

[16] Ellacuría is referring to the pastoral letter *Economic Justice for All* published by the United States Conference of Catholic Bishops in 1986.—*Eds.*

between the rich countries and the poor countries, and more attention is paid to the unity of language or learning than to the profound gap between the state of economic development and to the position occupied in the international economic order. There is a question here of two distinct inculturations, or two sources of profound diversification that inculturation ought to take into account. On one side is the tremendous difference of cultures, of fundamental modes of being, originating from a complex series of factors (racial, psychosocial, linguistic, educational, and of every sort). On the other side is the likewise fundamental difference in the gross national product and in per capita income, which renders impossible many of the cultural modes of the wealthy countries. It is not just a question of the indigenous populations or populations of color but of something that affects the whole continent, if we interpret the continent by looking at the mass of the people. Institutionally, the mentality is still that when it comes to theological thought, forms of religious practice, the world of rituals, and so forth, Latin America is still considered an appendage to Europe and a prolongation of Roman Catholicism, whereas it is a new reality and, what is more, the majority reality of the Catholic church.

This reality is one that itself becomes a prophetic denunciation. It summons to a profound transformation of the way the church sees itself and understands its mission. To ignore this summons, having recourse to the presumed unchanging and universal character of the faith and of Christian institutions, is to ignore the Spirit's voice of renewal, which always appears along with some degree of propheticism. This propheticism points out the limitations and evils that the institutional church has picked up as dead weight on its way through history. History has been fundamentally the history of the rich, dominant, and conquering peoples, not the history of the poor peoples, which should have been the fundamental matrix of the church but was lost from the time of Constantine. Although an important remnant of the gospel did not fall into the trap of either riches or of power, but always remained alive, and in the most vivid forms, it has always been poorly tolerated.

The propheticism of denunciation, within the horizon of the reign of God, marks out the ways that lead to utopia. The *no* of propheticism, the overcoming negation [*negación superadora*] of propheticism, continues to generate within itself the *yes* of utopia by virtue of the promise that is the reign of God already present among human beings, especially since the life, death, and resurrection of Jesus, who has sent his Spirit for the renewal (passing through death) of all people and all things.

The negation of reductive particularism leads to the affirmation that only a new global project that is universalizable can be acceptable for humanity. Independent of all ethical or theological consideration, the basic principle remains valid that any world order or conception that generates a constantly greater number of people in poverty, that can only be maintained by force and by the threat of humanity's total destruction through increasing ecological destruction and nuclear annihilation, that generates no ideals of qualitative growth, and that gets entangled with constraints of every kind is not acceptable. Out of purely selfish considerations, where the self is all of humanity along with the self of each individual person (nonviable in the long run without the former), substantial changes in the conception and in the dynamism of such so-called progress are necessary.

But above and beyond all selfish realism and realistic selfishness, it is clear that a world order favorable for a few and unfavorable for most is something that dehumanizes and de-Christianizes each person and humanity. From a human viewpoint, actions and projects must be measured by the classic quotation [from Terence] "I am human and nothing that is human is foreign to me," meaning that whatever alienation, action, or omission makes another human being a "foreigner" breaks down the humanity of the one who behaves this way. From a Christian viewpoint one is not to pass by the wounded person on the roadside, for then one refuses one's neighbor—the opposite of the "foreigner"—and that is the denial of both the second and the first of the commandments that the Father has renewed in the Son.

The principle of universalization certainly is not a principle of uniformization and, still less, of uniformization imposed from a powerful center on an amorphous and subordinated periphery. That, however, is the way to universalization proposed by those who wish to impose the model of existence that at the moment is more favorable to them. This uniformization is today ruled above all by the laws of the economic marketplace and is a most forceful statement that materialism, not historical but economic materialism, is what determines all else in the last analysis. Contrary to this a universalism must be generated that does not reduce but enriches, so that the entire wealth of peoples may be respected and developed, and their differences seen as the completion of the whole and not as the clashing of the parts. In this way all the members will complement one another, and in this complementing the whole will be enriched and the parts strengthened.

Universalization must result from the preferential option for the poor, for the universalization resulting so far from the preferential option for the rich and powerful has brought more ill than good to humanity. Until now, the historical world order and the church's institutions have been universalized from a preferential option for the rich and the powerful. In the secular order it has been made by the strong for the strong, and this has brought some advantages in scientific, technological, and cultural advances. But these advantages rest upon great evils for the majority, who are sometimes forgotten and at other times exploited. Also, the church has become worldly.

That is, it has followed this fundamental behavior of the "world" and has shaped its message and even its institutions more from the standpoint of a power that dominates and controls than from that of a ministry that serves. Both the secular order and the church have lived by the principle so contrary to the gospel, that devoting oneself to the rich and behaving so as to favor the more powerful is how the mass of the people, how humanity, is better served and how the gospel is better spread. Ecclesiastical pomp in imitation of royal pomp, the establishment of a state political power, submission to the laws of the marketplace, and so forth on the church's part show how it has submitted to the worldly principle that the option for power and for the powerful is what best secures institutions.

Now, this is not the Christian viewpoint. From the Christian viewpoint it has to be affirmed that the poor are to be not only the preferential passive subject of those who have power, but the preferential active subject of history, especially of the church's history. The Christian faith affirms—and this is a dogma of faith that cannot be contradicted under penalty of gravely mutilating that faith—that it is in the poor that the greatest real presence of the historical Jesus is found and therefore the greatest capacity for salvation (or liberation). The fundamental texts of the Beatitudes and of the Last Judgment, among others, leave this point settled with total clarity; many other things are affirmed as dogma with much less biblical support. How this historical subjectuality should be concretized and how it should be exercised is a question open to theoretical discussion and historical experimentation. But it does not for that reason cease to be an operative principle of discernment to ask oneself always what is most needed by the mass of the people so that they can really achieve what is due to them as human beings and as members of God's people.

In Latin America, propheticism puts more emphasis on the active and organized poor, on the poor-with-spirit, than on the passive poor—that is, the poor who suffer their destitution with resignation and hardly notice the injustice they suffer. It does not deny the importance, even the prophetic importance that belongs to the poor by the simple fact of their being the poor, for there is no doubt that as such they enjoy Jesus' special predilection and his very particular presence. But when those poor incorporate their poverty spiritually, when they become aware of the injustice of their condition and of the possibilities and even of the real obligation they have in the face of destitution and structural injustice, they are changed from passive to active subjects, and with that they multiply and strengthen the salvific-historical value that is theirs.

There is a further argument for searching for the new universal ideal of human being and of Christian, for the new ideal of world and of humanity coming out of the mass of the people (secular version) and out of the poor

(Christian version). In reality, they represent the greater part of humanity. This means, again, from the negative-prophetical viewpoint that many of the various past civilizations have not been really human but rather class and/or nationalist civilizations. From the prophetic-utopian viewpoint it means that the goal unavoidably must be the development-liberation of every person and of all people —but understanding that the ones who put conditions on the "every" of every person are the "all" of all people, and that those "all" people are mostly the poor. Until now, development-liberation has not been that of the whole of the person, nor is it going in that direction, as is shown in the fact that, far from leading to the development-liberation of all people, it has led to the underdevelopment-oppression of most of them. This is a long historical process, certainly, but the question is whether we are going in the right direction or instead are going toward humanity's dehumanization and de-Christianization.

In Latin America this prophetic march toward utopia is driven by a great hope. Beyond all rhetoric and in spite of all the difficulties, there are rivers of hope on the continent. Christian hope thus becomes one of the most efficacious dynamisms for going out of the land of oppression and toward the land of promise.

This march from oppression to promise is sustained on hope. It is received as grace (there would not seem to be many motives for hope, in view of the enormous problems and difficulties), but it goes on being nourished historically and growing in the praxis of liberation. It is a verifiable fact that hope, which animates the poor-with-spirit, inspires them in long and hard processes that to others seem useless and futureless. It is a hope that appears, therefore, with the characteristics of hope against all hope—a very Christian characteristic—although once it appears it is nourished by the results already achieved. It is not the secure reckoning that leads to making an investment with the calculated expectation of desirable fixed-term results; it is not an idealistic dream that removes one from reality. Rather, it is the accepting of God's promise of liberation, a fundamental promise that propels to an exodus in which historical goals and objectives unite with trans-historical certainties.

In contrast to the emptiness of non-meaning found in a life that tries to fill itself with activities and purposes without deep meaning, Latin America's poor-with-spirit are a real and effective sign that in the present-day world there are tasks full of meaning. Thus, in a real criticism—that is, criticism from hope-filled reality—of hopeless reality, of the confusion between being entertained or amused and being happy, between being occupied and being fulfilled, space opens for another form of life completely different from the one imposed today as ideal in a consumer society, a society for which improvements are proposed without consistency and without greater meaning.

That space is traveled by the poor-with-spirit in a new Christian disposition, which leads to giving their life for others, so that in giving it they find it and they find themselves. It leads to being able to despise the whole world, whose conquest means nothing if it means the loss of oneself, of the spirit of oneself (Mk 8:34–38 and parallels). It leads to emptying oneself to find oneself again after the emptying in the fullness of what one is and of what one can be (Phil 2:1–11).

The hope of the poor-with-spirit in Latin America—probably in other places also—is something qualitatively new. It is not a question of absolute despair that leads to a type of active desperation in persons who can go ahead and lose everything because they have nothing to lose but the all-nothing of their own lives—which have become unlivable. It is not despair, but hope. Hence, the attitude and the actions are not desperate actions but attitudes and actions that arise from life and that seek a greater life. This is a verifiable fact in thousands of men and women in refugee camps, in marginal communities, among the thousands of displaced persons, people for whom often it is not "political spirit" encouraging them [los alienta] but "Christian spirit" animating them [los anima]. That spirit will have to be historicized and politicized in order for it not to evaporate in fruitless subjectivisms, but politicization is not what is first, nor is it what is fundamental.

This hope arises from life, arises together with the promise of life and the negation of death, and it is celebrated festively. The sense of fiesta, as it exists in these poor-with-hope, indicates for now that they have not fallen into the fanaticism of desperation and of struggle for the sake of struggle. But neither do they fall therefore into the error of the fiesta purely for amusement that characterizes the Western world—fiesta lacking in meaning and lacking in hope. Fiesta is not a substitute for missing hope; it is the jubilant celebration of a hope on the march. The more or less explicit search for happiness is done in other ways, which do not simply mistake it for the forgetfulness drugged by consumerism or the mere consumption of entertainment. It is not simply in leisure that fulfillment is sought but in the gratuitous and gratifying labor of different liberating tasks.

In the search for a historically universalizable utopia, in which the poor, or the mass of the people, will have a determining role, and from out of the hope that urges them toward utopia, one glimpses a new revolution with the prophetic motto "begin anew." To begin anew a historic order that will transform radically the present one, based on the promotion and liberation of human life, is the prophetic call that can open the way to a new utopia of Christian inspiration.

"To begin anew" does not mean the rejection of all of the past, which is neither possible nor desirable, but it does mean something more than just setting out to make things new in linear development with the previous.

It means a real "beginning anew," since the old, as a totality, is not acceptable, nor is the principial dynamism [*dinamismo principial*] that drives it acceptable (Zubiri).[17]

Even in the most radical of revolutions, total rejection of the past is not possible and is not desirable, because it deprives humanity of possibilities without which it would find itself obliged to begin from zero—which is impossible. In addition, not all that has been achieved is bad, nor is it intrinsically infected with evil. There are elements of every type—scientific, cultural, technological, and so forth—whose malignity comes not from their essence but from the totality in which they are enlisted and from the finality to which they are subordinated. There are certainly unacceptable elements, but this is not sufficient to advocate an impossible and sterile nihilism. In this sense "begin anew" supposes neither previous annihilation nor creation of a new world from nothing.

But neither is it just a matter of making new things; rather, it is a matter of making all things new, given that the old is not acceptable. This belongs to the essence of utopian propheticism. The "if you are not born anew" (Jn 3:3), the incorporation in the death that gives life (Rom 6:3–5), the seed that needs to die to bear fruit (Jn 12:24), the disappearance and destruction of the old city so that the new one can arise in a different world (Rv 18:1ff.; 21:1ff.), and so many other Old and New Testament proclamations offer and demand a radical transformation. For in the Christian interpretation of the new life, death always intercedes as mediation. Certainly, the good news is a message of life, but a message of life that assumes not only the reality of death but the positive validity of the negation of death. To die to the old human being, to the world that is past, to the former age, and so on, is a fundamental part of the biblical message. Christian prophecy can go against one or other concrete fact, but in addition and above all it goes against the totality of any historical order where sin prevails over grace. As negation and as affirmation, Christian utopian prophecy proposes to make a radically new human being and a radically different world.

The fundamental principle on which to base the new order remains "that all might have life and have it more abundantly" (Jn 10:10). This is the utopian cry coming from historical prophecy. The historical experience of death, and not merely of pain, of death by hunger and destitution or death by repression and by various forms of violence, which is so living and massive in Latin America, reveals the enormous necessity and the irreplaceable value, first of all, of material life—as the primary and fundamental gift in

---

[17] Ellacuría, following Zubiri (as he indicates), makes use of a sophistical theologal term, *principial*, to refer to a dynamism that has its fundamental source in the principle of all things, God. This idea is central to the thought of the great medieval mystic Meister Eckhart.—Eds.

which must be rooted all other aspects of life, which in the final analysis constitute development of that primary gift. That life must be expanded and completed by internal growth and in relation to the life of others, always in search of more life and better life.

Not that it is evident in what the fullness of life consists, still less how fullness of life is to be achieved. But it is not so hard to see what it does not consist of and how it will not be achieved. And this not only by logical deductions from universal principles but by historical verification from the experience of the mass of the people. To seek life by taking it away from others or without concern for how others are losing it is certainly the negation of the Spirit as giver of life. From this perspective the basic Christian message of loving others as oneself, and not just that of not wanting for oneself what is not wanted for others (pragmatically formulated by the Declaration of the Rights of Man and of the Citizen of 1793 in its sixth article), of preferring to give rather than receive, and of resolving to give all one's property to those who are poorer, are utopian ideals. The prophetic historicization of these ideals can begin to generate that radical newness in persons and in institutions. With it, not only is there a drive to seek something radically new, but some lines are drawn for the attempts to begin anew, since what has been realized up to now is not on the right way to benefit the greater part of humanity, which is made up of masses with scarcely even access to life.

Latin American historical propheticism presents itself in our day as liberation. The utopia of freedom is to be attained by means of propheticism of liberation. The utopian ideal of a complete freedom for all human beings is not possible except through a liberation process; hence it is not primarily freedom that engenders liberation but liberation that engenders freedom, even though a process of mutual reinforcement and enrichment may occur between the two.

Thus it has been historically. The well-known English *liberties* of the Magna Carta or of the Bill of Rights are concrete achievements—fewer taxes, just judgments, protection against the arbitrary domination of kings, and so on—obtained by a process of liberating struggle through which definite rights are acknowledged and then formalized in agreements, laws, or constitutions. Basically, it is a process of liberation from injustice, from domination, from institutionalized and falsely justified abuse. Only later was the process of liberalism turned into the model of freedom and the way to preserve rather than obtain this freedom. But real freedom is obtained fundamentally through a process of liberation. This is so in the personal realm, in the communitarian, in the social, and in the political as well. On the other hand, liberalism, as it is contradicted by historical propheticism in Latin America, is the juridical and formal cover-up for those who have already been liberated from certain oppressions and dominations and who in turn see to it that others do not achieve the same through subsequent and more complex processes of liberation.

Both personal freedom and social and political freedom are effectively such only when one "can" be and do what one desires—or should or is allowed—to be and to do. Freedom without those very real conditions that make it really possible can be an ideal, but it is not a reality since without due and sufficient conditions one cannot be or do what one wants. But, if in addition to the absence of real conditions for exercising freedom, liberties, and formal rights, there is also positive oppression and domination that hinder that exercise even more, it is not only unreal but positively ideological and hypocritical to talk of freedom. There is no personal freedom when, for example, there is internal domination by very powerful internal preconditioning or external advertising and propaganda that is not duly counteracted. For example, there is no personal freedom in a child, who does not have the intellectual development and the minimum knowledge to be able to discern and counterbalance the weight of internal and external motivations. If parents or educators impose in all sorts of ways their own ideas, attitudes, or patterns of conduct, too, it is practically a mockery to talk of the child's freedom. The same should be said about economic and social freedoms. They can be enjoyed only by those who have effective access to them and for whom that access is not positively hindered by all sorts of means, at times covertly and other times openly. What freedom of movement is possessed by someone who has no roads, no means of transport, or even the ability to walk? What freedom is there to choose a job or type of studies when there are jobs or places for students for only 50 percent of the population? What freedom of expression is there when there is active access to the media for only 1 percent and only passive access—for lack of literacy, lack of receiver sets, lack of means, and so forth—for over 60 percent? What economic freedom is there when access to credit is for the very few? What political freedom is there when one lacks the resources to create a political party and when the apparatus of the state and of associations maintains a climate of terror—or at least of generalized fear? It will be said that liberalism ideally desires none of this, that it seeks to offer equality of opportunity for all individuals and all inclinations. But, in fact, this is not so, and the least exercise of historicization shows that freedoms and conditions of freedom are not given to but are won by people in a historical process of liberation.

Liberalization is one thing, and liberation is something very different. The processes of liberalization are only possible if the processes of liberation have taken place antecedently. Liberalization is a problem of and for the elite, whereas liberation is a process of and for the vast majority of the people [*mayorías populares*] that begins with liberation for basic needs and then builds positive conditions for the increasingly adult exercise of freedom and for the reasonable enjoyment of liberties. The fact that certain liberation processes tend to become new processes of domination of the many by the few is something we should very much take into account. But it does not invalidate the axiological priority of liberation over liberalization in the process of attaining freedom.

To want to pose the question of freedom apart from that of liberation is to want to evade the real question of freedom for all. In the realm of the personal, freedom is not actualized fully except by laborious processes of liberation confronting all sorts of more or less determinant necessities. There is an internal basis and an ideal of freedom that, up to a certain point and in a generic way, are given "naturally" to a person. But fundamentally this personal ideal is about capacities and freedoms that need to be actualized in order to become full realities, and quite precise conditions are required for that actualization to occur. With due distinctions, something similar must be said about social and political freedom. Such freedoms suppose a liberation from oppressive structures, which the classic liberals struggled against on the supposition that only the state limited or oppressed the individual without realizing that there were social groups that oppressed and exploited other social groups. It supposes, besides, the creation of conditions where the capacity and the ideal of political and social freedom can be shared equitably.

Liberation, therefore, is understood as "liberation-from" every form of oppression and as "liberation-for" a shared freedom that does not make possible or permit forms of domination. It makes little sense to talk of freedom when opportunity for its actualization is reduced because of unsatisfied basic needs, drastic limitations on real possibilities to choose among, and impositions of every sort, especially those depending on force and terror. But a mere "liberation-from" is not enough, since a "liberation-for" or a "liberation-toward" freedom is required, for freedom can be full freedom only when it is the freedom of all. The freedom of a few resting on the slavery of the rest is not acceptable, nor is a freedom resting on the non-freedom of the majority acceptable. Hence, here too, freedom must be seen from its historicization in the vast majority of the people within each country and within the oppressed peoples in the world as a whole. It is humanity that must be free, not a few privileged members of humanity, whether individuals, social classes, or nations.

From this perspective the question of the priority of justice over freedom or of freedom over justice is resolved by the unity of both in liberation. There can be no justice without freedom and no freedom without justice, even though in the social and political order there is a priority of justice over freedom, since one cannot be free unjustly. While justice, in giving to each what is due to each, not only makes freedom possible but also that which is moral and just. Liberation from every form of oppression whatever is a real process of "just-ification." This justification is the real means of promoting freedom and the conditions that make it possible. Thus, liberation is a process of "ad-just-ment" with oneself, in that it seeks to break one's internal and external chains. It is a "just" process in that it tries to overcome manifest injustice; and it is a "justifying" process in that it seeks to create adequate conditions for the full development of all and for an equitable use of the conditions.

In more explicitly Christian terms, liberation moves toward the utopia of freedom through a real, prophetic process of liberation, which implies liberation from sin, from the law, and from death (Rom 6—8). Its goal is to reveal what it is to be God's children, what the freedom and the glory of God's children actually mean—a goal only possible through a permanent process of conversion and liberation (Rom 8:18–26) that follows Jesus by means of the personal reproduction of the "features of his Son, so that he may be the eldest of many brothers" (Rom 8:29). A complete development of what is liberation from sin, from the law, and from death would give greater theological and historical clarity to how freedom is the result of liberation and how it is dangerous to pose the problem of freedom without regard to precise liberation tasks. This would demand a more extensive treatment of this question, but its mere suggestion points to the pressing need for processes of prophetic liberation so that the utopia of freedom can be really historicized.

4. Christian utopia is the forward-looking announcement, done in an historical manner, of the creation of the new human being, of the new earth, and of the new heaven.[18]

The *new human being* is sketched on the basis of the Christian ideal, but a historicized ideal that proposes to take the place of the old human being that has been the worldly and even Christian-worldly ideal, proposed as such or at least as a practically irresistible focus of attraction.

---

[18] This version of the fourth thesis is found both in the text of this essay in *Mysterium Liberationis*, vol. 1 (San Salvador: UCA Editores, 1993), 419; and also in the one in *Escritos teológicos*, vol. 2 (San Salvador: UCA Editores, 2000), 264. However, a longer version occurs in the first publication of "Utopia and Propheticism," in *Revista Latinoamericana de Teología* 17 (1989): 164. It reads, "La utopía cristiana, apuntada desde el profetismo de América Latina y, a su vez, orientada y regida por él, prenuncia de una manera histórica la creación del hombre nuevo, de la tierra nueva y del cielo Nuevo." A translation could be: "Indicated from the vantage point of Latin American propheticism and oriented and guided by it in turn, Christian utopia is a foreword-looking announcement, done in a historical way, of the new human being, the new earth and the new heaven."

This is done starting from the conviction, nourished both from faith and from historical experience, that the ideal and/or the dominant focus of the human person maintained in Latin America is anti-Christian and does not respond to the challenges of reality. Not everything in that ideal is imported to the extent that one can speak of an inculturation of that ideal, which transmits its own features to its historicization. Prescinding for now from which ones are imported features and which are native, a sort of catalogue of its traits can be made.

With respect to the ideal of the dominant, old human being in the so-called Christian, North Atlantic, and Western civilization, certain features have to be rejected. These include its radical insecurity, which leads it to take wild and irrational measures of self-defense; its lack of solidarity with what is happening to the rest of humanity; its ethnocentrism, along with its absolutizing and idolatrizing of the nation-state as fatherland; its exploitation and direct or indirect domination of other peoples and of their resources; the banal superficiality of its existence and of the criteria by which types of work are chosen; its immaturity in the search for happiness through pleasure, random entertainment, and amusement; the smug pretension of setting itself up as the elite vanguard of humanity; its permanent aggression against the environment shared by the rest of humanity.

To feel the multitudinous effects of this Northern-Western human being on the Latin American human being, effects that are oppressive on the one hand and disintegrating on the other, causes us to reject prophetically its false idealism and to sketch a different kind of human being on the basis of that negation. But before this, we must reject the proposition that Latin America simply belongs to the Western world and to the Westernized Christian world, for by means of this ideologization, Christ has been falsified; in addition, he is converted into a lure by a civilization that is not humanely universalizable, one that then attempts to export itself as the ideal model of humanity and of Christianity. When Hobbes wrote in *Leviathan* in 1651 that the causes of struggles among humans are three and that the three are written in human nature—insecurity, competition, and desire for glory—he was describing the experience of the emergent Western human being rather than anything necessarily innate to human nature. When official Christianity converts into optional and intentional virtues what ought to be the outright negation of anti-Christian attitudes and deeds, then it is giving a biased reading of the faith that nulifies its real truth and effectiveness.

Returning to the historical realism of the gospel proclamation, a historical realism that is by no means fundamentalist precisely because it is historical, obliges a return to the fundamental gospel theme of wealth-poverty. The biased reading of the faith has made it possible to reconcile material wealth with spiritual poverty, when the authentic reading, to which the church's greatest saints attest, is the opposite: the reconciliation of material poverty with spiritual wealth. Now, the historical verification of the dialectical relation of wealth-poverty reclaims the depth of the gospel message, making poverty not a purely optional counsel but a historical necessity. Correlatively, this makes wealth not something indifferent, easily reconcilable with the following of Jesus, but one of the fundamental hindrances to the building up of God's reign. Poverty and wealth are not here spoken of apart from each other but in their dialectical relationship: poverty as a correlate of wealth, and wealth as a correlate of poverty.

Not only from the viewpoint of faith but also from the viewpoint of history, one sees in wealth and in the lustful desire for wealth the fundamental engine of a heartless and inhuman culture, and the greatest resistance to the historical construction of the reign of God. The path of rapid and unequal enrichment has led to a Cainite rupture of humanity and to the formation of an exploitive, repressive, and violent human being.[19] The relationship of human beings with wealth, a question so essential in the gospel, again becomes a central point in defining the new human being, who will not come into existence until there is an entirely new relationship to deal with the phenomenon of wealth and the problem of unequal accumulation. Asceticism and individual and group spirituality have tried to resolve this problem, but it must be taken up again because it has become a historical necessity to curb the dehumanization of both rich and poor in their dialectical confrontation.

Enticed by the allure of wealth, of wealthy persons and peoples, one loses the marks of one's own identity. To seek one's own identity in the improper appropriation of these foreign models leads to dependencies and mimicries that impede one's own self-creation. The culture of wealth proposes models and establishes means to attain them, and it does so in a way that out-dazzles the possibility of seeking other models of fulfillment and happiness. It subjects to alienating dynamisms all those who devote themselves to adoring the golden calf that becomes the central idol of a new culture that in turn reinforces the central role that this golden idol plays in it. Where your treasure is, there is your heart, which ends up being shpaed by the features of your treasure.[20] Hence, the importance of the choice of one's treasure. When one's treasure is confused with the accumulation of wealth, the type of heart and the type of human being that result are subjected to a double alienation: one's very freedom is subjected to the deterministic and reifying dynamisms of money, and one's very identity is subjected to a model created not for liberation but for submission. Certainly, wealth does

---

[19] Ellacuría's reference to the "Cainite rupture of humanity" is an allusion to the biblical story where Cain murders his brother, Abel (see Gn 4:1–16).–*Eds.*

[20] Ellacuría alludes to Matthew 6:21.—*Eds.*

have some possibilities for liberation but at the cost of other possibilities of slavery for oneself and others.

All these evils, in great part induced from outside, are accompanied and reflected by others arising from within. Tendencies to machismo and violence are examples of these evils that degrade both men and women and are reflected in profound deviations in sexual and family life or in a whole interdependent combination of submission, fatalism, and inertia. How much of this is ancestral or even natural and how much is a reflection of external stimuli is a matter to be investigated in each case. But to place the origin of all evils in outside agents would not be the right way to recover one's own identity, because this would make harder the task of constructing the new human being from within.

The ideologization that corresponds to this set of real tendencies and deeds reveals itself to be negative and nullifying of one's own individual and collective conscience. This ideologization presents itself as religious, economic, and political, and what it does basically is reinforce fundamental interests, latent or explicit. Religious fatalism, the economic competition of free enterprise and the urge for profit, the democratic system offered as a controlled and mapped-out participation of the vast majority of the people: all are examples of this ideologization, which, although it rests on certain goods and values, transmits greater evils.

In its negativity the foregoing points to what should be positively the features of utopia. In the light of Christian inspiration, that negativity indicates what the new human being is to be, in contrast to the old human being. Since it is not primordially an intentional exercise but a praxis already under way, some of those features can already be appreciated in what is in existence.

The central point concerns the preferential option for the poor as a fundamental way to combat the priority of wealth in the shaping of human beings. There is a movement toward a greater solidarity with the cause of the oppressed, toward a growing incorporation into their world as the privileged place of humanization and Christian divinization. Such incorporation is not done in order to take perverse pleasure in miserable poverty, but in order to accompany the poor in their desire for liberation. Liberation cannot consist of passing from poverty to wealth by making oneself rich by means of the poverty of others. It consists rather of overcoming poverty through solidarity. We are, of course, talking about the poor-with-spirit, the poor who accept their situation as the foundation for constructing the new human being. Out of the materiality of poverty this construction of the new human being arises actively from the poor-with-spirit, impelling them toward a process of liberation in solidarity that leaves out no human being. In other words, these are active poor, whom necessity spurs to escape from an unjust situation.

Hence, this new human being is defined in part by active protest and permanent struggle. This new human being seeks to overcome the dominant structural injustice that is considered an evil and a sin because it keeps most of the human population in conditions of inhumane living. This unjust situation is negative, but its negativity propels escape from it as from a catapult. The positive aspect is the dynamic of overcoming. In that overcoming the Spirit breathes encouragement in multiple ways, of which the supreme way of all is readiness to give one's life for others, whether in tireless daily commitment or in sacrifice unto death violently suffered.

Typically, however, the motive of this new human being who is moved by the Spirit is not hatred but mercy and love, for all are seen as children of God and not as enemies to be destroyed. Hatred can be lucid and effective in the short term, but it is not capable of constructing a really new human being. Christian love is not exactly softhearted, but it does propose very decidedly not to let itself be entrapped and hardened in selfishness or hatred, and it has a very clear vocation to service. The lords of this world set out to dominate and to be served, while the Son of man, the new human being, has not come to be served but to serve and to give his life for the rest, for the many (Mt 20:25–28).

Along with love comes hope. To be really new, the new human beings must be persons of hope and of joy in the building of a more just world. They are not moved by despair but by hope, because despair tends toward suicide and death, and hope tends to life and to giving. It may at times be hope against all hope, but therein can be seen joy and the security of one who is above humans and their thoughts, the impulse of a vocation to build the reign, which fundamentally is the reign of God, because God is its final goal and its constant motive. Latin America, which has so often been called the continent of hope, is exactly that in multitudes of persons full of hope, and not merely just as a pure natural potentiality not yet developed.

It is an open and untiring hope. The new human being is an open human being who does not absolutize any achievement in the illusion of making something finite into something infinite. The horizon is necessary as a limit that gives orientation, but it is more necessary as a permanent opening for the one who moves forward. To absolutize wealth, power, the organization, the institution, and such is to make idols of them, and it makes the idolater a closed and subjugated person. Such a one is the opposite of the person who is open to a God who is ever greater and to a reign that is to be historicized in an ever-greater proximity to reality that, for various reasons, overcomes each partial achievement and overcomes it qualitatively by making out new developments that are logically and conceptually unforeseeable.

Thus one arrives at not only a new relationship among human beings but also a new relationship with nature. When the first inhabitants of Latin

America maintained that no one can own the earth, that it cannot be the property of anyone in particular, because it is a mother goddess that gives life to so many people, they maintained a respectful and worshipful relationship with nature. Nature cannot be seen merely as raw material or a place to invest; it is a manifestation and gift of God that is to be enjoyed with veneration and not ill-treated with contempt and exploitation.

To make all this possible, liberation theology outlines a new human being, at once contemplative and active, one who transcends both leisure and business. Activity is not sufficient, and contemplation is not enough. Against the temptation of sloth hidden in the leisure of contemplation, the urgency of the task impels to efficacious action, for the seriousness of the problems admits no delay. Against the temptation of activism concealed as the constant creation of new opportunities, the emptiness and destructiveness of its promises demand the wealth of contemplation. Action without contemplation is empty and destructive, while contemplation without action is paralyzing and deceptive. The new human beings are hearers and doers of the Word who discern the signs of the times and accomplish what is offered them as promise.

Other historical features of Jesus' life ought to be projected also on this new human being who dawns on Latin America's horizon already in the poor and in those who have cast their lot with them. But those features pointed out here, especially when they make explicit reference to a God ever present, in whom and to whom is confided the ultimate meaning of the seed sown, are those which unify and nuance those other features of Jesus' life that are taken on with distinct nuances, and especially with different concretions, according to the particular vocation of each person.

Between the negation that overcomes the old human being and the affirmation that realizes the new one, between the propheticism that denies by affirming and the utopia that affirms by denying, the Latin American praxis of Christian faith begins to open up new ways, good ways for all human beings, good ways to build a new earth and a new world.

The creation of *the new earth* implies the utopia of a new economic order, a new social order, a new political order, and a new cultural order. The so-called New World, far from being really new, became, especially in Latin America, an impoverished imitation of the old. Only now that the earlier model has failed is there a disposition to raise a really new world based on its negation.

This is not to remain on the level of voluntaristic idealisms. There are historical inertia, quasi-necessary laws, and a weight of tradition that cannot be abolished but that must be countered and, as far as possible, transformed by the force of the utopian ideal that arises from an objective and not merely intentional need to overcome the grave and universal evils of the present.

The existence of historical evolution's own dynamisms, never completely dominated by any historical subject whatever, cannot be ignored. But that is no reason to accept an absolute historical determinism that leads to fatalism or that, at best, merely permits an attempt to improve the structural whole by the improvement of each individual or of some of the social groups. The alternative proposal of "every man for himself" in this world disorder may be the momentary solution for a few, but it is the ruin of the majority. Hence utopia, the recourse to the utopian ideal as the effective force assimilated by many, is necessary to counteract and even to direct what otherwise becomes the blind and mechanical course of history. It is not correct that the freedom of each will lead to the freedom of all, when the inverse is much more real: general freedom is what will make possible the freedom of each one. And that ideal of realizing utopia can become the principle of freedom and of spirituality incorporated through the subjectivity of persons into the determinism and the materiality of the historical processes. From this perspective Marx's passage in "A Contribution to the Critique of Hegel's Philosophy of Right" could be read in a radically new form: "It is true that the weapon of criticism cannot substitute for the criticism of weapons, that material force must be overcome by material force; but theory also becomes material force as soon as it takes possession of the masses."[21] The utopian ideal, when it is presented historically as gradually realizable and is assumed by the mass of the people, comes to be a stronger force than the force of arms; it is at once a material and a spiritual force, present and future, hence able to overcome the material-spiritual complexity with which the course of history presents itself.

In the *economic order*, Christian utopia, seen from Latin America and arising from real historicized propheticism in a specific situation, proposes a civilization of poverty to take the place of the present civilization of wealth. From a more sociological than humanistic perspective, this same utopia can be expressed by proposing a civilization of work to take the place of the dominant civilization of capital.

If the world as a totality has come to be shaped above all as a civilization of capital and of wealth in which the former more objectively and the latter more subjectively have been the principal elements that propel, shape, and direct present-day civilization, and if this of itself has already contributed all that it had that is positive and is now causing constantly greater and graver ills, what must be favored is not its correction but its replacement by something better, by its contrary—that is, by a civilization of poverty. From the time of Jesus, whenever poverty is preferred to riches in order to enter God's reign, a powerful backlash [*un gran rechazo*] arises on the part of those who are rich or have made riches the essential foundation of their

---

[21] Marx, "A Contribution to the Critique of Hegel's Philosophy of Right."

lives. But what Jesus proposed as personal ideal can and must be expanded to socio-historical reality, with suitable adaptation.

The civilization of wealth and of capital is the one that, in the final analysis, proposes the private accumulation of the greatest possible capital on the part of individuals, groups, multinationals, states, or groups of states as the fundamental basis of development. Likewise, the possessive accumulation—whether by individuals or families—of the greatest possible degree of wealth, serves as the fundamental basis for their own security and for the possibility of ever growing consumption as the basis of their own happiness. We cannot deny that this kind of civilization—prevailing in the East as well as in the West and deservedly called capitalist civilization (whether state capitalism or private capitalism)—has brought benefits to humanity that as such should be preserved and furthered (scientific and technical development, new modes of collective consciousness, and so forth). But these civilizations have brought greater evils, and their self-correction processes are not sufficient for reversing their destructive course.

In consequence, seeing the problem in its worldwide totality from the perspective of real needs and of the expectations of the greater part of the world's population, that civilization of wealth and capital must be radically overcome. On this point the church's social doctrine, especially in its new formulation by John Paul II in *Laborem Exercens,* is to be added in a very significant way to the established demands of liberation theology. Materialist economism, which shapes the civilization of wealth, is not ethically acceptable in its own internal dynamism, and much less so in its real effects. Instead of materialist economism, a materialist humanism should be proposed, which, acknowledging and therefore basing itself on the complexly material condition of human beings, would avoid every type of idealistic solution to the real problems of people. This materialist humanism aims to overcome materialist economism, since it would no longer be economic matter that finally determines everything else, as is the case in any type of civilization of capital and wealth, but human material complex and open, which conceives human beings as the limited but real subjects of their own history.

The civilization of poverty, on the other hand, founded on a materialist humanism transformed by Christian light and inspiration, rejects the accumulation of capital as the engine of history and the possession and enjoyment of wealth as the principle of humanization. It makes the universal satisfaction of basic needs the principle of development and the growth of shared solidarity the foundation of humanization.

The civilization of poverty is so named in contrast to the civilization of wealth, and not because it proposes universal pauperization as an ideal of life. Certainly, the Christian evangelical tradition, in the strict sense, has an enormous distrust of wealth, following in this the teaching of Jesus, a teaching much clearer and more forceful than others might be that are presented as such. Likewise, the great saints of the church's history, often in open struggles for reform against church authorities, have incessantly preached the Christian and human advantages of material poverty. These are two aspects that cannot be ignored, because in the case of the great religious founders—for example, in the case of Saint Ignatius Loyola in his deliberations on poverty—explicit reference is made not only to the personal, but also to the institutional. But, even admitting and taking account of such considerations, which call into question wealth in itself, what is here meant to be emphasized is the dialectical relationship between wealth and poverty, and not poverty in itself. In a world sinfully shaped by the dynamism of capital and wealth, it is necessary to stir up a different dynamism that will overcome it salvifically.

This is achieved, for the moment, through an economic arrangement that relies on and directly and immediately addresses the satisfaction of the basic needs of all humans. Only this orientation responds to a fundamental right of human beings, without the observance of which their dignity is disrespected, their reality violated, and world peace endangered.

In regard to identifying basic needs, even accounting for cultural and individual differences that give rise to distinct subjectifications of those needs, not much discussion is needed if one looks at the conditions of extreme poverty or destitution of more than half of the human race. Such needs must be considered to be, first of all, proper nourishment, minimal housing, basic healthcare, primary education, sufficient employment, and so forth. This is not to say that this exhausts the horizon of economic development. It is simply a point of departure and of fundamental reference, a sine qua non of any sort of development. The great task remaining is for all people to be able to gain access to the satisfaction of those needs, not as crumbs fallen from the tables of the rich, but as the main portion from humanity's table. With the satisfaction of basic needs assured as the primary phase of a liberation process, people would be free to be what they want to be, provided that what they want is not a new mechanism of domination.

Rather than capital accumulation, the civilization of poverty proposes as dynamizing principle the dignifying of work, of work that will have as its principal object not the production of capital but the perfecting of the human being. Work, viewed at once as the personal and collective means to assure the satisfaction of basic needs and as a form of self-realization, would overcome different forms of the exploitation of self and other, and would likewise overcome inequalities that are both an affront and the cause of domination and antagonism.

It is not merely a matter of the new human beings ceasing to make wealth the fundamental idol to which they offer all they have: their ability to work, their moral principles, health, leisure, family relationships, and so on. It is, above all, a matter of making a society that, negatively, does not oblige one to make wealth the supreme value because without it one is lost. (For what does it profit them to save their soul, which is not seen and not esteemed, if they lose the world, which is seen and is most esteemed?)[22] Positively, such a society is structured so that one is not required to keep looking for wealth in order to have all that is needed for human liberation and fulfill-ment. It is clear that a society not structured by the laws of capital, but one giving primacy to the dynamism of humanizing work, would be shaped in a way very different from the present one, because the shaping principle is totally different. The humanistic and moral failure of present society, of the present earth, shaped according to capital's dictates, has begun in vari-ous ways to move those in the more or less marginal vanguards to shape a different society, even though for the moment that is by escaping from the structures and dynamisms that currently prevail. The definitive solution, however, cannot be in escaping from this world and confronting it with a sign of prophetic protest, but in entering into it to renew it and transform it in the direction of the utopia of the new earth.

In part, this will be gradually achieved if a fundamental characteristic of the civilization of poverty, shared solidarity, grows positively stronger, in contrast to the closed and competitive individualism of the society of wealth. To see others not as part of oneself, yet to see oneself in unity and communion with others, combines well with what is deepest in Christian inspiration and goes along with one of the best tendencies of Latin America's popular sectors, which unfolds in contrast to disruptive, individualistic tendencies. This solidarity is facilitated in the common enjoyment of com-mon property.

The private appropriation of common property is not needed in order to care for it and enjoy it. When the church's social doctrine, following Saint Thomas, holds that private appropriation of goods is the best practical manner for their primordial common destiny to be fulfilled in an orderly way, it is making a concession to "the hardness of their hearts," but "in the beginning it was not so."[23] Only because of greed and selfishness, connatu-ral to original sin, can it be said that private ownership of property is the best guarantee of productive advancement and social order. But if "where sin abounded, grace abounded more" is to have historical verification, it is necessary to proclaim in a utopian way that a new earth with new human beings must be shaped with principles of greater altruism and solidarity.[24]

---

[22] See Mark 8:36; Matthew 16:26.—*Trans.*

[23] Ellacuría alludes to a passage in the Gospel of Matthew dealing with divorce law (Mt 19:8).–*Trans.*

[24] Here the allusion is to Paul's Letter to the Roman (Rom 5:20).–*Trans.*

The great benefits of nature (the air, the seas and beaches, the mountains and forests, the rivers and lakes, in general all the natural resources for production, use, and enjoyment) need not be privately appropriated by any individual person, group, or nation, and in fact they are the grand medium of communication and common living.

If a social order were achieved in which basic needs were satisfied in a stable manner and were guaranteed, and the common sources of personal development were made possible, so that the security and the possibilities of personal development were guaranteed, the present order based on the accumulation of private capital and material wealth could be considered as a prehistoric and pre-human stage. The utopian ideal is not that all are to have much by means of private and exclusive appropriation, but that all are to have what is necessary and that the non-acquisitive and nonexclusive use and enjoyment of what is primarily common be open to all. The indispensable dynamism of personal initiative cannot be confused with the natural-original dynamism of private and privatizing initiative. Nor is excluding others as competitors to one's selfhood the only way to work for oneself or to be oneself.

An economic system that is oriented by these principles and that favors the development of the new human being should be the new utopian system of an economy at the service of human beings, which certainly would lead to a new earth. There is a common complaint today that human beings currently are subordinated to the economy and the economy is not subordinated to human beings. Although this phenomenon indicates, among other things, the predominance of what is common and structural over what is individual and integral, the way in which the phenomenon appears—the dominance of the economic over the human—is not acceptable as the utopian ideal and is far less compatible with the Christian ideal.

Which of the two great economic arrangements available today, capitalist or socialist, is better suited for the attainment of that utopian ideal?

Capitalist models have been patently dominant for decades in Latin America, and the failure of those models is utterly clear. It will be said that they have not been sufficiently capitalist. However, if that is so, it has not been because of opposition to capitalism, but because of the objective inadequacy of imposing a capitalist system in a situation like that of Latin America. Capitalist systems in Latin America have been unable to satisfy the basic needs of the greater part of the population. They have created bitter inequalities between the few who have much and the many who have little. They have led to a gigantic foreign debt imposed on human beings who in no way enjoyed or received benefit from the loans. They have frequently produced deep economic crises and they have promoted an immoral culture of consumption and of easy profit. Sadly, all this has been done by persons and classes that consider themselves Catholic and who see no contradiction between their economic praxis and their Christian praxis. From this reality, the least that can be said is that only a radical transformation of the capitalist economic arrangement is minimally reconcilable with what the Christian utopia is. Marxism, insofar as it is the great contradictor of that arrangement, insofar as it profoundly attacks the spirit of capitalism and analyzes the mechanisms that sustain it, and insofar as it proclaims in a utopian way the liberation of human beings through the liberation of labor, plays a far-reaching prophetic and utopian role in Latin America and offers a scientific method for puzzling out the profound dynamisms of the capitalist system.

In a different way, the economic results—later we will turn to the political ones—of the socialist arrangements are not satisfactory either, at least for entering the global competition. The recent attempts by the larger socialist nations to correct their economic systems with procedures more proper to the opposing system, without signifying the abandonment of what is principial in their own system, point to certain limitations that well deserve to be taken into account. On the other hand, it would be premature to condemn beforehand the failure of the reformed socialist models because of what is presently happening in Nicaragua, although it would be a mistake to ignore the real difficulties which that system has in the concrete way it exists, considering the places and the times. Even the Cuban model, although it has achieved the best satisfaction of basic needs in all of Latin America in a relatively short time, still has intrinsic difficulties that can be overcome only with a massive external support. Hence, there are also serious problems in the realization of the socialist model as the most effective instrument to historicize Christian utopia.

Nevertheless, it can be argued that, in economic matters, the socialist ideal is closer than the capitalist to the utopian demands of God's reign. The socialist economic ideal rests on profound values of the human being, but it does not prosper economically precisely because of its moral idealism, which does not take into account the empirical state of human nature. The capitalist economic ideal rests, at least in part, on the selfish vices of human nature. In this sense it is not more realistic, but it is more pragmatic, than its opponent. For that reason it has superior economic success. It could be said, therefore, that if the new human being were to be attained, the socialist arrangement would function better, whereas under the dominion of the old human being, structures that are fundamentally unjust for the greater part of the world's population work better. For this reason, although one cannot be naive in recommending one or other mediation of the reign, the Christian utopia, which strives for a new human being on a new earth, cannot help inclining in economic matters toward formulations that are closer to socialism than to capitalism as far as Latin America and, more generally, the Third World are concerned. It is not too much to recall that the church's social teaching has been drawing closer to this way of seeing things.

The objection can be made that the satisfaction of basic needs is better assured in the capitalist countries than in the socialist countries. But the objection is not so solid if one considers, first, that the capitalist countries take care of a much smaller part of the world population and, second, that this satisfaction is achieved at very high cost to a great part of that capitalist population and, third, that the system is not universalizable, given the limited world resources and the private appropriation of those same resources by a few privileged countries.

In both cases, although not equally because of differing situations, propheticism and Christian utopia need to be critical of the theory and the practice of the dominant economic systems. At times the church's social teaching has been too naive and tolerant toward the theory and, above all, toward the practice of capitalism for fear of losing patronages and for fear of the Marxist regimes. But liberation theology has also on occasions been naive and tolerant toward the theory and practice of Marxism because of a certain inferiority complex before the commitment of the revolutionaries. Without ignoring the difficult relationship of propheticism and utopia with the historical mediations—one that should not be anathematized from an unreal purism—what finally is important to underline is that, whatever the case, the civilization of work and of poverty must take the place of the civilization of capital and of wealth. And it would seem—and this is a most serious problem—that the civilization of capital and wealth is imposing itself worldwide, both where there is private capitalism and where there is state capitalism. Hence, Christian propheticism and utopia have a permanent task of leavening to do.

Corresponding to that new economic order, there needs to emerge *a new social order*—both vigorous and with multiple centers of power—in which it will be possible for the people to be increasingly the agents of their own destiny and to have greater possibilities for creative freedom and for participation. Just as it is the people of God that should have priority in the reign of God, and not a set of institutional superstructures, as sometimes happens, so in the history of this world it should be the social groups that carry the weight of history, and they should carry it on their own. In other words, the social should be given more weight than the political, without individualism thereby becoming the highest form of humanization. The social dimension should prevail over the political dimension but not take its place.

Between individualism and state interventionism [*estatismo*] a strong type of society should be built to overcome the licentiousness of the former and the dominating interference of the latter. It is not a question of compromising between two existing extremes but of finding new forms to overcome both existing models by negating them. Of course, undoing state interventionism must not be understood as a neoliberal demand for a lesser weight of the state before the demands of so-called private initiative and the laws of the marketplace. Rather, undoing state interventionism involves a socialization that promotes communitarian and social initiative delegated neither to the state nor to parties nor to vanguards nor to bosses. It is a question of overcoming social apathy in the management of historical processes without for this reason lapsing into either gremialisms or corporativisms.[25] Basically what is proposed, positively, is to give more life and decision-making to social enterprises and, negatively, to overcome the disruptive dynamisms of political power. It seeks the communitarian good [*el bien comunitario*] coming from communitarian pressures and through communitarian means without delegating this force to political enterprises, which become autonomous and can never adequately represent the social.

There is no reason to confuse the authority of the public sector with political authority, and there is no reason to accept the reservation of the entire public sector to the state and to political parties, to the detriment of social enterprises, for at bottom this represents a state centralization of social life. The social represents not a middle, or midpoint, but a mediation between the individual and the political, so that the essential communal dimension of the individual is primarily realized not in the political dimension of the state but in the public dimension of the social. At different moments in the Latin American political struggle there has been a certain disdain for parties for the benefit of the popular organizations. But this tendency has not contributed all it could when it has proposed that these popular organizations take on state political power, with the result that they have fallen again into the ill-advised use of politics to further their real interests. Likewise, the church has frequently abdicated its social authority by becoming an appendage of political power, thus impairing its mission and weakening thereby its historical potential to serve the vast numbers of common people.

Regarding the permanent problem of freedom and of equality-justice, the question does not reside in giving primacy to the individual over the state or vice versa. The union of liberty-justice-equality is better achieved in the mediation of the social, which is neither of the state nor of the individual. The mediation of the social permits individual-personal freedom that is not individualistic at the same time that it permits political freedom—that is, the freedom of individuals and groups vis-à-vis the power of the state. What generates real conditions for personal freedom is, first of all, social

---

[25] Gremialists, the main political faction in Chile under Pinochet, were founded at the Catholic University of Santiago by Jaime Guzmán after the failure of the Right in the elections of 1965. Corporativism refers to one or another economic or political model that favors some form of centralized state power.

freedom. In turn, it is not so much the individual as it is the community that becomes the best real and effective guarantee against the domination and oppression of politico-state structures.

This implies that excessive and conflict-producing inequalities are to disappear in the concrete sphere of the social without thereby giving rise to mechanical equalities that do not respond to different preferences in values and to the diversity of contributions by individuals and groups to social well-being. An obligatory equality does not respond to reality and is not demanded by ethical or religious considerations. What must be excluded, for the time being, is the present outrageous difference between those who squander and those who lack enough to subsist, even when there is no causal or functional relation between the poverty and the wealth. What is indeed a pressing obligation is that all be assured of the satisfaction of their basic needs. But beyond that minimal level respect should be given to greater particular choices, to labor, and to productivity, so long as respect is given to equality of opportunities and the processes that lead to pronounced and conflict-provoking inequalities are avoided.

These positions would be normal and reasonable ones for making possible an adequate freedom-justice-equality. But the utopian ideal of Jesus goes much further. Paradoxically, the follower of Jesus seeks to take the last place as the surest way to reach the first,[26] so that one would not be dominant but would be a servant, would not seek one's own honor but that of others. In general, what Jesus' message advocates is exchanging the real dynamisms of this old world, of this old earth, for the dynamisms of God's reign as the utopian ideal of the new earth and as the negation—death and resurrection—of the old one. The tremendous reservations in the New Testament regarding wealth, power, and worldly honors, along with its emphatic proclamation of poverty, service, and the humiliation of the cross, can and should be translated into the realms of the visible and the social. These represent not only a possible ideal for the individual but a model for society. That the realizations of this have not been totally satisfactory—for example, in the case of religious orders, social groups that bring individuals together without leaving them at the mercy of more globalizing institutions—does not keep them from raising the question of the need to give social, historical flesh to the invitation from Jesus to follow him. Social institutions, unlike political ones, can be impregnated with that spirit, which would seem to be reserved for individuals, and this is what the great founders of the religious orders have intended.

The *new political order*, prophetically sketched within the utopian horizon, is based on the attempt to overcome the political models that are

---

[26] "Thus, the last shall be first" (Mt 20:16).—*Eds.*

the result and at the same time the support of both liberal capitalism and Marxist collectivism.

What is being proposed is not a "third way" between liberalism and collectivism in the economic area or between liberal democracy and social democracy in the political. Such a "third way" does not exist in the latest documents of the church, not even as ideal solution.[27] In this historical phase, in which distinct forms of one or the other way can offer themselves, both in the economic and in the political sphere, some appear better than others in their applicability to a specific reality. It would not be hard to prove that some socialist political forms are much better than some capitalist political forms and, vice versa, that some capitalist forms are better than some socialist forms. This appraisal is indeed interesting. It is usually presented as an opening of one system to the other, which in practice brings them nearer to each other in spite of their fundamental differences. Of particular interest are recent, rather widespread efforts to democratize socialism, but there is hardly any equivalent effort toward a much-needed socialization of the democracies, perhaps because the more advanced ones had already done so in some way.

This two-way opening up of each of the systems could be evidence not only of the insufficiency of each but also of a possible leap forward to a now scarcely recognizable new political system. It is one of the few instances where one might appreciate a positive dynamism of history that goes against the blind dynamism of the demands of capital, subject to constant corrections by what might be called the dynamism of humanization-divinization. Signs like the increasingly spontaneous appreciation of human rights, of a greater democratic opening, of a more effective world solidarity, are, among other things, manifestations of the struggle between good and evil, between the closure of the systems and the openness of humanity. They are positive and hopeful signs that can scarcely hide the heaviness and inertia of their opposites, but they nevertheless point toward possibilities of change through reform.

From Latin America, however, the search has been and continues to be for revolutionary change rather than for reformist change. Hence, on occasions the effort has been made to take advantage of the subversive dynamism of the Christian faith, just as the dominant systems have tried to take advantage of the conservative dynamisms of the same faith. The reason is obvious. On the one hand, there is such a degree of structural injustice affecting the very structure of society that it appears indispensable to demand a quick and profound change of structures—that is, a revolution. On the

---

[27] See John Paul II, *Sollicitudo rei socialis*, no. 41.

other hand, the prevailing dynamism does not, in fact, lead to a reform that might build a revolutionary change but instead to a deepening and widening of the structural injustice—and this under the guise of reformism whose path is development.

From this viewpoint it can be affirmed both from the theory about and from the verification of historical reality—and of course from the utopian propheticism—that a revolution in the present dynamisms and structures is needed, an anti-capitalist revolution—"anti" to the capitalism found in the underdeveloped and oppressed countries—and an anti-imperialist revolution that is "anti" to every type of external empire that tries to impose its own interests. The question is not, then, if a revolution is needed or not, but what revolution is needed and how to bring it about.

The revolution that is needed, the necessary revolution, will be the one that intends freedom deriving from and leading to justice and justice deriving and leading to freedom. This freedom must come out of liberation and not merely out of liberalization—whether economic or political liberalization—in order to overcome in this way the dominant "common evil" and build a "common good," a common good understood in contrast to the common evil and sought from a preferential option for the vast majority of the people.

The dogmatic imposition that says liberal democracy is the best path for combining freedom and justice in whatever time and circumstance is simply presumptuous, many times concealing elite and vested interests. Likewise, the dogmatic imposition of the so-called social or popular democracies as the best and only way adequately to join freedom and justice does not square with some of the forms in which they have actually appeared. It would be better to stick to the more radical principle that it is reality as experienced by the vast majority of the people—and not dogmatic principles or even historical models—that should be set as the criterion of selection in the process of authentic self-determination. The real measure of a duly ordered and quantified system of human rights takes precedence over the formal criteria of one or other type of democracy.

From this perspective social liberation appears more necessary and urgent than political liberation in the Central American countries and in the greater part of the Third World, something that is perhaps not the case in other situations in the First World and the Second World. Of course, they are not mutually exclusive and, even less, contradictory. But social liberation, which rests on satisfying the basic needs of the masses and supports the autonomous exercise of social life, is above political freedom, which intends equality of opportunity for attaining political power, and above what are called strictly political freedoms, as distinct from fundamental freedoms.

This is because, in order to be enjoyed by most people, political freedoms require liberation from basic needs and they also require social freedom, even though these in turn demand arenas of political freedom.

For all that, in the present stage of the realization of God's reign, with the greater part of the population living in extreme poverty and oppression, the socialist ideal appears more connatural to the profound inspiration of the Christian message than the capitalist ideal, although neither of them is to be identified with the Christian utopian ideal. Another matter altogether is the possibility of actually realizing each of these two ideals.

Many trials and attempts to formulate a Christian correction of capitalism have already been made, and the results have not been good even for satisfying basic needs, not to mention the area of ethics—of forming a new human being and a new earth better conformed to the utopian ideals of God's reign. Although in the church's social teaching useful corrections of capitalism have been formulated, frequently the mistake has been made of thinking that capitalism is fundamentally good and is the system more conformed to Christian values. On the other hand, while the influence of the Christian faith and even of the historical forms of Christendom in correcting capitalism (as it has existed in Latin America, where the official faith has been Christian since the time of the conquest) has not been completely ineffective, it shows notable weaknesses. These, in turn, have made the church worldly and capitalist more than they have made the structures and behavior of the world Christian and evangelical.

The attempt to make the Christian faith the yeast and leaven of Marxist positions has been put to the test much less. Something has been done in this regard, as Latin American revolutionaries from Fidel Castro to the Sandinista leaders and those of the Salvadoran FMLN have acknowledged. Liberation theology in different forms has sought to contribute important corrections to Marxism, as the church's social teaching had sought to do until recently with capitalism. Not that liberation theology proposes that the church surrender its social and political function into the hands of movements, parties, or vanguards that would represent it. On the contrary, liberation theology demands a direct and independent commitment of the church to the defense of human rights and to the promotion of greater justice and freedom, especially for those most in need. But it does propose that the Marxist forms of revolution be profoundly transformed—and not only the human beings who bring them about—because in their theory and, especially, in their practice, Marxists tend toward reductionisms and knee-jerk reactions [efectivismos] little in accord with the Christian utopian ideal. In turn, the experience of the best of Marxism has served to spur the church and has obliged it to turn—to be converted—toward radical points in the Christian message that the passage of years and inculturation into capitalist forms had left merely ritualized and ideologized without historical value for individuals and peoples.

The *new cultural order* ought to free itself from the models of Western culture, for these leave much to desire when it comes to achieving the perfection of the human person and the happiness of the human family. Only by removing and freeing oneself from the deception of the Western culture it has already encountered can it begin to seek another type of culture, at least as a way to true human progress.

The consumer cultural order is a product of the consumer economic order. Hence it is not adequate for mobilizing a civilization of poverty, which should have its corresponding cultural development. The cultural tradition will not be enlarged by following the road of permanently evolving entertainments. To confuse being entertained with being happy favors and promotes the consumption of products by inducing needs through the marketplace, but at the same time it invents and fosters an enormous inner emptiness. The civilization of poverty, far from provoking consumption and activity in the cultural sphere, tends to further what is natural and to facilitate attitudes of contemplation and communication more than attitudes of activity-consumption in some and of pure passivity-receptivity in others.

The huge cultural wealth amassed through thousands of years of human life, diversified in multiple forms and in various times and places, cannot be permitted to be overwhelmed by cultural modes that seek in what is new the affirmation and consolidation of human beings that are not new and only try to sell newness. It is necessary to recover this secular wealth, not to remain immersed in it conservatively but rather to move toward novelties that do not just substitute for former ones but surpass *(superar)* them. Many of the technological and consumerist models are losing sight of and losing the use of reality—if not actually murdering it—along with the deep meaning of the great cultural achievements born of a true cultural identity. It is through one's own identity that one can assimilate the values of other cultures without becoming lost in them. For example, the case of the inculturated assimilation of the Christian faith made by the liberation theology movement is a good demonstration of how a universalizable reality can, at the same time, be historicized, particularized, and enriched.

Culture, above all, must be liberating. It must liberate from ignorance, from fears, from inner and outer pressures, in search of a fuller and fuller truth and more and more fulfilling reality. In this liberation process culture will continue generating real freedom. This freedom will not be reduced to picking—rather than thoughtfully choosing—from among different deals offered under this or that set of conditions. Rather, this freedom will be oriented toward the construction of its own being, as persons, as communities, as peoples and nations, in an effort of creation rather than passive acceptance. Everywhere in the world there is a tremendous cultural imposition from powerful centers that universalize the world's vision and values with the most varied communications media. In various ways this cultural imposition keeps the huge masses of Latin America and of other lands alienated from understanding themselves and from understanding and valuing the world. Something that ought to favor a pluriform unity becomes an impoverishing uniformity. At the same time the facility of the communications media leads to another kind of alienation. These media promote the leap from a primitive state of culture, which is at times a very valuable and healthy state, into sophisticated and decadent phases of a culture imposed more by its milieu—and by its attendant baggage—than by its own basic content.

Here too the question is one of seeking a culture for the majority and not a culture for the elite with much form and little life. That all, if possible, and not just a few, have life and have it in abundance should be the motto of the new culture on the new earth.[28] This is a really utopian task but one that is propelled—and the propulsion is seen in many places—by the real propheticism that repudiates and overcomes the open ulcerous sores of an alienating and, at bottom, dehumanizing culture.

The creation of *a new heaven* supposes achieving a new presence of God among humans that will let the old Babylon be transformed into the New Jerusalem.

Certainly, all of the foregoing, expressed under the headings of new human being and new earth, is a very special presence of the Spirit of Christ in the world, sent by the crucified and risen One. But it needs to be made more explicit and more visible, which is what is expressed in the new heaven, not as something superimposed on human beings and on the earth, but as something integrated and structured with them.

So, by *new heaven* there must be understood here that presence of God on the new earth that continues to make possible and to animate God being all in all and in everything (1 Cor 15:28), because Christ is all for all (Col 3:11). It is, therefore, a christological new heaven and not simply the heaven of an abstract God, univocal in his abstraction. Neither does it mean heaven as the final place of those resurrected in grace but the heaven present in our history, the historical and increasingly operative and visible presence of God among human beings and in public human structures. The historical Jesus must be constituted not only the Christ of faith but also the Christ of history. That is, the visible and efficacious historicization of the Pauline affirmation that he is to be all in all and for everything, that the real life of

---

[28] Ellacuría alludes again to the Good Shepherd discourse (Jn 10:10), but he has adapted it. —*Eds.*

humans and institutions—with the essential differences that this life must have in humans and institutions—must no longer be the life that arises from its limited and sinful immanent principles, but the life that arises from the principles that make all things new, that create, regenerate, and transform whatever is insufficient and even sinful in the old creature.

Viewing things in this way, the new heaven exceeds what is habitually understood as church, although not what should be understood as the city of God, and of course as the reign of God. Nevertheless, the reference to the church is indispensable for adequately describing the new heaven, under and in which to live historically, while God's history continues its journey, or God continues to journey through history as the historical Christ.

Indeed, one of the principal forms in which this new heaven ought to be historicized is the church of Christ as the historical body of Jesus crucified and risen.

It is not enough to affirm that the church makes the divine life present to us, transmitted sacramentally. This is important, but it is not enough. For the present, that sacramental presence of the church as a whole and of the distinct sacraments, in which that fundamental sacramentality is actualized (Rahner), needs to be revitalized beyond what is ritual and formal until the effectiveness of the Word and the active correspondence of the one who receives the grace of the sacrament are recovered. To confuse the mystery, which is the sacrament, with a process given in the interiority of the person is to devalue the mysteriousness of the sacrament's efficacy through a sheer assertion that cannot be verified and has no efficacy. Even from this point of view a profound renewal, without which revitalizing sacramental life is unthinkable, is indispensable, prophetically and utopianly.

But the church must go beyond the sacramental realm or, at least, its sacramentality must be understood more widely. For this it needs to be permanently open and attentive to the newness and the universality of the Spirit, which breaks the fossilized routine of the past and the limits of a restricted self-conception. Only a church that lets itself be invaded by the Spirit, the Renewer of all things, and that is attentive to the signs of the times can become the new heaven that the new human being and the new earth need.

The church as institution tends to be more conservative of the past than renewing of the present and creative of the future. Certainly, there are things to preserve; but nothing vital and human, nothing historical, is preserved if it is not maintained in constant renewal. Fear of what is new, of what is not controllable by already established institutional means, has been and still is one of the church's permanent characteristics. When one reviews the positions of the different ecclesiastical authorities previous to the religious renewal movements that have afterward proved to be fundamental for the church's advance (for example, the founding of the great religious orders, new forms of thought, new methods and even new fruits of biblical research, and so on), not to mention positions taken in the face of scientific and political advances, it is difficult to argue that church authority and its institutional organs have been open to the newness of history and to the creative breath of the Spirit.

This opening out from our worldliness toward the Spirit of Christ from earthliness, which entails the following of the historical Jesus, is, however, absolutely indispensable. There is no ecclesiastical authority that can replace this need, for the Spirit of Christ has not delegated the totality of its presence and of its efficacy to any institutional authorities, although their historical corporeity is also a demand of the Spirit. What often happens is that this institutionality configures itself more from the law than from grace, as if the ecclesial institutionality should configure itself more according to sociological and political laws of a totalitarian nature, which are disguised as God's will and proper obedience to God's will, rather than according to the dictates and power of the Spirit. On the other hand, this is not just about any spirit at all that some charismatic might come up with, but it is the Spirit of Jesus, which animated his own conception, was manifest at his baptism, and was evident in his person and in his living, and which he finally promised to send to us when he should no longer be with us.

It is in this context that the signs of the times become present, some in one epoch and some in another, some in certain regions of the world and others elsewhere. It is precisely the signs of the times that provide the element of future and without which an essential element for the interpretation of the word of God, along with of one of the greatest forces of renewal, is lacking. But these are signs of the times framed here and now in the utopia-prophecy dialectic, without which one would fall back into ineffective idealism.

Looking at the current situation of Latin America, the church's renewal and its projection toward the future must be as the church of the poor if it is to become the new heaven. On the one hand, to be a church that really has a preferential option for the poor will be proof and manifestation of the renewing Spirit present in it. On the other, it will be a guarantee that it can become the new heaven of the new earth and of the new human being. But the utopian exercise of prophecy can lead to a church (up to now configured in great part by the dynamisms of Western capitalism as a church of the rich and of the powerful that, at best, directs toward the poorest the crumbs falling from the table of abundance) to become converted—in a genuine "conversion"—into a church of the poor that really can be the heaven of a new earth where a civilization of poverty becomes dominant and where humans are not only intentionally and spiritually poor, but really and materially so, that is, detached from what is superfluous and from the constraining dynamisms of individual monopolizing and collective accumulation. Money can be an incentive for material development for human beings and for states, but it has always been, and it continues to be more and more, a deadly poison for an authentic humanism and, of course, for an authentic Christianity. That this arouses a powerful rejection from the world, that this is a scandal and even an affront to the civilization of wealth, is one more proof of the continuity of these ideas and of this practice with the fullest way of the gospel, always attacked with the same reproaches.

It is in this sense that the church of the poor becomes the new heaven, which as such is needed to overcome the civilization of wealth and build the civilization of poverty, the new earth where the new human being will live in a welcoming and not in a degraded home. Here there will be a great confluence of the Christian message without disfiguring glosses and the present degraded situation in the greater part of the world. This is certainly true of Latin America, still for the most part a repository of the Christian faith, even if this faith has not up until now done very much to make of this region a new earth, regardless of the fact that it was initially presented as the new world. Prophetically negating a church that is the old heaven for a civilization of wealth and power, and utopianly affirming a church as a new heaven for a civilization of poverty, constitute together an irrefutable claim pressed by the signs of the times and by the soteriological dynamism of Christian faith that is historicized in new human beings. These new human beings, for their part, keep on announcing, firmly and steadfastly although always in darkness, a future that is ever greater, because beyond all these futures, following one upon another, they catch sight of the God who saves, the God who liberates.

—Translation by James Brockman,
J. Matthew Ashley, and Kevin F. Burke, SJ

3

Monseñor Romero's Impact on Ignacio Ellacuría

JON SOBRINO, SJ

You have developed important themes in the thought of Ignacio Ellacuría at this meeting.[1] Upon asking me to say a few words at this point, I thought that I would take up a theme that is not normally the object of academic lectures. I mean the impact that Monseñor Romero had on Ignacio Ellacuría, and this at the profoundest depths of his person. I am talking about that dimension of reality where a human being finds himself or herself before a mystery, before God, and the faith that makes it possible for him or her to correspond to God. Or before an enigma, with questions that have no answer, or with the silence that can come with it.

It is not easy—in the end, it is not possible—to penetrate adequately into this ultimate dimension of another person. Neither does it seem to me to be possible to talk as if the words *God* and *faith* were univocal, words that we could understand and manage adequately. Saying these things will always be a sort of stammering, then, although I think that it is, indeed, possible to find some pathways for doing it responsibly. This is what I will try to do in what follows.

To be precise, we are going to investigate the impact that Monseñor Romero had on Ignacio Ellacuría's faith: on the content of his *fides quae*, if and how he understood the reality of God; and on his *fides qua*, if and how he gave himself to God. We will speak about this faith using traces. But in fact, when it comes to the impact that Monseñor Romero had on Ellacuría there are more than traces; rather, we can construct more of an argument.

---

[1] This is the written text of a reflection shared with the members of the International Colloquium on the Thought of Ignacio Ellacuría at its meeting held in San Salvador on August 12, 2013.—*Eds.*

I have already reflected and written on this theme some years ago.[2] I said then that when it came to what was ultimate, to his faith, Ellacuría was carried by Monseñor Romero. Now I would like to add a few reflections that can offer something a little bit new. It will have to do with something that Ellacuría himself said on various occasions—something novel and audacious—about the relationship between Monseñor Romero and God. In my opinion this was his most radical way of formulating it: "With Monseñor Romero God passed through El Salvador." I will use this perspective to organize our reflections as well.

1. Ellacuría showed his conviction that God, to be precise, the God of Jesus—and, in principle, that which is ultimate and good in reality—made Godself present in Monseñor Romero. And at the same time he saw that Monseñor responded and corresponded to this God—to this ultimate and good reality.

2. For this reason, above all, Monseñor Romero had an impact on Ignacio Ellacuría in a way that was distinct from, and more definitive than, the impact that other persons in his life, and from whom he learned, had on him. He came to be—and I think he remained—a disciple of Monseñor Romero more than of any other person.

3. Ultimately, in my opinion, Ellacuría "was carried" in his own faith by the faith of Monseñor Romero. By this I want to express the dimension of gift and of grace that became present in his life, and the way that it became present in him.

It wasn't always this way. Up until 1977 the two failed to meet for years. Let just one example suffice to show this. Under the charge of the Episcopal Conference of El Salvador, Monseñor Romero wrote a critical review of Ellacuría's book *Freedom Made Flesh* in 1974.[3] Ellacuría was for his part a critic of Monseñor, since, although the latter accepted Medellín in theory

---

[2] Jon Sobrino, "Monseñor Romero y la fe de Ignacio Ellacuría," in *Ignacio Ellacuría: Aquella libertad esclarecida,* ed. Jon Sobrino and Rolando Alvarado (San Salvador: UCA Editores, 1999), 11–26; in English as "Archbishop Romero and the Faith of Ignacio Ellacuría," in *Witnesses to the Kingdom: The Martyrs of El Salvador and the Crucified Peoples* (Maryknoll, NY: Orbis Books, 2003), 208–17.

[3] The critique was based on theological arguments, but without the spirit of Medellín. It was a serious and educated work and not done just out of prejudices (often offensive). I mention this because it does not always happen this way when it comes to critiques by some members of the hierarchy of those who consider themselves to be liberation theologians. The Spanish original of the book that Monseñor Romero critiqued was Ignacio Ellacuría, *Teología Política* (San Salvador: Ediciones del Secretariado Social Interdiocesano, 1973); it also appeared as *Freedom Made Flesh: The Mission of Christ and His Church,* trans. John Drury (Maryknoll, NY: Orbis Books, 1976).—*Trans.*

because it was a document of the Latin American hierarchy, he did not feel comfortable with the documents and showed a great deal of mistrust for and criticism of those priests, seminarians, and those communities (the UCA too) that were trying to put its teachings into practice.

Everything changed on March 12, 1977, with the assassination of Rutilio Grande.[4] From that moment the encounter of Romero and Ellacuría saw more and more of a coincidence of historical vision for Salvadoran society, more and more agreement on what following Jesus and the praxis of the church had to be. At the base of everything there was an understanding of God as a God of life, struggling against the idols of death. Personally the two came to be very close. In the case of Ellacuría, whom I knew more closely, his relationship with Monseñor went very deep. Ignacio Ellacuría ended up venerating Monseñor Romero.

I continue now by developing the three points given above, quoting at length from Ellacuría from time to time.

The God Who Passed Through El Salvador with Monseñor Romero

Ellacuría spoke about Monseñor Romero on a number of occasions and, in order to speak adequately about him, Ellacuría felt the need to speak about "something else" at the same time. In a programmatic text he wrote, "It is difficult to talk about Monseñor Romero without finding oneself compelled to talk about *the people*."[5] He used to insist in this way on the intimate relationship between Monseñor Romero and the people, the historical Salvadoran people.

Following the logic of this formulation my assertion is that, for Ellacuría it is difficult to talk about Monseñor Romero without finding oneself compelled to talk about *God*.

Let us make a slight clarification. It is not just by a personal whim that I use an identical way of speaking to relate Monseñor Romero to "the people," a historical reality, and to relate him to God, a transcendent reality. Ellacuría himself made a point of doing this, and took advantage of it in a speech that he gave when the UCA conferred, posthumously, an honorary doctorate

---

[4] See Jon Sobrino, *Monseñor Romero* (San Salvador: UCA Editores, 2013), 16–22; idem, *Archbishop Romero: Memories and Reflections* (Maryknoll, NY: Orbis Books, 1990), 6–13.

[5] Ignacio Ellacuría, "El verdadero pueblo de Dios según Monseñor Romero," *ECA* 392 (1981), 530; also in *Escritos Teológicos*, vol. 2 (San Salvador: UCA Editores, 2000), 357–96.

on Monseñor Romero, on March 22, 1985. Speaking of Monseñor's hope, Ellacuría said:

> His hope was supported by two pillars: a historical pillar, which was his familiarity with the people and to which he attributed an inexhaustible capacity to find solutions for the most serious problems; and a transcendent pillar, which was his conviction that ultimately God is a God of life and not of death, that what is ultimate about reality is good and not evil.

Let us analyze now what Ellacuría said about God passing through El Salvador with Monseñor Romero.

That Ellacuría—an intellectual, philosopher, and above all a theologian—would talk about God is something we can take for granted. He did it in a multitude of theological writings very much in a biblical vein, dealing with themes in Christology and ecclesiology, and themes such as justice, spirituality, liberation, and faith. And, as I just said, he talked about God by talking about Monseñor Romero.

All of this could be taken as the most natural thing in the world, but we need to take one more step. Ellacuría understood and formulated the relationship between God and Monseñor Romero in a novel way. It was a way that, in my opinion, theologians and people in the church are not accustomed to using. Ellacuría certainly talked about Monseñor Romero as good news, as a prophet, as a follower of Jesus, and as a man of God. But without any kind of excessive piety at all (which he was not given to anyway), but rather with existential and intellectual conviction, he discerned in Monseñor Romero "the true signs of the presence of God or of God's plans."[6] Monseñor Romero was a theologal sign of the times.[7]

---

[6] This is how *Guadium et spes* describes the meaning of "signs" (no. 11).

[7] *Theologal* is a technical term used by both Ellacuría and Sobrino (coming ultimately from Zubiri), not to be confused with *theological*. A first approximation of what it means can be reached by means of an analogy with other disciplines and what they study. For example, just as the relevance and relative autonomy of sociology are premised on the existence and relative autonomy of a social dimension to reality that is not reducible to other dimensions (to the realms studied by biology and psychology, for instance), so too the relevance and relative autonomy of *theology* presume the reality of a "theologal" dimension to all reality, which is most definitely related to all the other dimensions in the most intimate way imaginable, but cannot be reduced to them without distortion. Just as sociology must determine the appropriate tools and loci to gain access to the social dimension of reality it wishes to understand, so too must theology find the tools and loci to gain access to the "theologal dimension," which ultimately has to do with the whole trinitarian sweep of God's relationship to reality in creation, redemption, sanctification, and ultimate consummation. Saying that Monseñor Romero is a "theologal sign of the times" can be taken, then, to mean, among other things, that he provides a privileged

With all the requisite analogies and without falling into any facile literalism, Ellacuría's way of talking about Monseñor calls to mind what the first Christians did with Jesus of Nazareth. They *proclaimed* the life and praxis of Jesus as good news: "he went around doing good." They *explained* in a succinct way in what this good news consisted: "healing those possessed by the devil." And from having confirmed this historically, and because of that, *they found themselves compelled to talk about his special relationship to God*: "God was with him." This is what Peter says in Cornelius's house (Acts 10:38ff.).

Ellacuría saw that Monseñor also "went around doing good." He talked about this in great detail, as we will see later. And he concluded, "God was—especially—present in Monseñor Romero." The words might be surprising, or even shocking; but for anyone who knew Ellacuría it is unthinkable that in speaking this way about "God," and much less about "God and Monseñor Romero," he was speaking off the cuff, without thinking about it. He was speaking in all seriousness.

I am going to recall three texts in which Ellacuría puts Monseñor Romero in relationship to God. The first is from the beginning of his ministry as archbishop. The second, a few months after his murder. The third, and most radically formulated, from Monseñor's funeral mass at the UCA. In each of these we will consider *a theologal affirmation, brief and lapidary*, on the relationship between Monseñor Romero and God, and *explanatory affirmations about the historical reality of Monseñor*, in which Ellacuría found a foundation for the lapidary affirmations, theologal and doxological,[8] once again, applying all requisite analogies.

"I have seen the finger of God in your action."

"From this far-off exile I want to let you know of my admiration and my respect." This is from his letter of April 9, 1977, to Monseñor Romero, written from exile in Madrid, concerning his reaction to the murder of Rutilio Grande on March 9.[9] And he continues, "I have seen the finger of God in

---

locus for attaining to, understanding more deeply, and responding more faithfully to this God-world relationship.—*Trans.*

    8 By "doxological affirmation" I understand one that affirms what God *is* in Godself (without human reason now being able to gain mastery over what it affirms) on the basis of an affirmation that is in principle historical, positing an action on God's part—God *does* something. This follows Pannenberg's line of thinking. Ellacuría grasped that Monseñor Romero *did* many things, and based on this, he made a leap to what Monseñor *was*.

    9 In 1976, as in every other year, Ellacuría went to Madrid for the winter months. He was unable to return to the country until August 1978, secretly, and at no little risk to himself.

your action." This is a *theologal* assertion, and he adds three reasons *that explain* why this expression should not be reduced to a mere literary flourish.

I will transcribe the basic points of these reflections, and I will do so almost in their entirety, although lightly edited, since this text sheds a great deal of light on what it was about Monseñor that had an impact on Ellacuría and the degree to which it did. I do this as well because the text is not well known. As I see it, it is one of the best texts of Ellacuría's. Here is what he wrote to Monseñor Romero:

> *The first aspect* that impressed me is *your evangelical spirit.* I understood this from the first moment through Father Arrupe's communication. . . . You immediately perceived the clear meaning of Father Grande's death, the meaning of religious persecution, and you put yourself behind this meaning with all your energy. This shows your sincere faith and Christian discernment.
>
> This brings me to see *a second aspect: a clear Christian discernment.* You, who are familiar with the *Exercises of Saint Ignatius,* know how difficult it is to discern and make decisions following the spirit of Christ and not the spirit of the world, which can present itself *sub angelo lucis,* as an angel of light. You were able to listen to everyone, but ended up deciding for that which seemed most risky to prudent eyes. When it came to the single Mass, to the cancellation of all activities in the schools, to your keeping clear distance from every official act, and so on, you discovered how to discern where the will of God was and how to follow the example and the spirit of Jesus of Nazareth.
>
> I see *the third aspect* as a conclusion from the earlier ones and their confirmation. On this occasion you have built a church, and you have built unity in the church. You know how difficult it is to do these two things in El Salvador today. But the Mass in the Cathedral and the almost complete and unanimous participation of the clergy, of religious, and of so many people of God show that on this occasion you succeeded. You could not have started off on a better foot to build a church and to build unity in the church in the archdiocese. It will not have escaped you that this is hard to do. And you succeeded. And you were able to do it not by taking the paths of flattery or cunning, but by the Gospel path: being faithful to it and being courageous on it. I think that while you continue in this vein and have as your primary criterion the spirit of Christ, lived in a martyrial way, the best part of the church in El Salvador will be with you, and those who need to pull away will do it.
>
> In this hour of trial we can see who are the faithful sons of the church, which continues the life and mission of Jesus, and who are

the ones who want to use the church. It seems to me that in this we have an example in the closing years of Father Grande's life, far removed from the extremisms of the Left, but much more distant from the oppression and from the blandishments of unjust wealth, as Saint Luke says.[10]

In Monseñor's way of acting, full of the gospel and of discernment before God, being everybody's archbishop, but an archbishop with the people and on the people's side, independent of the government, distant from the powerful who wanted to get him on their side, someone who denounced their misdeeds, as well as those of the government: in all of this Ellacuría saw how Monseñor Romero was a follower of Jesus. A man who, listening to everyone, asked himself what it was that God wanted and how he would do it. This is "to discern."[11] A man who was walking with God in history, as Micah asks, and who followed Jesus of Nazareth, the historical and unmanipulable Jesus. A man who, in this walking and in this discerning of fundamentals, laid the groundwork for numerous specific discernments.

Ellacuría saw that, being and acting in this way, Monseñor Romero *responded* to God the way Jesus did. And he saw that by responding in this way to the will of God, Monseñor *corresponded* to God, created an affinity between himself and the reality of God. And this is what allowed Ellacuría to speak of "the finger of God."

Ellacuría scrutinized, to be sure, the signs of the times—signs in a *historical* sense (see *Gaudium et spes,* no. 4) that characterized the Salvadoran reality at that time. But he also discerned "authentic signs of God's presence and purpose in . . . happenings, needs, and desires" (*Gaudium et spes,* no. 11)—signs in the *theologal* sense. For Ellacuría, these signs became present in the being and in the actions of Monseñor Romero. And this same Monseñor, "a man with an evangelical spirit," turned into a theologal sign. In this Monseñor Ellacuría saw the "finger of God."

When it comes to Monseñor Romero's discernment, I think that for Ellacuría—and for me—the greatest historical sign that impressed itself on him was the martyrdom of Rutilio Grande and of many other priests of the crucified people over the course of three years. I think that they became

---

[10] For the full text of this letter, see Chapter 1, "Letter from Ignacio Ellacuría to Monseñor Oscar Romero," in the present volume.–*Eds.*

[11] For a member of the ecclesiastical hierarchy to make discernment before God, and in the end, only before God, is not impossible, of course; but it is not an easy thing because the discernment has to coexist with a special obedience to his superiors in the hierarchy. There are few, like Don Pedro Casaldáliga, who make a free discernment before God "in rebellious fidelity."

for him a theologal sign. In the martyrs and in the crucified people God became present to him.

Concluding his letter, Ellacuría said to Monseñor: "I ask God that all these things continue for the good of all. It has been nothing more than a beginning, but it has been an extraordinary beginning." And he adds, "I pray that he grants you to go forward in the midst of such exceptional difficulties."

"These things" continued for three years. The *beginning* that Monseñor Romero made in Aguilares, next to the bodies of Rutilio Grande, a little boy, an old man, *began* many realities that have come down even to our own days. Some of them have come to us weakened, sometimes greatly weakened. Others have kept their vigor and keep on bearing fruit.

"Monseñor Romero, one sent by God to save his people."

In November 1980, after Monseñor's martyrdom, the journal *Sal Terrae* asked Ellacuría for an article on Monseñor Romero. So he wrote "Monseñor Romero, One Sent by God to Save His People."[12] The theologal affirmation is "Monseñor Romero, one *sent by God*."

The texts that explain this, which I will not analyze as extensively as the prior ones, insist on three things. One, self-evident, given the circumstances, is Monseñor Romero's *martyrdom*. The second is that Monseñor Romero was and brought *salvation*. The third is that Monseñor Romero was *grace* for the people.

Martyrdom

I will present what Ellacuría has to say about the *martyrdom* of Monseñor Romero almost literally, quoting the beginning of the article:

> It has been eight months—since March 24—that Archbishop Romero was killed on the altar while saying Mass. It took only one bullet to the heart to end his mortal life. Even though he had been threatened for months, Romero never sought out the least bit of protection. He drove his car himself and lived in a small apartment adjacent to the chapel in which he was assassinated. Those who killed him are the same ones who kill the people, the same ones who in this year of Romero's martyrdom have exterminated almost 10,000 persons. The majority of these persons are young peasants, workers, and students, but also

---

[12] Ignacio Ellacuría, "Monseñor Romero, un enviado de Dios para salvar a su pueblo," *Revista Latinoamericana de Teología* 19; also in *Escritos Teológicos*, vol. 3 (San Salvador: UCA Editores, 2002), 93–101. This essay appears in English as "Monseñor Romero, One Sent by God to Save His People," in *Ignacio Ellacuría: Essays on History, Liberation, and Salvation*, ed. Michael E. Lee (Maryknoll, NY: Orbis Books, 2013), 285–92.

elderly women and children, who are taken from their homes and appear shortly thereafter: tortured, destroyed, and often unrecognizable.

It is not important to determine who shot Romero. It was evil; it was sin; it was the anti-Christ. However, it was a historical evil, a historical sin, and a historical anti-Christ, which have been incarnated in unjust structures and in those who have chosen to take on the role of Cain. Romero had only three years of public life as archbishop of San Salvador. They were enough to sow the seeds of God's word and to make present the countenance of Jesus to his people. This was too much for those who cannot tolerate the light of truth and the fire of love.[13]

These words need no commentary. They are vintage Ellacuría. They recall three things with great precision and lucidity: the affinity that Monseñor Romero bore to Jesus of Nazareth; his solidarity with the crucified people; and the three years of his life from the perspective of the cross—which brings to mind what the German theologian Martin Kähler wrote years ago: "The Gospel is the story of the passion with a long introduction."

Salvation

In his first letter to Monseñor Romero, Ellacuría had already related the most basic elements of this "long introduction" to the passion of Monseñor. Now, in the article that I am quoting, he begins with the passion but goes on by asking *what Monseñor Romero had done in his life*.[14] And in a very concentrated formulation—and a favorite one for Ellacuría—what Monseñor Romero did was *to bring salvation to his people*.

Ellacuría says that he did not bring salvation like a political leader, or like an intellectual, or like a great orator. He began to proclaim and to realize the gospel, fully incarnate and in all its fullness, and began to produce the historical power of the Gospel. He understood "once and for all"—says Ellacuría forcefully (and critically with respect to those who do not grasp this)—that the mission of the church is the proclamation and realization of the reign of God, which unavoidably passes by way of proclaiming the good news to the poor and liberation to the oppressed.

Monseñor searched for and brought a *real salvation* of the historical process. He spoke on behalf of the people so that they themselves could construct critically a new earth in which the predominant values would be justice, love, solidarity, and freedom. Time and again he set his eyes on Jesus as the principle for faith and for Christian transcendence. And the people

---

[13] Ellacuría, "Monseñor Romero, One Sent From God to Save His People," 286.
[14] In what follows I quote freely from the article.

opened themselves to that faith and that transcendence. In this way, too, he brought salvation.

Grace

Ellacuría saw in Monseñor Romero gift and grace. "He was one sent," he says, not the mere product of our hands. He became—not to the same extent for everyone—the great "gift of God," a very special gift.

> The wise and the prudent of this world, in the church, in society and in the military, the rich and the powerful of this world, used to say that he was engaging in politics. But the people of God, those who hungered and thirsted for justice, the pure of heart, the poor with spirit, knew that all of this was false. . . . They had never felt God to be so close, the spirit so apparent, Christianity so authentic, so full of grace and of truth.

But it was not a *cheap* grace, one that did not commit one to something, but a *costly* grace that committed one and saved.

> All of this gained him the love of the oppressed people and the hatred of the oppressor. It gained him persecution, the same persecution that the people suffered. This is how he died and this is why they killed him. Because of this Monseñor Romero became just as much an exceptional example of how the power of the Gospel can be turned into a historical power for transformation.

"With Monseñor Romero, God passed through El Salvador."

Ellacuría's thought on Monseñor reached its culmination in the homily that he gave in the funeral at the UCA. I cite it as the third theologal text: "With Monseñor Romero, *God passed through El Salvador.*"

I have spoken of the *presence* of God in Monseñor, and of the *"one sent"* that God made of him. Now Ellacuría expresses himself with the greatest linguistic and conceptual radicality. With Monseñor Romero, God made Godself present in Salvadoran history.

There is a brilliance of thought in these words, and I do not know any pastors, theologians, philosophers, or politicians who conceptualize and formulate realities with this kind of radicality. The words can startle and surprise believers, and certainly nonbelievers. They could seem to be not very scientific and not very academic; although they are theologal, perhaps they don't sound so very religious and pious. But I must confess that, for me, they are authentic and fruitful. At the least they express greater truth and produce more fruit than others I have heard about Monseñor Romero. I will explain.

In the God of Monseñor Romero, Ellacuría saw an ultimacy and a radicality that he never found to the same degree in any other reality, even though these are good realities such as truth and freedom, democracy and socialism (when these are authentic). He saw this ultimacy in Monseñor's history and did not mention, as I recall, other persons from the past—some very venerable—with this radicality.

He saw that the passage of God in Monseñor produced personal benefits, as well as, in a novel way, social benefits that are difficult to obtain, and once obtained, difficult to maintain. It produced justice without yielding before injustice, the defense and liberation of the oppressed. It produced compassion and tenderness toward the defenseless. It produced truth without political maneuvering, a truth not imprisoned by the lie or by the unending danger of yielding to the politically correct. And it sustained a hope that did not die.

Monseñor spoke to Ellacuría, on the one hand, of a God of the poor and the martyrs, certainly, a liberative God, demanding, prophetic, and utopian. In a word, he spoke to him of how much "this-sidedness" there is in God. But he also spoke to him of how much there is in God that is ineffable, that cannot be adequately historicized, of how much there is in God that is "beyond," of a mystery that cannot be plumbed, and that is blessed.

And to anyone for whom the word *God* sounds alien or strange, think about the words of Ellacuría that I just quoted: "what is ultimate about reality is good and not evil." *That* is what passed through El Salvador with Monseñor Romero.

Ignacio Ellacuría: A Disciple of Monseñor Romero

When Ellacuría was forty-seven years old and had been working in the UCA for ten years, Monseñor Romero "appeared" *(opthē)* to him. I am intentionally using the term "appear," the language in which the resurrection appearances are narrated, to express, with all the requisite analogies, how much there was in this of the unexpected, the powerful, perhaps the disorienting, and of blessing.

This was not the first time he encountered persons whom he considered his teachers, mentors, or fathers in spirit, and people who were going to have an important influence on his life. Among these are Miguel Elizondo, in the novitiate; Aurelio Espinosa Polit, during his humanities studies in Quito; and the Basque-Nicaraguan poet Ángel Martínez Baigorri. When it comes to theology, he was a student of Karl Rahner for four years in Innsbruck. And when it comes to philosophy he studied and worked with Xavier Zubiri. He was his closest intellectual collaborator and inspired him in various ways until Zubiri's death.

Ellacuría was always grateful to them, and he could recognize superiority in intellectual work—he said this clearly in Zubiri's case. But in some way he was also able to consider himself a colleague of those who had once been his mentors. Nonetheless, he never considered himself to be Monseñor Romero's colleague.

Romero's impact on Ellacuría was specific. Certainly, as for many others, Monseñor's prophecy and his denunciations had an impact on him, as well as his compassion and hope, his closeness to the poor and his struggle for justice, his readiness to have his life taken from him, and his keeping faith until the end without letting himself be diverted by any risk or threat.[15]

We looked at all of this in the prior section, but I think that the most novel impact and most powerful one was the impact produced by the faith of Monseñor Romero. Accepting the other aforementioned impacts, this faith meant for Ellacuría some kind of even greater discontinuity. To put it graphically, and using two sentences that Monseñor Romero used in his final homilies, Ellacuría succeeded in grasping, certainly to his amazement but in continuity with his own way of being and acting, what Monseñor said in his homily just before he was assassinated, the homily from March 23: "In the name of God, then, and in the name of this suffering people, whose cries rise up more and more loudly to heaven, I ask you, I beg you, I order you in God's name: Stop the repression!"

Ellacuría also succeeding in grasping—although with some measure of discontinuity—what Monseñor had said in a homily six months earlier, on February 10: "Nobody knows himself as long as he has not encountered God. . . . Oh, let it be, beloved brothers, that the fruit of today's preaching would be that each one of us would be going to encounter God and that we would live in the joy of God's majesty and of our smallness!"

I think that in these words Ellacuría felt something different and superior in Monseñor Romero, not only quantitatively but also qualitatively. It did not belittle Ellacuría, but I think it helped him understand himself and find his place more adequately in reality.

Said in a graphic way now, speaking of the work that the church has to do—and we ourselves, within the church—I heard Ellacuría tell him: "Monseñor, you've already gone ahead of us." And in 1985 he recognized publicly,

---

[15] It is certain that, in contrast to what some of Monseñor's friends were saying, Ellacuría approved of the risks that he was taking and insisted on this. Once I heard him say: "Monseñor must take risks. It is what he has to do."

explicitly, and solemnly, Monseñor Romero's superiority. Six years after his martyrdom the UCA conferred on Monseñor a posthumous doctorate, *honoris causa*, in theology.[16]

On this occasion Ellacuría gave an important speech. Countering the accusations of manipulating Monseñor Romero, the UCA publically confessed the importance and the superiority of Monseñor Romero for its own existence and activity. This is how Ellacuría put it:

> Some people have maliciously said that Monseñor Romero was manipulated by our university. It is time to say publicly and solemnly that this was not the case. To be sure, Monseñor Romero asked for our collaboration on many occasions and this represents, and will continue to represent, a great honor, both because of the one who asked and because of the cause for the sake of which he asked . . . but in all these collaborations it was absolutely clear who was in charge and who was assisting, who was the pastor who laid down the guidelines and who was carrying them out, who was the prophet who unraveled the mystery and who was the follower, who animated and who was animated, who was the voice and who was the echo.[17]

Ellacuría would confess humbly (something he was not given to doing) and gratefully (something he was given to doing) the debt that the UCA had to Monseñor Romero. What rings through these words as well is a personal recognition of his own debt to Monseñor, from the most profound depths of his person.

And we can understand this unequivocal recognition of Monseñor better if we remember the following. Ellacuría was demanding and critical by temperament, sometimes excessively so, and always in search of the good. Thus, I heard his criticisms of many people when, in his judgment, they had made a mistake in concept or in praxis, sometimes too because of the objective limitations of even very good people and good friends. I never heard him criticize Monseñor Romero, perhaps out of a sense of reverence that was growing in him. I think that it was a way of respecting this mysterious superiority that he saw in Monseñor. In this sense I have called Ellacuría "a disciple of Monseñor Romero."

---

[16] Ellacuría asked me to give a lecture on the significance of Monseñor Romero for theology, in which I developed an idea that is somewhat similar to the one that he had in mind about Monseñor: "Monseñor Romero as a theological event: word of God and word of the people." I ended up saying that Monseñor was not only a theologian but was also a theological reality.

[17] Ignacio Ellacuría, "La UCA ante el doctorado concedido a Monseñor Romero," *ECA* 437 (1985); also in *Escritos Teológicos*, 3:101–14.

Ellacuría Was Carried in the Faith and by the Faith of Monseñor Romero

What I am about to say could be reformulated, simply and a little audaciously, by saying that Ellacuría was "a disciple in faith of Monseñor Romero." However, I think that we have to go one step further: "Ellacuría was carried in the faith and by the faith of Monseñor Romero." I would like to reflect on this a bit.[18]

Ellacuría "struggled with God."

At a meeting in Madrid in 1969 I heard him say to a small group of people that "Rahner carried his doubts about his faith elegantly." I am convinced that with this he was saying that faith was not something obvious for him either. I was not surprised at his words, because those were tough years for the faith, my own, that of other companions of mine, and even for our professors.

The environment that predominated during the years that Ellacuría came to his intellectual maturity was one of open and serious engagement with modern philosophers—most of them, with the exception of Zubiri, nonbelievers—and of the rise of critical theology, including death-of-God theology.[19] His own critical and honest bent, which did not make him at all well-disposed toward credulities or toward unpersuasive arguments and apologetic nuances, along with the massive question put to God by the misery and the scandal of the Latin American continent, could not have made faith in God obvious to an Ignacio Ellacuría.[20]

Like many others, I think that Ellacuría was someone who struggled with God. Using the words of scripture, he wrestled with God, like Jacob. I am convinced that he let himself be conquered by God, although the victory, or the defeat, is always something very personal. One can only speak of it with great care and, at the end of the day, it cannot be grasped from the outside. Said more simply, what I think happened was that, without El-

---

[18] See also Sobrino, "Monseñor Romero y la fe de Ignacio Ellacuría."

[19] It is enough to recall, from a Christian perspective, books like that of Charles Moeller, *Literatura del siglo XX y cristianismo* (Madrid: Gredos, 1964), and Heinz Zahrnt, *A vueltas con Dios* (Zaragossa: Hechos y Dichos, 1972), translated into English as *The Question of God; Protestant Theology in the Twentieth Century* (New York: Harcourt, Brace and World, 1969).

[20] Recall the book by Gustavo Gutiérrez, *On Job: God-talk and the Suffering of the Innocent* (Maryknoll, NY: Orbis Books, 1987) and his article, "How God Can Be Discussed from the Perspective of Ayacucho," in *On the Threshold of the Third Millennium*, *Concilium* 1990/1 (Philadelphia: Trinity Press International, 1990): 103–14.

lacuría intending this, Monseñor Romero drove him forward and made it possible for Ellacuría to place himself actively before the ultimate mystery of reality, and to stay there.

I already said that for Ellacuría, Monseñor was a guide who *went in front*. I think that what impressed Ellacuría deeply about Monseñor was the way he turned to God, not only in his reflection and in his preaching, but in the most profound reality of his life. For Monseñor, God was absolutely *real*. And Ellacuría saw that with this God, Monseñor was humanizing people and bringing salvation to history.

Monseñor Romero's faith won Ellacuría's respect as something good and humanizing. It made him happy that Monseñor was a man of faith, and this faith was contagious. I think that some of this, or a lot of it—in the end God alone knows—rubbed off on Ellacuría. The mystery was made new and made close.

There aren't apodictic arguments to defend this assertion, but there can be *ways*, as Saint Thomas used to say, to make it reasonable. While in exile in Madrid (1980–83), when he had more time, and during his last years in El Salvador (1983–89), despite all the work and all the responsibilities that pressed on him with the greatest urgency, he always found time to write texts that were theo-*logical*, especially about the church and in ecclesiology. Some were more specifically theo-*logal*.[21] In these texts he took up, directly or indirectly, the reality of God.

It was second nature to him to mention God in order to give greater force to an idea, even when there was no real reason to do it. In a savage critique he wrote: "All of this matters more than really listening to the voice of God that . . . is heard in the sufferings of the people as well as in their struggles for liberation."[22] Above and beyond these concrete themes, turning to the thought of Monseñor Romero, Ellacuría found it completely natural to talk about transcendence. I cite a text, significant because it includes many important themes, that culminates with the transcendence of God.

Monseñor Romero never tired in repeating that political processes, as pure and idealistic as they may be, can never be enough to bring

---

[21] Ignacio Ellacuría, *Conversión de la Iglesia al reino de Dios. Para anunciarlo y realizarlo en la historia* (Santander: Sal Terrae, 1984).

[22] See Ignacio Ellacuría, "Discernir 'el signo de los tiempos,'" *Diakonia* 17 (1981): 59; see also *Escritos Teológicos*, 2:133–36, here 133. [The "all of this" refers to the prior sentence, which is not quoted here: "Our conscience being content with this pious exercise of lament or of compassion (regarding the fate of the crucified people), we immediately turn to what we are really worried about: to lowering the price of gas . . . or to playing the lottery of life to see if we hit the jackpot of power, of money, of domination, or success or of entertainment."—*Trans.*]

integral liberation to men and women. He understood perfectly the saying of Saint Augustine that to be human one must be "more" than human. For Romero, history that was only human, that only attempted to be human, would promptly cease to be so. Neither humanity nor history is self-sufficient. For that reason he never stopped appealing to transcendence. This theme emerged in almost all of his homilies: the word of God, the action of God breaking through human limits.[23]

Monseñor Romero came to be like the face of the mystery that rises in our world, a mystery ultimately more *fascinans* than *tremendum*. And in the presence of that Monseñor, Ellacuría felt himself made small—he, who was not accustomed to this. But this was a being-made-small that does not humiliate but that places one adequately in history and confers dignity. With exquisite delicacy Monseñor offered to him that in which Monseñor excelled, but in which others are much more limited.

His Final Years

After returning from his second exile Ellacuría entered into the last six years of his life. The fundamental task in which he spent his greatest efforts, his time, and his health was putting an end to the war by means of a dialogue that would lead to negotiation. And because of this he had to listen to criticisms from both sides—more from the Right than from the Left—since each faction wanted to triumph over the other. And they had reason, or self-deceptions, that led them to hope that victory was still possible.

Ellacuría was in the middle of all this. Now I only want to recall a few moments, most of them in the form of brief, personal encounters, with his health getting worse and worse, although he maintained his iron will. As I perceived it, in those moments he was showing himself more and more as someone who was grasping the meaning, or the lack of meaning, of the history of his life. As the reader will see, Ellacuría showed himself at times courageous and at other times was brought low. Allow me to mention some of these moments.

One day in 1983, having returned from his second exile, the community having taken refuge in Santa Tecla, Ellacuría presided at the Eucharist and spoke to us of the "Father in heaven." It was not language very typical of him, but the Ellacuría who was so cerebral and critical wanted to say something important and good with these words. Other times he told me, as in passing, "all that is left is aesthetics." Things were not going well for the country, for the kingdom, and Ellacuría did not seem able to sense any firm foothold for his struggle for dialogue.

---

[23] Ellacuría, "Monseñor Romero, One Sent by God to Save His People," 290–91.

Another time he told me, once again in passing, something that the reader may not immediately understand and that will bring a smile. For those born in Vizcaya, in the Basque country, the soccer club Athletic de Bilbao is close to their hearts. Every Sunday Ellacuría used to follow faithfully the results of its games on the radio. One day he told me, "Not even the Athletic anymore." I understood perfectly. The meaning of things was slipping from his hands.

Some months before his death he told me that now that he was working for dialogue his life was at greater risk than it was when he used to defend the oppressed so vigorously and would attack the oligarchy, the army, the government, and the US empire so vehemently. And he had to think about this in all seriousness. Like a stoic master he commented: "I have heard that the pain of being shot only lasts twenty seconds."

In the midst of these personal experiences of the meaning or meaninglessness of life Ellacuría kept on fighting. And he kept on thinking. He wrote articles on the military, economic, and political situation, and he wrote various theology articles that he published in the *Revista Latinoamericana de Teología*, which we founded in 1984. They were theological articles, but with a theologal undercurrent. Here I want to focus on a dimension of his thought that has to do with *totality* and with *ultimate realities*, sometimes explicitly religious, a dimension that I think is related, explicitly or implicitly, to the theologal.[24]

Personally, what impresses me is that because of his honesty with the real, he insisted on the negativity of reality. Thus, in 1985 he asserted against Martin Heidegger that "perhaps instead of asking why there is something rather than nothing, he should have asked why there is nothing—no being, no reality, no truth, etc.—instead of something."[25] And the historical dimension of negativity had an impact on him to the end. He thought and wrote continuously about the *crucified* people, the human rights of *oppressed peoples*.

This propensity and talent for seeing and unmasking negativity stayed with him to the end of his life. In his last speech, on November 6, 1980, upon accepting the Comín prize in Barcelona, he said: "Our civilization is

---

[24] See Ignacio Ellacuría, "The Historicity of Christian Salvation," in *Ignacio Ellacuría: Essays on History, Liberation, and Salvation*, 136–68; "Voluntad de fundamentalidad y voluntad de verdad: conocimiento-fe y su configuración histórica," *Revista Latinoamericana de Teología* 8, also in *Escritos Teológicos*, vol. 1 (San Salvador: UCA Editores, 2000), 107–38; and "Aporte de la teología de la liberación a las religiones abrahámicas en la superación del individualismo y del positivismo," *Revista Latinoamericana de Teología* 10, also in *Escritos Teológicos*, 2:193–232.

[25] Ignacio Ellacuría, "The Liberating Function of Philosophy," in *Ignacio Ellacuría: Essays on History, Liberation, and Salvation*, 101.

gravely ill . . . and if we are to avoid a bad outcome we have to try to change it from within.[26] Hence the pressing need to turn back history.

Nonetheless, Ellacuría also insisted there can be a beginning [*principio*][27] of salvation in negativity. He wrote repeatedly about the salvation that the servant of Yahweh brings, suffering and crushed; the *assassinated* martyrs and a church of the oppressed and the poor. In his last speech in Barcelona, to heal a dehumanized society he turned to that which is *low in history.* "Only out of hope and in a utopian way can one believe and have the courage to try to turn history back together with the poor and the oppressed of the world, to subvert history and launch it in a different direction."[28]

In this final speech he also turned to—or at least made a strong allusion to—the theologal plane, certainly to "what is Christian" *(lo Cristiano)*, a formula he frequently used. He did this by putting faith and justice into tension with one another. "Christian faith has as its necessary condition, although perhaps not a sufficient one, its confrontation with justice; but the justice that one seeks is profoundly illuminated in turn from the perspective of a faith that is lived out in the preferential option for the poor.[29]

During this last period of his life Ellacuría, surrounded by countless problems, and in rather unfamiliar words, said, "I wanted to think El Salvador." He wanted to think *the whole* in which he found himself. And he had since 1982 been thinking about how there needed to be a *totalizing* civilization as a solution to that exhausted totality that is our world. One day he commented to me: "The theoretical formulation of the solution, that's clear. Making it a reality is very difficult. It is the *civilization of poverty.*" And he was convinced of the originality of this concept.

To define or at least to describe what a particular civilization was, he focused on two essential things, although he formulated them in various ways: what is the *fundamental engine of history* and what is the *principle for humanization.* In the civilization of wealth the *engine* of history is the accumulation of capital, and the *principal of (de)humanization* is the possession-enjoyment of wealth. In the civilization of poverty the *engine of history*—sometimes

---

[26] Ignacio Ellacuría, "El desafío de las mayorías pobres," *ECA* 493–94 (1989); also in *Escritos universitarios* (San Salvador: UCA Editores, 1999), 297–306.

[27] The Spanish word *principio* can also mean "principle."—*Trans.*

[28] "El desafío de las mayorías pobres." He also talked about the serious knowledge needed to think through development projects and projects for social justice.

[29] Ibid., 79. As I conclude this brief analysis of his last speech I would like to add what I heard from him in one of his private conversations. "Alfonso Comín, a convinced Christian and a convinced Communist, was bedridden and defeated by cancer. In his final days he asked for tapes of the homilies of Monseñor Romero." Ellacuría recalled this as an expression of Comín's faith. And he could not resist adding that in *his* death, "Pius XII had asked that they put on music by Beethoven."

called the principle of development—is the universal satisfaction of basic needs and the *principle of humanization* is the increase in shared solidarity. Starting in 1982 he wrote four articles on this fundamental theme.[30] He insisted on the dialectical character of both civilizations, sometimes adding the dialectical formulation of the *civilization of capital* and *civilization of work*. But he held on to the term *poverty* to the end, despite the scandal created by defining an ideal for a truly human civilization in this way.

To assert the necessity of the civilization of poverty, and in addition to historical reason, Ellacuría went back to the spirit of the gospel. This is another sign of how the theological and the theologal undercurrent had become connatural for him.

"Catching sight of the God who liberates."

I end this chapter by citing (with some slight editing) the conclusion of his last article, which was published in the *Revista Latinoamericana de Teología*:

> The church of the poor becomes the new heaven, which as such is needed to overcome the civilization of wealth and build the civilization of poverty. It will become the new earth in which the new human being will live in a welcoming and not in a degraded home.
>
> This is where a great confluence will happen of the Christian message, without distorted glosses, and the current situation of the greater part of the world, and certainly of Latin America, still the repository, for the most part, of the Christian faith, which up until now has not helped very much to make this area a new earth, even though it was originally presented as the new world.
>
> Prophetically negating a church as the old heaven of a civilization of wealth and the affirming utopianly of a church as the new heaven of a civilization of poverty is an irrefutable claim pressed by the signs of the times and by the soteriological dynamism of the Christian faith historicized in new human beings.[31]

---

[30] Ignacio Ellacuría, "The Kingdom of God and Unemployment in the Third World," in *Unemployment and the Right to Work*, ed. Jacques Pohier and Dietmar Mieth, *Concilium* 1982/10, English ed. Marcus Lefébure (New York: Seabury Press, 1982), 91–96; "Misión actual de la Compañía de Jesús," *Revista Latinoamericana de Teología* 29; also in *Escritos Teológicos*, 3:173–76; "La construcción de un futuro distinto para la humanidad," available at http:/mercaba.org (FICHAS/Teología latina); "El desafío de las mayorías pobres."

[31] Ignacio Ellacuría, "Utopia and Propheticism," in this volume, 55. Note that slight changes from Ellacuría's text, including the introduction of the separate paragraphs, are from his "slight editing."—*Eds.*

This is Ellacuría's fundamental thesis, unifying the analysis of history—the signs of the times—and salvation.

The last words are historical and theologal: "These new human beings keep on proclaiming, firmly and steadfastly, although always in the darkness, an ever greater future, because beyond all the futures following one on the other, they catch sight of the God who saves, the God who liberates."

"They catch sight of the God who liberates." In these words it is possible to perceive the spirit of Monseñor Romero.

—TRANSLATED BY J. MATTHEW ASHLEY

4

The Cost of Discipleship

GUSTAVO GUTIÉRREZ, OP

Before long it will be twenty years since a horrendous event: the murder of six Jesuit priests and two humble women, a mother and her daughter, who for safety's sake had sought refuge in the same house, thinking it more secure. I heard the incredible news a few hours later on the radio; the faces of these friends, and the conversations we had, came to my memory. This community had given me lodging on various occasions when I visited El Salvador; I remember in particular the days when Monseñor Romero was buried. At that same moment I found out that Jon Sobrino was still alive, and I wondered how he was doing.

For decades we had been witnesses to the murders of laypeople, of bishops, of religious, committed to our continent's poorest and most insignificant, a painful saga that put its stamp on the life of the church.[1] This book, dedicated to the testimony and the thought of Ignacio Ellacuría, inevitably brings us to the memory of all those who died with what Monseñor Romero called "a martyrial sign" (which was true in his own case). A memory that keeps us mindful in a particular way of those who accompanied Ignacio in his life and the path he took, and of these two women who belonged to the poor of El Salvador, cruelly murdered that night—without these Ellacuría would not have been the same, and neither would we.

Along these lines, as a first stage, I reflect on an important text from the conference at Aparecida,[2] which, going beyond the vacillations and brief allusions of Puebla and Santo Domingo, recognized the martyrdom of so

---

[1] One of the first cases (in 1969) was the murder of Henrique Pereira Neto, a young priest of African descent in the Diocese of Olinda and Recife, a coworker with Dom Hélder Câmara.

[2] Fifth General Conference of the Latin American and Caribbean Bishops' Conferences, which met in Aparecida, Brazil, in May 2007. An English translation of the documents is available on the celam.org website; referred to hereafter as Aparecida. The earlier two general conferences were held in Santo Domingo (1992) and Puebla (1979).

many on the continent. In a second stage, among the numerous points from his writings (which surely will be material for the other collaborators to this book) I limit myself to a brief commentary on a contribution that I consider to be essential in his work: the historical perspective.

With the Martyrial Sign

"We wish to recall the courageous testimony of our men and women saints, and of those who, even though not canonized, have lived out the gospel radically, and have offered their life for Christ, for the church, and for their people."[3] These lines show an open recognition of the meaning and the significance of giving up one's life for proclaiming the gospel in our times. Ignacio—a philosopher and a theologian who has a very unique place in the context of liberation theology—contributed to it with "blood and ink," to say it in the expressive terms used as the title of an important book on his work.[4]

Following Jesus requires a permanent change of mind and of heart. This is what the Gospels call conversion, an indispensable condition for accepting the reign of God. This is a demand that is not limited to the personal dimension but refers to the church's ongoing and permanent conversion in its entirety *(Ecclesia semper reformanda est)*.[5] Only a church in a humble process of conversion will be in a position to be a sign of the reign of God in a changing history.

Walking in the footsteps of Jesus sometimes means confronting difficulties, open or hidden, the hostility and the lack of understanding that make up part of the disciple's path. These are not sought after or desired, but neither can they be avoided or feared—this is a matter of fidelity and personal consistency. Many in the church of Latin America and of the Caribbean have had the experience that Bonhoeffer refers to when he talks about "the cost of discipleship," the title of one of his books. This situation—in which things even get to the point of extreme scandal, where some people who proclaim themselves to be Christians torture and murder others whose Christian faith inspired their commitment, or are indifferent or even complicit in these acts—is one of the most painful and tragic in the life of this continent and of the church present in it.

---

[3] Aparecida, no. 98.

[4] Robert Lassalle-Klein, *Blood and Ink: Ignacio Ellacuría, Jon Sobrino, and the Jesuit Martyrs of Central America* (Maryknoll, NY: Orbis Books, 2014).

[5] "We affirm the need for conversion on the part of the whole Church to a preferential option for the poor, an option aimed at their integral liberation" (Puebla documents, no. 1134, in *Puebla and Beyond: Documentation and Commentary*, ed. John Eagleson and Phillip Scharper, trans. John Drury (Maryknoll, NY: Orbis Books, 1979), 264.

Being on the side of the forgotten, participating in what Pius XI called the "combat for justice," worries the powerful of the world. Many are those who know about the mistrust and intimidation that comes because of their solidarity with the poor and their defense of their rights. Nonetheless, those who take on this commitment see it to be anchored in faith in the God of life, and because of this they recognize the face of Jesus in the faces of the poor, as the Bishops' Conference of Latin America and the Caribbean never ceases to repeat. In some cases this attitude has led to a violent death for those seeking to be in solidarity with the poor and the insignificant. They are privileged witnesses ("even though not canonized") of the gospel and of hope, and, despite everything, of that Easter joy that comes from being a disciple of Jesus Christ.

This testimony has made its mark on the church of this continent. The text of Aparecida quoted earlier recognizes this; in it the violence suffered by these people is rejected, and yet at the same time new realities and dimensions are perceived in the events. Let us take note of the final point, which speaks of those who "have offered their life for Christ, for the church, and *for their people*." What we have here is a clue for understanding the meaning of martyrdom in our times and in our continent. It is true that martyrdom has traditionally been seen as something motivated by "hatred for the faith" *(odium fidei)*; for the martyr it is a testimony of faith in Christ lived out in the church, a giving of one's life for what one believes. Aparecida adds something important to the fundamental points made about Christ and the church: "for their people." And it bears saying: for love and service of people that ask for justice and that demand to be recognized in their dignity as human beings and sons and daughters of God.

Establishing justice is a clear gospel requirement; it forms part of the heart of the Christian message insofar as it is a manifestation of love for the other. Not a few have lost their lives because of this commitment; hence the proposal to keep in mind what this implies for the way we understand martyrdom. The cases of Monseñor Romero and of Ellacuría and his companions, among others, suggest this clearly and urgently. They risked their lives in this service. Love of neighbor is united to love of God and make up a single commandment. This is what we are pointed toward by the affirmation, "for their people," for justice—a central biblical theme.[6]

To affirm that establishing justice forms part of the proclamation of God's reign is not an attempt to introduce surreptitiously a social or political element into a religious discourse but is rather an attempt to see the evangelical dimension of justice and put it into practice. Actually, what we

---

[6] See Benedict XVI, *Deus caritas est*, nos. 15, 18.

are confronting is a way of understanding the Christian faith, the faith in the Son of God, who became one of us, one whom we have to encounter in history, especially in the most forgotten and marginalized. This is what Aparecida has in mind; it is what Oscar Romero affirmed with absolute clarity; and it is the case for many more—members of the laity, of religious orders, bishops, priests—who are in solidarity with their people who are the objects of their friendship and their respect. Not a few of them have been close friends and companions on the road with these people for a long time. These events call us to deepen and extend the notion of testimony for the faith, martyrdom, taking it beyond a strictly "religious" sphere in order to bear in mind the different dimensions of Christian faith and everything implied in testifying to Christian faith in our times.[7]

The following of Jesus, that is to say, what we call spirituality, is not a kind of oasis in the midst of everyday commitments; it is even less an escape or refuge from storms and conflicts. As Benedict XVI said and as Aparecida recognized, "Holiness is not a flight toward self-absorption or toward religious individualism, nor does it mean abandoning the urgent reality of the enormous economic, social, and political problems of Latin America and the world, let alone a flight from reality toward an exclusively spiritual world."[8] Quite to the contrary, we live out the gospel and give testimony to it in the midst of historical situations that are complex and difficult. The text of Aparecida is clear on this and it makes us understand what people have lived through and reflected on in this continent over the last several decades.

Nonetheless, the inevitable obstacles that one will encounter in following Jesus Christ, and even the sorrows and the desolations that can confront someone who does this, should not make us forget that this path is equally a font of profound joy, an Easter joy that produces the love that is received and that is given away, and a love that reaffirms life in communion with others. As Ignacio himself said years earlier: "All the blood of martyrs that has been spilled in El Salvador and throughout Latin America, rather than causing discouragement and despair, is infusing a new spirit of struggle and new hope in our people."[9]

---

[7] See the reflections by Karl Rahner, Jon Sobrino, Juan Hernández Pico, and Matthias Barth in *Martyrdom Today*, ed. Johann Baptist Metz, Edward Schillebeeckx, and Marcus Lefébure, *Concilium* 163 (New York: Seabury, 1983).

[8] Aparecida, no. 148; cf. Benedict XVI, "Address to the Inaugural Session of the Fifth General Conference of the Bishops of Latin America and the Caribbean," Aparecida, no. 3.

[9] Ignacio Ellacuría, "The Latin American Quincentenary: Discovery or Cover-up?" in *Ignacio Ellacuría: Essays on History, Liberation, and Salvation*, ed. Michael E. Lee (Maryknoll, NY: Orbis Books, 2013), 38.

Salvation and Transformation of History

Ignacio put his wealth of intellect creatively at the service of the understanding of a faith lived by a people that is poor and mistreated—but does not lose hope—in the complex and at times turbulent conditions of our continent.

The murders of the Jesuit community make clear, as if this were necessary, a decision of long standing that this community had made: to be in full solidarity with the Salvadoran people and to make, as Pope Francis says, "a Church that is poor and that is on the side of the poor." This was something that meant taking on the sufferings of the people with whom they had decided to share their lives. This choice brought them to an early and violent death. They did not seek it; martyrdom is not sought. They met it on the road of fidelity and of solidaristic love. George Bernanos reminds us of this, in unforgettable terms, in his 1956 opera, *Dialogues des carmélites*.[10] The life that Ignacio chose makes us understand the meaning of the death he had. As a disciple of Jesus he was able to take up what was said by the Lord: "No one takes my life from me; I lay it down of my own accord" (Jn 10:18).

He gave up his life for love of the God of life and of the people that he made his own. Proximity to the poor made him see the scandal of poverty and its interminable suffering. He understood in this way the key role that justice has in the evangelical message, and he understood that without it there is no authentic social peace or fraternity; he understood just as clearly that to walk in the footsteps of Jesus means committing oneself to the history of a people, accompanying them in their will to see their dignity as human beings respected. Ignacio exercised this accompaniment with specific commitments in a diversity of situations in the historical progression of his country and with his theological reflection. A key theme for him was the history of salvation and its link with the history of humanity. A point that was broached in the theology of the twentieth century, that is present in Vatican II and, with a particular contour, in liberation theology, this vision allowed him to understand the reality of Latin America better and to work out a theology that opens up a fruitful approach to the biblical message. This will be of service, providing a "north star" to what he used to call "becoming aware of the weight of reality" *(hacerse cargo de la realidad)*, a phrase rich in consequences and one that he liked to repeat, inspired by his teacher, Zubiri.

History was a key notion for him in view of an anthropology and a theology in conformity with the message of a God who became one of us, entering into time. He was convinced that a markedly ahistorical under-

---

[10] George Bernanos, *The Carmelites* (London: Fontana Books, 1961).

standing of the Christian message was alien to its biblical sources and made it difficult, if not impossible, to understand what was happening in Latin America.[11] This is one of the most powerful points in his thought, and truly a vision that would be fertile soil in which the seeds of other perspectives of his theology would germinate—and a crucial one for outlining the task of the church in the world, insofar as it is a sign of communion with God and between human beings, that is to say, of a salvation that embraces the totality of human existence (and of creation) and that reveals the theological challenge represented by poverty, to the extent that it is an exclusion and oppression of those who were first in Jesus Christ's life.

In this vein Ignacio took up, insistently, the perspective of the unity of history. He said in this respect: "Jesus' salvation, which far from divorcing itself from historical liberation processes, mandates those very processes on account of the transcendental unity of the history of salvation." Moreover, he insists on the affirmation that "there are not two histories, but one single history in which the presence of the liberator God and the presence of the liberated and liberator human being are joined together."[12] This is a unity that is not monolithic, that recognizes diversity, and that has serious consequences speaking practically. For him, the history of salvation happens within human history, in which the people of God makes its pilgrimage. This is the concrete field within which human beings encounter one another and God, the space in which we have to learn to find God in all things, according to Ignatius of Loyola's rule.

The perspective of the history of salvation has a close tie with the biblical data on the reign *(reino)* or reigning *(reinado)* of God. What we have here is a notion that speaks to us of the presence of the kingdom in history ("thy kingdom come") and that, at the same time, reaches beyond it ("your will be done on earth as it is in heaven"). Ignacio spoke correctly, thus, that liberation theology is a theology of the kingdom and said more precisely that "it is not a theology of the political, but a theology of the kingdom of God." It is a total theology in breadth because it does not leave out "any part of the actual revealed message" and always "alludes to the reigning presence

---

[11] Ellacuría makes reference to this kind of theology in his article "Salvation History," in *Ignacio Ellacuría: Essays on History, Liberation, and Salvation,* 170–73.

[12] Ignacio Ellacuría, "Liberation Theology and Socio-historical Change in Latin America," in *Toward a Society that Serves Its People* (Washington, DC: Georgetown University Press, 1991), 21. In his excellent study on Ellacuría's work, Michael Lee comments on this point and cites another text that adds a further nuance: "There are not two levels of problems (the profane level on one side and the sacred on the other), and neither are there two histories (one profane and the other sacred); there is only one level and one history" (quoted in Michael Lee, *Bearing the Weight of Salvation: The Soteriology of Ignacio Ellacuría* (New York: Crossroad, 2009), 30–38.

of God in this world."[13] The reign is a gift; it expresses the gratuity of God's love, the God "who first loved us" (1 Jn 4:19). It is a gift that leads to a certain way of acting, to love of the other. This is the ethics of the reign. Keeping it alive prevents us from getting lost in purely formulaic rules for acting or distorting it in abuses of power.

But we have to take a further step. In history we encounter many peoples and many persons who live in inhuman conditions. Their poverty and the suffering that follows from it challenge Christian faith in a God of love. Those who believe in this God have to ask themselves how they can testify to God's love and mercy (in its original sense) on behalf of those who lead a life stamped by an injustice that renders them insignificant, socially speaking, and that discriminates against them for a variety of reasons—an injustice that constitutes a sin, that is, a rupture of communion with God and among persons.

We are not talking about something merely social. We are facing an essential element of the history of salvation. Jesus talks about the poor as "the least of my sisters and brothers," and adds that whatever is done for them is done for him (Mt 25:31–46). The primacy of commitment to the poor has a central place in Ignacio's life and takes up a lot of space in his writings. The proposal that John XXIII presented to the council about what he called "the church of the poor" hardly touched the conciliar documents, but it was accepted a little later in Latin America and is returning today with freshness and energy in the magisterium of Pope Francis. Ignacio refers to this theme, insisting again and again on the preferential option for the poor (a formulation first worked out in Christian communities in the 1970s and taken up later by the Puebla Conference), and relating it to faith and justice: "Only from faith can one affirm that the preferential option for the poor, the partiality in favor of the most needy, is from (Christian) justice."[14] From the perspective of this practice the liberative character of the love of God is perceived with clarity, a liberation that encompasses the different dimensions of the human being and that, for this reason, we call integral liberation, as Ignacio always recalled.

Faced with the difficult exigencies that all of this represented, Ignacio never distanced himself from everyday life to take refuge in an intellectual life that would carry on its discourse in a purely academic sphere, a way of life in which there might from time to time be echoes of what was happening to the marginalized of the Salvadoran people, but which really would be far from them and their anguish. He was well equipped to excel in the

---

[13] Ellacuría, "Liberation Theology and Socio-historical Change in Latin America," 20–21.

[14] Ignacio Ellacuría, "On Liberation," in *Ignacio Ellacuría: Essays on History, Liberation, and Salvation*, 47.

world of the university, we know this well. Possessed of a solid philosophical and theological formation, the doors to the academy were open to Ignacio. Neither did he succumb to the other tempting easy path: he did not put aside his intellectual abilities on the pretext of the urgencies of commitment. There was no lack of such pretexts, and even serious reasons, for him to do this. He need only have brought to mind the memory of theoretical disquisitions that are barren from the outset and that only serve to cover up one's fears or to swell one's personal prestige and give something to the library catalogues. If they don't have any purchase on reality, they will wilt and disappear as soon as the sun rises.

Ignacio valued the contribution of intellectual work to the cause of the poor; he did not immerse himself in a short-term pragmatism that is alien to a critical reflection. He acted and he thought. He was in solidarity with the poor, and at the same time, he delved tirelessly into the gospel message. He knew what could happen. In a text from 1981 he wrote with great lucidity: "The preferential option for the poor that urges one to accompany the people in their struggles for liberation and to introduce the Christian spirit into its heart, can in today's world have only one response: persecution, and even death."[15]

We will never know for certain how many tensions and perplexities, how many vacillations and misunderstandings, how many low moments and painful impasses he experienced on the complex road that he chose to follow. But, as is normal, his could not have been a path that was either calm or triumphal. It never is. What is certain is that he put his intelligence, his analytical lucidity, at the service of that discernment that was necessary to find the appropriate path in the midst of the jumble of events that El Salvador and Latin America was living through—a discernment of the signs of the times that is important for anyone who takes a steady historical perspective, which was the case for him. Not only did he not forget his philosophical formation, but he made of it a source of criteria for maneuvering in a changing and surprising situation. In this way he made the most of his academic formation and showed that distrust of reflection without qualification is one of the subtlest and most paradoxical forms of intellectualism.

He learned by trial and error, as everyone does. How could there be any other way of doing this when one wants to be faithful to everyday life and from that perspective get some idea of what is coming? How else, if one is not bent on being right all the time at the price of distancing oneself from the present moment and of avoiding the demands to commit oneself that this moment poses? According to the gospel, the path of discipleship passes,

---

[15] A text published by the Centro Pastoral of the Universidad Centroamericana in April 1990.

in one way or another, through the cross of Christ. The Latin American experience tells us this on a daily basis. Ignacio left us profound reflections in this respect, but above all, he gave personal testimony. An Easter testimony that increases a hope that, according to Pope Francis, is called to "generate history."[16]

—Translated by J. Matthew Ashley

---

[16] Pope Francis, *Evangelii gaudium*, no. 181.

PART II

ELLACURÍA AND THE DYNAMISM OF A NEW THEOLOGICAL METHOD

5

The Praxical Character of Theology

Francisco de Aquino Júnior

The expression *liberation theology* covers both an ecclesial *movement more or less conscious and reflexive* (theologal praxis) and also its *more explicit and strictly theoretical moment* (theological theory). From the beginning, liberation theology was understood and developed in this structural tension of theory-praxis, although the link between theory and praxis has been more affirmed and presupposed than made explicit and justified.

Here my aim is to explain and justify, from a strictly theoretical point of view, this fundamental epistemological presupposition of liberation theology. To do so I (1) outline the problematic of the theory-praxis relationship, (2) situate the discussion about the process of theological knowledge in liberation theology within the horizon of the aforementioned problematic, and (3) make explicit the praxical character of theology.

The Problematic of the Theory-Praxis Relationship

Certainly, no one denies the existence of some linkage between theory and praxis, at least insofar as praxis becomes subject or object of theory and the theory can guide or assist the praxis. This is clear. The question is discovering what kind of linkage this is and if it is the only possible nexus between the two.

It could be that theory and practice are complete and self-sufficient realities and that between them there is no more than a mere *relationship* between *relata* that, in and of themselves, would be completely independent of each other. In this case we would have two realities or relata (theory and praxis) that might or might not come into any contact with each other (relationship). If this were the case, it would be a purely external linkage, to the extent that theory would not be a constitutive moment of praxis, and praxis would be even less a constitutive and determinative aspect of theory. This is not to deny the possibility and even the necessity of the linkage between theory and praxis, but it determines the type of bond that exists between them: a relationship between already constituted relata.

Basically, this position is rooted and grounded in the radical dualism that has constituted and characterized Western civilization from its origins to the present day (intelligence vs. sensibility), a dualism that gives rise to many other dualisms (sensible vs. supra-sensible; material vs. spiritual).[1] In fact, according to Zubiri: "Classical philosophy has always opposed intellection to sensation. Even when it has tried to unify them, as once with Kant, it has always been a matter of a 'unification' but not of a structurally formal 'unity.'"[2] This way of approaching sensibility and intelligence contains a fundamental and decisive statement: "Intellection comes after sensibility and this coming-after is an opposition. This has been philosophy's initial thesis since Parmenides, a thesis that has been having its gravitational effect, imperturbably, and with a thousand variations, on all European philosophy."[3] The strangest thing is that this opposition occurred without making explicit what are the proper meanings of sensation and of intellection.[4] And, "given that what intellection and sensibility as such are has not been determined, the result is that their alleged opposition remains ungrounded."[5]

In fact, when human sensibility and intellection are analyzed more closely, as Xavier Zubiri does in his trilogy *Sentient Intelligence* (reality, logos, and reason),[6] one reaches a different conclusion:

> Human sensibility and intellection are not only not opposed, they constitute, in their intrinsic and formal unity, one single act of apprehension. That act insofar as it is sentient is an impression of reality; and, insofar as it is intellective, it is an apprehension of reality. Therefore, the single unitary act of sentient intellection is an impression of reality. Intellection is a mode of sensibility, and in the human being sensibility is a mode of intellection.[7]

---

[1] Xavier Zubiri, *Inteligencia sentiente: Inteligencia y realidad*, vol. 1 (Madrid: Alianza, 1980, 2006), 24; Ignacio Ellacuría, "La superación del reduccionismo idealista en Zubiri," in *Escritos filosóficos* (San Salvador: UCA Editores, 2001), 3:312.

[2] Zubiri, *Inteligencia sentiente*, 79.

[3] Ibid., 11.

[4] Ibid., 24–25, 79.

[5] Ibid., 25.

[6] The second and third volumes are published as Xavier Zubiri, *Inteligencia sentiente: Inteligencia y logos*, vol. 2 (Madrid: Alianza Editorial, 1982); and *Inteligencia sentiente: Inteligencia y razón*, vol. 3 (Madrid: Alianza Editorial, 1983).

[7] Zubiri, *Inteligencia sentiente*, 1:13.

In other words, the human animal senses by intelligizing (intellective sensing) and intelligizes by sensing (sentient intellection).[8] There is, therefore, between intellection and sensibility "a radical structural unity through which sensibility itself is intellective and intellection is sentient." Thus, Ellacuría writes, "from the sentient intellection one radically overcomes all forms of dualism between intellection and feeling."[9] Similarly, if we consider the linkage between theory and praxis as constituent and not as mere relation, we can also overcome the also classical separation and/or opposition between them.

From this perspective *theory* and *praxis* do not constitute complete and self-sufficient relata between which a relationship could, or even should, be established. Rather, they would be *constitutive moments of each other*: theory would be a moment of praxis, and praxis would be one determinant aspect of theory. So there would be no praxis without theory or theory without praxis. In fact, praxis, as human action, has intellection as one of its constituent notes.[10] There is no praxis that in some manner or to some degree is not intellective: "Some kind of theory is inevitable in any human praxis and even in any socio-historical praxis."[11] And theory, insofar as it is intellection, is *one* fundamental note of human action that, however irreducible it is, only acts "in a primary unity with all the other notes of human reality."[12] It is "a moment of a unitary praxis from which it receives its final determination."[13] Therefore, we are talking about an *internal linkage*, in which theory and praxis constitute each other in respectivity prior to and outside of any relationship (theory is a moment of praxis, and praxis has theory as one of its fundamental notes).[14]

Instead of speaking about a *relationship* (between relata), one should speak, therefore, about *respectivity* (of notes). And, in this sense, it is not

---

[8] Ibid., 82–81.

[9] Ignacio Ellacuría, "La nueva obra de Zubiri: *Inteligencia sentiente*," in *Escritos filosóficos*, 3:336.

[10] Zubiri, *Sobre el hombre* (Madrid: Alianza, 1998), 11–18; *Inteligencia sentiente*, 282ff.

[11] Ellacuría, "Relación teoría y praxis en la teología de la liberación," in *Escritos Teológicos*, vol. 1 (San Salvador: UCA Editores, 2000), 235.

[12] Ignacio Ellacuría, "Laying the Philosophical Foundations of Latin American Theological Method," in *Ignacio Ellacuría: Essays on History, Liberation, and Salvation*, ed. Michael E. Lee (Maryknoll, NY: Orbis Books, 2013), 79.

[13] Ellacuría, "Relación teoría y praxis en la teología de la liberación," 235–45.

[14] According to Zubiri, "Respectivity is a metaphysical character of reality, and not simply one relationship or property among others of real things" (Xavier Zubiri, "Respectividad de lo real," in *Escritos menores: 1953–1983* [Madrid: Alianza, 2006], 173). The distinction between relationship and respectivity made by Zubiri is fundamental in Ellacuría's philosophy and theology, because it allows him to overcome many forms of dualism and to apprehend reality simultaneously in its irreducible richness of elements, aspects, and dimensions, and in its radical unity.

enough to state that the praxis *can* become an issue or object of theory and that theory *can* guide or assist praxis, as if this would be simply to relate relata already established that, in principle, have nothing to do with each other. We must recognize that every praxis has intellection as one of its fundamental constituents and determinants, and that all theory, as intellection, is constituted as a fundamental, constitutive, and defining *moment* of praxis, structured by a variety of notes (intellection, sentiment, and volition) coherently or systematically articulated together.

Liberation Theology Within the Horizon of the Problematic of the Theory-Praxis Relationship

After outlining the problematic of the theory-praxis relationship, I now situate the discussion about the process of theological knowledge of liberation theology within the horizon of that problematic; that is, I circumscribe and formulate the question of the doing of theology in theory-praxis terms.

Actually, this new theoretical horizon of doing theology begins to be outlined in the context of the theological renewal that took place after the Second World War and that was consolidated in the renewal movement of the Second Vatican Council, particularly in its reception and development in Latin America with liberation theology.[15] Whether it was due to the necessity and urgency of social, political, economic, cultural, and religious transformations (postwar Europe, liberation movements in Latin America, Vatican II, Medellín, among others), or whether it was due to the discovery of the historical character of knowledge (hermeneutical philosophies, philosophies of language, of life, of action, of praxis, social, historical, cultural sciences, and so on), theology, little by little, started to make its praxical origin and goal explicit and to emphasize them, although it has not always adequately perceived and formulated the praxical nature of knowledge as such. This happened first in Europe (Moltmann, Metz, and Schillebeeckx),[16] and later in Latin America with liberation theology.[17] In this, particular emphasis was put on the theory-praxis linkage. Although with different conceptions of praxis (Christian life, popular culture, social and political activity, the reigning of God, and so on) and its linkages with theory (first act–second act, mediations, hermeneutical circle, moment of praxis),

---

[15] Enrique Ruiz Maldonado, *Liberación y cautiverio: Debates en torno al método de la teología en América Latina* (México: Venecia, 1976), 409.

[16] Ibid., 421–29.

[17] Antonio González, "La vigencia del 'método teológico' de la teología de la liberación," *Sal Terrae* 983 (1995): 667–75.

the liberation theologians have always understood liberation theology as a theology of praxis: "a moment of the process by which the world is transformed;"[18] a kind of praxeology of liberation;[19] a conscious and reflex moment of the ecclesial praxis;[20] "political theology and its mediations;"[21] "intellectus amoris;"[22] among others. The problem is that this was always much more presupposed than made explicit and elaborated, as if it was something obvious and indisputable, as if everyone thought and said the same in talking about theory and praxis. With a few exceptions the liberation theologians rarely came to grips more deeply and more consistently with that problematic. And the few who did, Clodovis Boff and Ignacio Ellacuría, started from theoretical assumptions that were so different that they arrived at conclusions that were not only different but, in certain cases, contradictory.

Boff,[23] driven by an idealistic conception of knowing and of knowledge (Aristotle, Thomas Aquinas, and Althusser) even stated that "the real things remain behind the cognitive process,"[24] that "praxis is not a theoretical mediation at all,"[25] and that "a theological practice as such is only 'responsible' for the criteria for its grammar, that is, the set of rules that govern its speech."[26] It is as if knowledge were self-sufficient, completely independent from reality, reduced to its discursive moment, as if the truth could be reduced to the internal coherence and rigor of argumentation, regardless of whether or not this discursive system, however coherent and logical it might be, expresses (translates) reality as it is and as it is disclosed. From this perspective, praxis is not a constitutive aspect of the process of theological knowledge as such. According to Boff's way of putting it, it can be "prime matter" of theology

---

[18] Gustavo Gutiérrez, *A Theology of Liberation: History, Politics* (Maryknoll, NY: Orbis Books, 1988).

[19] Hugo Assmann, *Theology for a Nomad Church* (Maryknoll, NY: Orbis Books, 1975).

[20] Ignacio Ellacuría, "La teología como momento ideológico de la praxis ecclesial," *Escritos Teológicos*, 1:163–85.

[21] Clodovis Boff, *Theology and Praxis: Epistemological Foundations* (Maryknoll, NY: Orbis Books, 1987); originally published as *Teologia e prática: teologia do político e suas mediações* (Petrópolis: Vozes, 1993).

[22] Jon Sobrino, *The Principle of Mercy: Taking the Crucified People from the Cross* (Maryknoll, NY: Orbis Books, 1994), 27–45.

[23] Clodovis Boff, *Teologia e prática*, 22, 29f; ídem., "Como vejo a teologia latino-americana trinta anos depois," in *O mar se abriu: Trinta anos de teologia na América Latina*, ed. Luis Carlos Susin, 79–95 (São Paulo: Loyola 2000), 86.

[24] Clodovis Boff, *Teologia e prática*, 147.

[25] Clodovis Boff, "Teologia e prática," *Revista Eclesiàstica Brasileira* 36, no. 144 (1976), 796.

[26] Clodovis Boff, *Teologia e prática*, 60.

and/or "medium in which" the theologian lives *(medium in quo)*, but never "medium with which" theology is made *(medium quo)*.[27] Consequently, for Boff the starting point and the fundamental principle of theology can only be the positivity of faith *(fides quae)*,[28] although he acknowledges that, in its own way of doing theology, Eastern theology has privileged its experiential dimension *(fides qua)*, while liberation theology has favored its praxical dimension.[29] Boff assumes, therefore, a conception of knowing and of knowledge in which praxis does not interfere directly in theological theory: it is there before (presupposed) or after (as goal).[30] Thus, in addition to reducing theological knowledge to its discursive moment and to not consistently assuming the praxical dimension of all language (theological language too), he ends up denying the "epistemological density of praxis" that he admits, at least theoretically, elsewhere.[31] Accordingly, he denies one of the intuitions and most fruitful and effective theoretical principles of the "new way of doing theology" that liberation theology determines: the primacy of praxis. By denying the praxical nature of knowledge, he ends up denying the other fundamental and weighty intuition of liberation theology as theoretical, namely, the perspective of the poor and oppressed as a fundamental theological place, as if knowledge were neutral and situated above social conflicts.

Ellacuría, in turn, based on Zubiri's realistic-praxical conception of knowing and knowledge,[32] (a) understands human intellection as apprehension of reality and the confrontation with it,[33] (b) states that "the principal source of light [for theory] is certainly reality and not some a priori condition of the human subject," although he makes clear "that reality is only a source of light in the context of intelligence; and clearly intelligence must be directed at reality,"[34] (c) speaks of the theory as a moment

---

[27]   Ibid., 157, 377, 385.

[28]   Clodovis Boff, *Teoria do método teológico* (Petrópolis: Vozes, 1998), 111; idem, "Retorno à arché da teología," 148.

[29]   Clodovis Boff, "Teología," in *Nuevo diccionario de teología*, ed. Juan Tamayo-Acosta (Madrid: Trotta, 2005), 866–67.

[30]   Clodovis Boff, *Teologia e prática*, 147.

[31]   Ibid., v.

[32]   Ignacio Ellacuría, "Laying the Philosophical Foundations of Latin American Theological Method," in *Ignacio Ellacuría: Essays on History, Liberation, and Salvation*, 90n7.

[33]   Ibid., 80.

[34]   See Ignacio Ellacuría, "The Liberation Function of Philosophy," in *Ignacio Ellacuría: Essays on History, Liberation, and Salvation*, 104. Ellacuría continues, "Reality does its part, but so does intelligence, and their respectivity functions in different ways. This does not deny or annul the priority of reality, but that priority does not annul the dynamism and even the activity proper to the human mind in its zeal to extract all the

of praxis, the "theoretical moment of praxis,"[35] and, consequently, treats "theological theory" as a moment of "theological praxis."[36] Obviously, this is *one* irreducible moment with its own structure and dynamics, as well as with specific requirements, activities, and technical apparatus, but it is a *moment* of a broader process, namely, theologal praxis—the historical realization of the reigning of God. From this perspective theologal praxis is not simply behind (presupposed) or ahead of (as goal) theological theory, as Boff maintains, but is part of the process of constructing theological theory *(medium quo)*. This might happen when the theologal praxis constitutes the reality to be theologized and thus determines, in some way, its intellective access; or when it produces and/or mediates the intellective possibilities (thought structure, concepts, and so forth); or when it directs doing theology, based on certain interests, more or less legitimate, from the evangelical point of view; or when it constitutes itself as the place of historicization and verification of the theological theory. Therefore, Ellacuría starts from a conception of knowing and of knowledge that allows the overcoming of the traditional and dominant idealistic vision of theological knowledge, of which Boff is an example, and to assume consistently, theoretically and theologically, the "epistemological density of praxis" and, with it, the decisive character of the social place of the poor and oppressed in the doing of theology.

From this point of view, opened up by Ignacio Ellacuría, we will examine the praxical character of theology. Our intention is to show how the theological praxis is crucial and constitutive of the theological theory, that is, how the process of theological knowledge is a constitutively praxical process.

The Praxical Character of Theology

The problematic of the relationship theory-praxis has been adequately formulated, and liberation theology has been located within the horizon of this problematic. What is necessary now is to make explicit the praxical character of theology. This has to do with the reality that will be intellected *(inteligida)* by theology, with the development of the intellective activity, with the interested character of that activity, and with the process of verification and historicization of theology.

---

light it can from reality by looking at it in the different ways that intelligence itself is able to generate."

[35] Ibid., 110.

[36] Ellacuría, "Relación teoría y praxis en la teología de la liberación," 235; idem, "La teología como momento ideológico de la praxis ecclesial," *Escritos Teológicos,* vol. 3 (San Salvador: UCA Editores, 2002), 171.

The Reality to Be Intellected by Theology

The praxical character of theology refers to the proper reality to be intellected by it. Contrary to what is usually thought and to what a purely etymological approach to the word suggests (*Theos*: God, and *logia*: word), theology is not about God, without any further ado. It is concerned with God, indeed, but insofar as God is present and acts in history. It is concerned, therefore, with the *action of God in history*, which is always, in some way and to some extent, *re-action* to certain situations and events (salvation) and *inter-action* with persons and concrete people (people of God–church). Hence Ellacuría's insistence that the matter or object of Christian theology is not God, simply, but the *reigning of God*.[37]

"Evidently this is not about the materiality of the term,"[38] as if it were not possible to formulate the object of Christian theology otherwise. But neither is about a mere "verbal formula or a stylistic detour for talking about God,"[39] as if there were not objective reasons to prefer this term over others. Ellacuría opts for the expression *the reigning of God* because of its praxical character (action of God in history), its direct reference to Jesus Christ (center of its life and mission), and his church (people of God–church), its salvific character (partiality for the poor and oppressed) and even its capacity to encompass and totalize the object of Christian theology (God and God's reigning in history).[40]

But with this not all has been said. The praxical character of theology, as theory, cannot simply be deduced from the claim that what is at issue is the reigning of God or God's salvific action in history. Therefore, it cannot

---

[37] Ignacio Ellacuría, "Fe y justicia," 3:307–73, in *Escritos Teológicos*, 3:311; "La teología como momento ideológico de la praxis ecclesial," 175–76; "Relación teoría y praxis en la teología de la liberación," 235, 240–41; "Liberation Theology and Socio-Historical Change in Latin America," in *Toward a Society that Servies Its People: The Intellectual Contribution of El Salvador's Murdered Jesuits*, ed. John Hassett and Hugh Lacy (Washington, DC: Georgetown University Press, 1991), 19–20; "Aporte de la teología de la liberación a las religiones abrahámicas en la superación del individualismo y del positivismo," 2:193–232, in *Escritos Teológicos*, vol. 2 (San Salvador: UCA Editores, 2000), 202.

[38] Ignacio Ellacuría, "Recuperar el reino de Dios: Desmundanización e historización de la Iglesia," in *Escritos Teológicos*, 2:312.

[39] Ellacuría, "La teología como momento ideológico de la praxis ecclesial," 1:176.

[40] Ellacuría, "Laying the Philosophical Foundations of a Latin American Theological Method," 84–85; "Recuperar el Reino de Dios," 313ff.; "La teología como momento ideológico de la praxis ecclesial," 1:167–84; "Aporte de la teología de la liberación a las religiones abrahámicas en la superación del individualismo y del positivismo," 2:202ff.; "Relación teoría y praxis en la teología de la liberación," 1:317–42; "Iglesia como pueblo de Dios," in *Escritos Teológicos*, 2:317; "Liberation Theology and Socio-Historical Change in Latin America," 20.

be deduced from a praxis. What is at issue is the determinative character of the reality to be intellected *(inteligida)* in the process of intellection itself, because the mode of intellection depends in large measure on the reality to be intellected *(inteligida)*. The intellection of a purely biological reality is different from the intellection of a personal reality; the intellection of a purely spiritual reality (if possible) is different from the intellection of a historical reality, however spiritual it may be. Given this, to determine the reigning of God to be the object of theology is, to a large degree, to determine the proper process of intellection, given that the intellective access to a reality depends largely on the way in which this reality is constituted and the way in which it allows its intellection.

The praxical character of theology is concerned, therefore, with the reality to be intellected *(inteligida)* (the reigning of God as praxis) and with the determination of the process of intellection itself by the reality to be intellected *(inteligida)* (the reigning of God as determinative of its own intellective access). Thus, both due to *its object* as well as the *way to treat it,* theology is a fundamentally praxical activity.

The Development of the Intellective Activity

The praxical character of theology it is not only concerned with the reigning of God as a theological matter and as determinant of its intellective own access. It is also concerned with the doing of theology itself, as intellective activity, because the intellective activity is an inherently praxical activity.

This is the case, first, because the intellective activity is "one of the essential moments of every possible praxis."[41] Theology is a moment of the praxis of the reigning of God. As we saw before, regardless how irreducible and important and determinative it might be, intellective activity is only one note of human action and occurs only in respectivity and interaction with other notes of human action. Strictly speaking, we should not even speak about intellective activity, as if it were an action complete in itself compared with non-intellective activities. We should always speak about a note or a moment of human action. And this leaves to the side for the moment the fact that, depending on the reality to be intellected, as in the case of the reigning of God, knowledge, in addition to being a moment of praxis, is in need of praxis "not only for its scientific verification but also so as to put it in touch with the source of many of its contents."[42]

Second, this is the case due to the intrinsically praxical character of the intellective moment of human action. Its development depends largely on

---

[41] Ellacuría, "Laying the Philosophical Foundations of Latin American Theological Method," 83.
[42] Ibid.

the available intellective possibilities at a determinate time, on their appropriation, and also, on this basis, on the creation of new intellective possibilities. On the one hand, in every moment the intellective moment depends on the available theoretical "possibilities," that "are constituted as the result of a historical journey and represent the substratum from which it thinks."[43] This varies according to the age, the people, and the situation. One cannot always count on the same theoretical possibilities. But one can always count on some possibilities and only from them and with them does the process of intellection happen. They condition it positively (making it possible) or negatively (hindering or preventing it). On the other hand, "intelligence, even in the most theoretical cases, has a moment of option."[44] And herein lies the fundamentally praxical character of the intellective moment of human action. It is necessary to opt between the available possibilities in each intellective moment and, from them, create new intellective possibilities. The process of *appropriation of intellective possibilities* is being constituted, thereby, as a process of intellective capacitation *(capacitación)*, "the constitution of the real possibility is itself part of a process *(procesual)* and is what should formally be understood as capacitation; capacitation is a process through which a being able–to be able *(poder-poder)*, a being able to make possible *(un poder posibilitar)*, a being able to make things possible *(un poder hacer posible)* is incorporated into the subject in question."[45] Consequently, no theoretical formulation, no matter how abstract and speculative it might be, can simply be explained by itself. It always depends, to some extent, on the available and appropriate intellective possibilities and on the capacitation to create new intellective possibilities.

As a constitutive moment of praxis or as a process of appropriation and creation of intellective possibilities, the development of intellective activity is constituted, therefore, as a fundamentally praxical process. Thus, besides being a *moment of the praxis*, it is a praxical moment.

The Interested Character of the Intellective Activity

In addition to the reality to be intellected (the reigning of God as a subject for theology and as determinant of theology's intellective access) and the process of intellection itself (the moment of praxis and the praxical moment), the praxical character of theology is concerned too with the interests inherent to any intellectual activity.

---

43 Ibid., 81.

44 Ibid., 82.

45 Ignacio Ellacuría, *La Filosofía de la realidad historica* (San Salavador: UCA Editores, 1990), 554.

Insofar as it is a moment of praxis (intellection-feeling-volition) and insofar as it is a praxical moment (appropriation and creation of intellective possibilities), intellection has an origin and a goal that are praxical and, as such, it is conditioned by interests that are more or less explicit. Just as all praxis is conditioned by certain interests and responds to them, so too its intellective moment.

There is no such thing as disinterested praxis. Not even the praxis of the reigning of God. Every action, every praxis, is structured and dynamized from and in function of certain interests, which may or may not be explicit, interests that can be more or less legitimate from the point of view of the gospel. Even the most gratuitous action is an interested one. When one reacts to certain events or situations in one way or another, opting for certain possibilities of reaction or interaction within the range of available possibilities, one always acts according to some reason or interest that may be in conflict with other interests. And this conditions and determines, in large measure, the intellective activity, insofar as it is a moment of praxis. It could not be otherwise. If intellection is a moment of praxis and praxis is structured from and in function of certain interests, it is clear that those interests, in some way and to some extent, structure and determine the most properly intellective moment of praxis.

First, given its praxical origin and goal. "Human knowing . . . above all in disciplines such as theory, with explicit reference to human realities, performs, together with its contemplative and interpretive functions, a praxical function that comes from and returns to the configuring of a specific social structure. Human knowing not only comes from an interested praxis, but it ends up favoring the interests inherent to that same praxis insofar as it "ends up either favoring or resisting certain social forces."[46] This happens with theology as well; it not only comes from the praxis of the reigning of God (origin), but it is at the service of that same praxis (goal). In one way or another it is conditioned and dynamized by a very concrete interest: the realization of the reigning of God.

Second, given its praxical character. We already saw that the process of intellection occurs through the appropriation and creation of intellective possibilities. And that process is conditioned "by a multitude of elements, which are not purely theoretical"[47] but depend on biographical and historical conditions and interests. The choice to investigate a concrete reality or some aspect or dimension of that reality and the option for certain theoretical and conceptual mediations is never neutral; neither occurs for purely theoretical

---

[46] Ibid., 82, 86.
[47] Ibid., 81–82.

reasons. This, which is true of thought in general, is particularly true for theological thinking, much more prone to "distortions and manipulations that are not always conscious," given the "apparently" unverifiable character of many statements.[48] Hence the need for "an ongoing and thematically focused investigation into the social world to which these formulations respond, since not even a purely theoretical formulation is fully explained only from itself."[49] Now, "besides being subjected to multiple pressures of the social order, which if they are not unmasked mystify their results, theological activity, has to take advantage of theoretical resources that may result from more or less hidden ideologizations." Either way, implicitly or explicitly, theological activity is always conditioned by more or less legitimate interests, from the point of view of the Gospel.

Whether due to its origin and praxical goals (the reigning of God) or due to its praxical character (appropriation of conceptual-theoretical possibilities), the doing of theology is always conditioned and dynamized by certain interests, which make it a constitutively praxical activity.

Verification and Historicization of Theology

In the end the praxical character of theology has to do with its verification and historicization. Insofar as it is an intellective praxis of the reigning of God, theology is at the service of that praxis and in it theology has its place and its principle of verification.

On the one hand, theology has in the praxis of the reigning of God its place and principle of fundamental verification. Insofar as it is the intellection of a praxical-historical reality (the reigning of God), it verifies its veracity in that praxis and it does so praxically. Consequently, praxis, in addition to being the *place* for experiencing or confirming the theory (the where), becomes the principle according to which its veracity is measured or weighed (the how). If it is a theory of a praxis, the theology can and must be confirmed in that praxis (the place) and can and should be made praxis and history *(ser practicable-historizable)* (the principle). Indeed, says Ellacuría:

> A theological theory that is not verifiable in theologal praxis, lacks at least one essential dimension, namely, historicity. There may be parts or aspects of a theory that are not verifiable directly and it could even be that their indirect form of verification is underdetermined. But, in being a way of theorizing a faith that is salvific, theological theory

---

[48]   Ellacuría, "La teología como momento ideológico de la praxis ecclesia," 1:165.

[49]   Ellacuría, "Laying the Philosophical Foundations of Latin American Theological Method," 82.

must, as a totality, find some form of historical verification for that salvific character.[50]

On the other hand, theology is at the service of God's reigning and must find some way to make it a reality. It is not only interested in its intelligizing it, but also in making it a reality. And that interest conditions and determines, in some way, the process of intellection itself. Insofar as it is an intellective moment of a concrete praxis (the reigning of God), theology is conditioned and guided by the inherent interests of that praxis (its historical realization). It is not a neutral or uninterested activity, and neither does it develop in an absolutely objective way. Its theoretical-conceptual possibilities are closely tied to its praxical interests. Theology not only arises out of the praxis (its intellective moment), but it is oriented to that same praxis (its goal). Therefore, it must find some form of realization (historicization). It is not the case that first one does theology (theory) and then one tries to make it real (praxis), as if the praxical interest was not inherent to the development of the intellective moment of praxis. For this reason Ellacuría maintains that "a theology that is absolutely irrelevant to a particular historical situation, besides diminishing the power of the required theologal praxis, stops being an *intellectus fidei* and becomes a study of inertness *(inoperatividades)*."[51]

Whether due to its place and principle of verification (the praxis of the reigning of God) or due to its goal (the realization or historicization of God's reign), theology as intellection has an intrinsically praxical character.

Conclusion

Discussing the praxical character of theology may seem overly speculative, abstract, and ironically, of little or no praxical relevance or impact. However, it is much more determinative and decisive for the doing of theology and has many more practical implications than it might seem at first glance.

Indeed, as noted by Antonio González:

A theology's starting point decisively determines the theological perspective used to address [any given problem] theologically. If theology starts, for example, from the question of the meaning of life, the cultural dialogue between different worldviews would be a matter of

---

[50] Ellacuría, "Relación teoría y praxis en la teología de la liberación," 241.
[51] Ibid., 241ff.

primary interest, while other human problems would be relegated to secondary importance or excluded from the field of theology. The adequate choice of the starting point of theology can decisively determine the formulation of the message that Christianity wants to convey to a humanity haunted by enormous conflicts.[52]

Furthermore, when theology consciously and consistently assumes its praxical character, it becomes more critical, more biblical, and more historically relevant. After all, what does it mean to know God but to love him (1 Jn 4:8), to do his will (1 Jn 2:3ff.), and do justice to the poor and oppressed (Jer 22:16; Mt 25:31–46)?

—Translated by J. Matthew Ashley,
José Adrés Fayos, SJ, and Raúl Zegarra

---

[52] Antonio González, "La vigencia del 'método teológico' de la teología de la liberación," *Sal Terrae* 983 (1995): 669.

6

Respectivity and a Theology of Signs

THOMAS FORNET-PONSE

With Vatican II's stress on the significance of the signs of the times, the need for a theology of signs increasingly comes into focus, although this is far from a new concern for theology. Besides the explicit references to the signs of the times in *Gaudium et spes*, the renewed understanding of the church as a sacrament—or, as *Lumen gentium* states, "as sign and instrument both of a very closely knit union with God and of the unity of the whole human race" (no. 1) —calls for a renewed analysis. What does such a sign look like from a given philosophical or theological perspective? How can it be distinguished from other signs? What are the consequences of one's position on signs?

In this chapter I address the contribution a philosophy and a theology in the footsteps of Ignacio Ellacuría can make to these questions. Therefore, after a short discussion of the need for and main contents of a theology of signs based on Vatican II, I show that Ellacuría's theology can be summarized as a theology of signs. Second, regarding his treatment of Zubiri's concepts of sentient intelligence [*inteligencia sentiente*] and respectivity [*respectividad*], I deal with the philosophical ground for his theology of signs. On this basis it is possible to take a closer look at Ellacuría's understanding of Jesus Christ as the perfect sign for God and of the church as a sign for God's reign.

The Need for a Theology of Sign

Gaudium et spes teaches:

> To carry out such a task, the Church has always had the duty of scrutinizing the signs of the times and of interpreting them in the light of the Gospel. Thus, in language intelligible to each generation, she can respond to the perennial questions which men ask about this

present life and the life to come, and about the relationship of the one to the other. We must therefore recognize and understand the world in which we live, its explanations, its longings, and its often dramatic characteristics. (no. 4)

Although, as Hans-Joachim Sander notes, the term "signs of the times" only appears at this point in *Gaudium et spes*, it nevertheless represents its fundamental perspective. Because it is necessary that every generation address anew the ultimate questions of humankind, recognizing that there is no contradiction between the temporal and the eternal. "The signs of the times stand for this non-contradiction. They are determined by a non-exclusion of the historical pole from the enduring deposit of faith and by a non-exclusion of the time-transcending position from the concrete contemporary."[1] Thus, the signs of the times mark incidents, events, or facts that provide a look at broad developments—whether humanizing or dehumanizing—which at once represent what is essential about the human and what is significant in a given current situation. They are precarious appearances, in which the weal and woe of the men and women of this age become visible, and through which people have to struggle for the recognition of their dignity. By referring to them, it is possible to stress the significance of faith. "What the signs of the times reveal from the outside, the light of the gospel enables from the inside. Both are producing a difference necessary for not being completely absorbed or drowning in hope and anxiety of the people of this age."[2] *Gaudium et spes* uses the pastoral spiral (see–judge–act) with regard to the signs of the time by mentioning the duty to scrutinize them, interpret them in the light of the gospel, and respond to the existential questions of human beings. The signs of the times thus become *loci theologici*.

This fundamental perspective of *Gaudium et spes* expresses clearly the semiotic character of theology and the need for a theology of signs, which is not restricted to a theology of symbol but regards other everyday symbolic representations as a mediation of our encounter with the mystery of God's self-offer.[3] All signs arise out of the difference between inside and outside and enable us to work with this difference.

---

[1] Hans-Joachim, Sander, *Theologischer Kommentar zur Pastoralkonstitution über die Kirche in der Welt von heute Gaudium et spes*, in *Herders Theologischer Kommentar zum Zweiten Vatikanischen Konzil*, vol. 4, ed. Peter Hünermann and Bernd Jochen Hilberath, 581–886 (Freiburg i.Br. et al., 2005), 716; hereafter Sander, *Kommentar*.

[2] Sander, *Kommentar*, 717, trans. emended.

[3] See Robert Lassalle-Klein, "Rethinking Rahner on Grace and Symbol: New Proposals from the Americas," in *Rahner Beyond Rahner: A Great Theologian Encounters the Pacific Rim*, ed. Paul Crowley, 87–99 (Lanham, MD: Rowman and Littlefield, 2005), 94.

A semiotic perspective may appear as a perspective from the outside of theology, yet it leads into its center since theology, too, works with signs. *God* is first and foremost a generally accessible name and embodies a public resource of speech. "God is present with his name and at the same time independent from those who have learned to address him."[4] The sign is not restricted to theologians, because all who have learned to work with it are able to do it. With reference to C. S. Peirce's conception of the semiotic triangle as a universal constellation for every cognitive act, Sander stresses that the Firstness, the reference to reality, cannot be excluded, and that is the representational problem for theology since it cannot be restricted to the internal discourse. "Without signs, [theology] is speechless external of itself, but if it really has signs for its own concerns available, it can present the content of reality of its statements."[5] Addressing this semiotic necessity is not only one of the most important dogmatic achievements of Vatican II but also something about which Ignacio Ellacuría was deeply concerned.

In fact, based on Rahner's theology of symbol and his own conviction that historical reality is the proper object of philosophy and theology, Ellacuría applies a "more complex, nuanced theology (and ontology) of sign"[6] in which not only the sacraments but also sacramentals or other everyday symbolic representations can be considered as a mediation of our encounter with God. A very short description of his understanding of a sign can be found in one of his ecclesiological writings:

> The sign, by its very nature, should be something visible and verifiable; the sign should, also by its nature, refer to something that is both in relation to the sign, but which is not the sign itself. The sign does not have to resemble what it signifies; e.g. the linguistic sign does not resemble the message it wants to transmit but its effectiveness lies in transmitting the message. The sign is nothing but an active mediation between two extremes, whose connection cannot be immediate.[7]

Theologically speaking, there is no union between God and humankind but in a historical process, the history of salvation, one encounters the visible and effective presence of God among humans. Thus, by unifying—not

---

[4] Hans-Joachim Sander, "Die Zeichen der Zeit erkennen und Gott benennen: Der semiotische Charakter von Theologie," *ThQ* 182 (2002): 30.

[5] Sander, "Die Zeichen der Zeit erkennen und Gott benennen," 32.

[6] Lassalle-Klein, "Rethinking Rahner on Grace and Symbol," 95.

[7] Ignacio Ellacuría, "Iglesia y realidad histórica," *Escritos teológicos*, vol. 2 (San Salvador: UCA Editores, 2000), 505, translated by Lassalle-Klein, "Rethinking Rahner on Grace and Symbol," 95.

identifying—its theologal and historical character, the apparent duality of the church is overcome.

Although Ellacuría uses the category of sign mainly in his ecclesiological writings, his whole theology can be summarized as a "theology of sign."[8] In an unpublished letter defending his book *Teología Política* (1973) against criticisms expressed by an unnamed reviewer for the office of the apostolic nuncio in San Salvador, he not only stresses the impact of Rahner's theology of symbol for his own work but also its fundamental perspective. According to Ellacuría, this reviewer "ignores and passes over what is essential in my work: salvation in history is a sign of the plenitude of a salvation that is meta-historical." This theology of sign "dominates the entire publication. . . . Everything that is presented as salvation in history . . . is regarded as a sign of the history of salvation. It comes from that, and it moves toward that. My work tries to demonstrate the connection between the sign and what constitutes it as a sign."[9] This leads us to the philosophical basis of his theology of sign, which he does not mention explicitly but which can be found in his appropriation of two central and closely connected notions of his mentor, Xavier Zubiri: the epistemology of sentient intelligence and the metaphysical idea of respectivity.

Sentient Intelligence and Respectivity as Philosophical Fundament for a Theology of Sign[10]

Both concepts provide a philosophical basis for a theology of sign: the sentient intelligence addresses the epistemological issue of the relationship of *intellection* (reasoning) and reality, and the possibility of anything referring to something else based on the *respectivity* of the real.

Zubiri's epistemology of "sentient intelligence" is the result of his reconstructive critique of a reductionist idealism he diagnoses in Western

---

[8]   See Lassalle-Klein, "Rethinking Rahner on Grace and Symbol," 95.

[9]   This letter is quoted in Lassalle-Klein, "Rethinking Rahner on Grace and Symbol," 95.

[10]   See Xavier Zubiri, *Sentient Intelligence*, by Thomas Fowler (Washington, DC: The Xavier Zubiri Foundation of North America, 1999), trans. from *Inteligencia sentiente: Inteligencia y realidad*, vol. 1 (Madrid: Alianza, 1980, 2006); Xavier Zubiri, "Respectividad de lo real," *Realitas III–IV* (1979), 13–43. For Zubiri's impact on Ellacuría, see Robert Lassalle-Klein, "Ignacio Ellacuría's Debt to Xavier Zubiri: Critical Principles for a Latin American Philosophy and Theology of Liberation," in *Love That Produces Hope: The Thought of Ignacio Ellacuría*, ed. Kevin Burke and Robert Lassalle-Klein, 88–127 (Collegeville, MN: Liturgical Press, 2006); Kevin F. Burke, *The Ground Beneath the Cross: The Theology of Ignacio Ellacuría* (Washington, DC: Georgetown University Press, 2000), 43–97.

philosophy.[11] To overcome the distortions of the logification of intelligence and the entification of reality, Zubiri proposes to understand human intellection as a structural unity of intellection and sensing, as two dimensions of one single intellective act: "I believe that understanding consists formally in apprehending the real as real, and that sensing is apprehending the real in impression."[12] Thus, human sensing—that is, the perception by means of the senses—and intellection are not in opposition but constitute a single and indivisible act of apprehension. "Intellection is a mode of sensing, and sensing in the human is a mode of intellection."[13] This act is not only an apprehension of reality but an impression of reality, thus combining the intellective moment with the experience of the senses. Therefore, the intellection of reality is not simply produced by affirmative, propositional, or predicative judgments about data given by the senses. "Reality is already actualized in sensing itself, in the sensible actualization itself."[14] This is not meant to reduce the subsequent or other intellective functions to sensing since the sentient character of intellection does not only produce contents; sensing is the impression of the formal dimension of reality itself.

On this basis Ellacuría develops his philosophy of historical reality with its focus on historical reality as the proper object of philosophy.[15] Thus, he stresses not only the contextuality of his own work but regards it as necessary for a truly authentic philosophy to arise out of its own historical reality and to fulfill its critical and liberating task with regard to this historical reality.[16] Furthermore, it provides the basis for his theological emphasis on the historical dimension of salvation and for proclaiming the historical crucified people as the principal sign of the times that should orient the "universal historical mission" of the church.[17] With the signs of the times the revelation of God is put in relationship with real history which does

---

[11] See Ignacio Ellacuría, "La superación del reduccionismo idealista en Zubiri," *Escritos filosóficos,* vol. 3 (San Salvador: UCA Editores, 2001), 403–30.

[12] Zubiri, *Sentient Intelligence,* 4.

[13] Ibid., 4, trans. emended.

[14] Ellacuría, "La superación del reduccionismo idealista en Zubiri," 422, trans. in Lassalle-Klein, "Ignacio Ellacuría's Debt to Xavier Zubiri," 100.

[15] See Ignacio Ellacuría, *Filosofía de la realidad histórica* (San Salvador: UCA Editores, 1990).

[16] See Ignacio Ellacuría, "Función liberadora de la filosofía," *Veinte años de historia en El Salvador (1969–1989); Escritos políticos,* vol. 1, 93–121 (San Salvador: UCA Editores, 2005), 121; English trans., "The Liberating Function of Philosophy," in *Ignacio Ellacuría: Essays in History, Liberation, and Salvation,* ed. Michael E. Lee, 93–119 (Maryknoll, NY: Orbis Books, 2013).

[17] See Ignacio Ellacuría, "Discernir 'el signo' de los tiempos," *Escritos teológicos,* 2:133–35; idem, "Los pobres, lugar teológico en América Latina," *Escritos teológicos,* vol. 1, 137–61 (San Salvador: UCA Editores, 2000).

not displace the gospel as the most important source of theology but rather takes the signs of the times seriously as a theological place, to relate them to the deposit of faith. "The word of God reveals its true contents through historical reality. In this way, the word of God is alive and creative, and it is capable of saying new things in new historical situations."[18] With regard to Zubiri, Ellacuría considers the deposit of faith as a system of possibilities that are actualized according to the necessities of historical events. In addition, Ellacuría transforms the reciprocal actualization of reality and the subject developed by Zubiri into an ethical imperative by pointing out that "the formal structure of intelligence and its differentiating function . . . is not to comprehend being or capture sense but to apprehend reality and to face up to that reality."[19] This has a triple dimension: first, the noetic moment of *realizing the weight of reality* [*el hacerse cargo de la realidad*], which implies being in the reality of things (and not merely being before the idea of things or being in touch with their meaning); second, the ethical nature of intelligence, *shouldering the weight of reality* [*el cargar con la realidad*], since intelligence must respond to the demand of reality; and third, the *taking charge of the weight of reality* [*el encargarse de la realidad*], which indicates the praxis-oriented nature of intelligence.[20] In particular, the last dimension explains why Ellacuría writes that a sign should be something visible and verifiable, why the credibility of the church as a sign of God's reign depends on its dedication to realize salvation historically, and why the historical reality "leads to the truth of reality and to the truth of the interpretation of reality" and that this concerns rather the equivalency between *verum* and *faciendum* than between *verum* and *factum*.[21]

Both Ellacuría's stress on this triple dimension of apprehending reality and his reasoning for the historical reality as the proper object of philosophy are based on his reception of Zubiri's idea of respectivity (one of Zubiri's neologisms) as the expression for the unity of reality and its dynamic structure. The core of this philosophical idea is expressed in Ellacuría's first thesis about the proper object of philosophy: "The totality of intramundane reality constitutes a single physical unity that is complex and differentiated

---

[18] Martin Maier, "Karl Rahner: The Teacher of Ignacio Ellacuría," in Burke and Lassalle-Klein, *Love That Produces Hope*, 136.

[19] See Ignacio Ellacuría, "Hacia una fundamentación del método teológico latino-americano," *Escritos teológicos*, 1:187–217, quotation at 1:207; see "Laying the Philosophical Foundations of Latin American Theological Method," trans. J. M. Ashley and K. Burke, in Lee, *Ignacio Ellacuría*, 63–91.

[20] Burke, *The Ground Beneath the Cross*, 100. For a detailed analysis of meaning and function of praxis in Ellacuría's theology, see Michael Lee, *Bearing the Weight of Salvation: The Soteriology of Ignacio Ellacuría* (New York: Crossroad, 2009), 105–33.

[21] Ignacio Ellacuría, "El objeto de la filosofía," in *Escritos políticos*, 1:63–92, quotation at 1:89.

in such a way that the unity does not nullify the differences and the differences do not nullify the unity."[22] This thesis emphasizes the totality of reality by pointing out a prior, primary, and systematic unity of reality—called respectivity—that is prior to all relations (static aspect) and functions (dynamic aspect) and constitutes all things as things and as real. Reality *qua* reality is characterized by a foundational intraconnectedness; any real thing is linked to every other real thing in the cosmos. Furthermore, this intramundane reality is intrinsically and constitutively dynamic: "Reality is dynamic from itself [*de por sí*], it is dynamic of itself [*de suyo*], and its moment of dynamism consists initially in a giving-of-its-own [*dar de sí*]. The world, as the respectivity of reality *qua* reality, does not have dynamism, nor is it in dynamism, but rather, it is itself dynamic: worldly respectivity is essentially dynamic."[23] The intrinsic dynamism of reality is prior to movement or process and is closely interrelated to the balance of identity and multiplicity since dynamism breaches identity and non-identity actualizes dynamism. Furthermore, it is the basis for the movement from lower to higher forms of reality culminating in historical reality as the supreme manifestation of reality. In this systematic and structural unity of reality, each part receives its reality from the whole, although the parts themselves constitute it as a whole.

The foundational intraconnectedness of all real things *qua* real is based on another important aspect of Zubiri's notion of respectivity: the openness of a real thing. "The formality of reality is in itself, *qua* 'of reality,' something open, at least with respect to its content. . . . By being open this formality is that by which a real thing *qua* real is 'more' than its actual content. Reality is not, then, a characteristic of the *content already completed,* but is *open formality.*"[24] Above all, the formality of reality is open to a content which is "in its own right" [*de suyo*] and thus constitutes its-own-ness [*suidad*] as such. Furthermore, it is open to being a moment of the world that is not a conjunction of real things but the physical unity formally constituted by the character of being purely and simply real. "This respectivity has two moments: it is *own-making* and *world-making.* That is, each thing is 'this' real thing; in a further sense it is 'its own' reality (own-making); in a still more ulterior aspect it is pure and simple worldly reality (world-making)."[25] Since all kinds of relations are references of a real thing to another, all presuppose a transcendental respectivity that consists primarily and

---

[22] Ellacuría, "El objeto de la filosofía," 76, trans. K. Burke, in Burke, *The Ground Beneath the Cross,* 54.

[23] Ellacuría, *Filosofía de la realidad histórica,* 591, trans. K. Burke, in Burke, *The Ground Beneath the Cross,* 55.

[24] Zubiri, *Sentient Intelligence,* 45.

[25] Ibid., 46.

radically in the intrinsic and formal openness of the moment of reality. "It is possible for there to be relations precisely because reality is respectively open."[26] In particular the openness of a real thing and this determination of the relationship of a real thing to the whole of reality can be successfully applied for the question of grounding a theology of sign that can best be shown by discussing specific examples like Christ as the sign in which God revealed himself in history or the church as a sign of God's reign.

Christ and the Church as Examples for a Theology of Sign

Although Ellacuría joins a long tradition in understanding Christ as a sign of God and the church as a sign of God's reign, his remarks nevertheless show his particular perspective as a liberation theologian with a focus on historical reality. Like Rahner, he stresses the close connection between salvation history and world history. Historical reality understood as a respective totality contains all that leads to God's reign and all that opposes it and is thus not something to be wholly overcome or negated. "Salvation history and so-called profane history both belong to a single history that they serve: God's history; what God has done with all of nature; what God does in human history."[27] By emphasizing salvation history as a salvation in history and the historical life of Jesus as the culminating point of the history of revelation, he concludes concerning salvation: "1) It will differ according to the time and place in which it is fleshed out; 2) it must be realized and brought about in the historical reality of human beings, in their total concrete reality."[28] The church remains loyal to its mission by taking fresh readings of revelation and by proclaiming salvation in different ways corresponding to different situations, thus acknowledging the concrete needs of the particular situation and demonstrating its openness to other realities and especially historical reality. "Christians must insist that history is the locale of God's revelation, and that this revelation is meant to show us here and now that God is revealing himself in history. . . . God revealed himself in history, not directly but in a sign: humanity in history. There is no access to God except through this sign in history."[29] The Christian belief therefore stresses that it is only possible to communicate with God the Father

---

[26] Zubiri, "Respectividad de lo real," 40.

[27] Ignacio Ellacuría, "The Historicity of Christian Salvation," in Lee, *Ignacio Ellacuría*, 137–68; from "Historicidad de la salvación cristiana," *Escritos teológicos*, 1:535–96, quotation at 571.

[28] Ignacio Ellacuría, *Freedom Made Flesh: The Mission of Christ and His Church* (Maryknoll, NY: Orbis Books, 1976), 15.

[29] Ibid., 18.

through the sign of Jesus' humanity. Jesus is the perfect sign and showed us in a historical way the need for mediation both in the presentation of God to us humans and of us gaining access to God. "He also shows us what the historicization of this mediation can and should be."[30] Thus, a reflection of Jesus and his prophetic mission and its political character is indispensable for understanding the nature of salvation in history. Because the presence of salvation becomes manifest in and through history, the relationship between Christian salvation and historical liberation can be described as historical soteriology.[31] Burke points out the correspondence between Ellacuría's historical soteriology and the triple dimension of apprehending reality: The noetic dimension is to interpret theologically the relationship of transcendence to history, the ethical option is to take the crucified people down from their crosses and the praxis-oriented dimension concerns the "ecclesial praxis that participates in God's saving action and constitutes God's people as a historical sacrament of liberation."[32]

Ellacuría emphasizes the sociopolitical dimension of Jesus' prophecy by pointing out his rooting in and transcending from the prophetic tradition with his rejection of a ritualized religion, his attack on the oppression exercised by religious authorities, and his preference for the universalism of the prophets—in short, his "shift of religious emphasis to operative faith."[33] It is truly Christian to follow Jesus in our concrete lives, for example, by giving up material wealth and distributing it to the poor. Ellacuría refers to the comparison between the three miracles of Moses in Exodus 4 and three corresponding miracles by Jesus and points out the need for signs or amazing deeds that show or prove God's presence or will, depending on the situation. Independent of the signs being consequences or presuppositions of believing in Christ, they show the inner connection between the sign and the signified. "Furthermore, the sign can be understood as the unity of the signifier (the historical event that points to salvation) and the signified (the salvation made present in the historical event)."[34] In view of the whole praxis of Jesus' life—which leads him to oppose oppressing and idolatrous worldly powers, and finally ends in his violent death—Ellacuría stresses the novelty of Christian historical transcendence: "The historical

---

[30] Ibid., 87.

[31] For more on the meaning of *historical soteriology*, see Michael Lee, "Toward a New, Historical Evangelization," in the present volume.—*Eds.*

[32] Burke, *The Ground Beneath the Cross*, 152. See also Lee, *Bearing the Weight of Salvation*, esp. 48–50.

[33] Ellacuría, *Freedom Made Flesh*, 30. See also Ellacuría, "Historicidad de la salvación cristiana," 552.

[34] Ellacuría, "Historicidad de la salvación cristiana," 565.

praxis of Jesus reveals in him a new and definitive presence of God, which in turn lends new perspectives and new dimensions to transcendence in its specifically and fully Christian sense."[35] The preeminent place for reflecting this interrelatedness of transcendence and historical reality is the cross on which Jesus was crucified. It must not be separated from the crucified, which would make it an abstract or dehistoricized symbol.

Regarding this last point Ellacuría emphasizes the close connection of two questions concerning Jesus' death: Why did Jesus die? Why was he killed?[36] While the first question addresses the theological-historical and thus the soteriological perspective, the second question is concerned with the historical reality and the political dimension. These questions cannot be separated, but the historical priority must be sought in the second one. Jesus was killed because of the life he lived and the mission he carried out. "If, from a theological-historical point of view it can be said that Jesus died for our sins and for human salvation, i.e. that his death has a soteriological character; from a historical-theological point of view it must be maintained that they killed him for the life he lived."[37] This underlines that history of salvation is salvation in and of history. The necessity of Jesus' death mentioned in the Gospels (Lk 24:26) is explained as a historical necessity, which refers to historical-theologal reality with both historical sin and God's salvific will affecting the structures of society and history. Particular historical reasons—a conspiracy of religious and political elites threatened by Jesus' preaching and his prophetic actions—led to his death. "It was not accidental that the life of Jesus was what it was; neither was it accidental that this life brought him to the death that he suffered. The struggle on behalf of the reign of God necessarily presupposes a struggle in favour of the human unjustly oppressed; this struggle leads one into confrontation with those responsible for this oppression. Because of this he died."[38]

Thus, it is not only his death that has salvific weight but the continuity of his life with his death. The life gives ultimate meaning to his death, which only as a consequence of this life is the meaning of his life. Therefore, it is necessary that the events of Jesus' earthly life and death continue as "a historical continuation which continues realizing what he realized and how he realized it."[39] This leads Ellacuría to establish the crucified people as the most

---

[35] Ibid., 567.

[36] See Ignacio Ellacuría, "¿Por qué muere Jesús y por qué lo matan?" *Escritos teológicos,* 2:67–88.

[37] Ibid., 2:86.

[38] Ibid., 86–87.

[39] Ellacuría, "El pueblo crucificado: Ensayo de soteriología histórica," *Escritos teológicos,* 2:137–70, quotation at 2:152; see also "The Crucified People: An Essay in Historical Soteriology," in Lee, *Ignacio Ellacura,* 195–224.

urgent of all contemporary signs of the times. It is the historical continuation of the Servant of Yahweh in Isaiah and is distinguished not by suffering alone but by a situation of crucifixion due to the way society is organized and maintained by an oppressing minority. By representing the historical continuation of Jesus' saving death, the crucified people become themselves a sign of God's will. "On the basis of the similarity between the passion of Jesus and the passion of the crucified people, Ellacuría concludes that the people appear not only as victim of the sin of the world, but as savior and judge of the world."[40]

With regard to our interpretation of Jesus Christ as the sign of God, it is very important to note that the concrete experiences of his life enabled Jesus "to learn how he was to understand the kingdom that he had come to proclaim and how access to this kingdom was to be provided."[41] Not only does salvation takes place in and through history, but also Jesus' own messianic consciousness and our knowledge of it are mediated by it. It is indeed necessary to move from salvation in history to a meta-historical salvation, and human beings can recognize authentic salvation in history because of the proclamation of this meta-historical salvation. However, "authentic salvation in history will be the one and only valid sign, comprehensible to human beings, of what meta-historical salvation means."[42]

Referring to the short definition of *sign* by Ellacuría quoted above, Jesus' humanity (in view of the unity of his life and death) represents the sign in which God has revealed himself as he is through something visible and verifiable. It refers to something that is both not the sign itself but in relation to the sign since on the one hand, the Word became flesh in historical reality and not God the Father or the Holy Spirit, and on the other hand, the two natures are unconfused, unchangeable, indivisible, and inseparable. It is an active mediation between the two extremes, God and humankind, whose connection cannot be immediate but needs the mediator, Jesus Christ, with his two natures. The triple dimension of apprehending reality with its focus on the praxis-oriented nature of intelligence is clearly reflected in Ellacuría's insistence on an operative faith and concretely following Jesus. It further founds the possibility of the church to be a sign of God's reign: Acting in the world is acting in accordance to this sign character. An observer would not be able to recognize something that only deals with one dimension of apprehending reality and does not follow Jesus' life as a sign for God's reign. Because of the historicity of the church's mission, the church has to proclaim and realize salvation historically and

---

40 Burke, *The Ground Beneath the Cross*, 185.
41 Ellacuría, *Freedom Made Flesh*, 54.
42 Ibid., 68–69.

in a more and more secularized world it has to make clear the credibility of its mission.

The human, Jesus, is the perfect sign and shows us a possible historicization of the mediation between God and humankind. "In continuing the work of Jesus Christ, therefore, we must seek out the specific kind of mediation that will signify God and make him present in a sign way."[43] The fundamental sign of God is the history of the chosen people, the history in the fullness of time that is Jesus and Christ and the church insofar as it continues his life and mission, insofar as it is a historical sacrament of liberation. The church only does justice to its character as a mediating sign if it is at work in history, "when it strives wholeheartedly to be itself a sign, and only a sign, of the God who has revealed himself in history."[44] The starting point is historical reality, which assumes both the personal intersubjectivity and the objectivism of nature in a positive way, thus corresponding to the total reality of the human person as nature and history. The sign of credibility should be fleshed out in historical praxis and salvation must be proclaimed in a signifying way:

> And the nature of signs requires us to consider both what should be signified and to whom it is to be signified. What should be signified in this case is the total salvation of human beings in and through their intrinsic deification; and the addressee of this effort is the world of today, which is engaged in the salvation of the history that it bears on its shoulders. Thus salvation in history is the present-day sign of salvation history.[45]

The historicity of salvation has the triple dimension as real-life authenticity, as actualization in history, and as hope in an eschatological future. As a historical reality the church itself influences the configuration of salvation in history. Combining the essential historicity of salvation and the need of mediating salvation in history through the church, it is possible to explore the proper incarnation of the sign—between the extremes of signifying nothing beyond itself (angelism) and not intrinsically signifying what it should signify (secularism). Liberation, justice, and love are essential dimensions both of the historical world and of the gospel message and thus "offer an adequate channel for mediating salvation in a historical way, and for allowing the church to present itself as the sign par excellence of the God who saves the world."[46] On the basis of the connection of salvation and

---

43 Ibid., 87–88.
44 ibid., 89.
45 Ibid., 93, trans. emended.
46 Ibid., 95.

history, Christian liberation is concerned about evading the tendencies to view liberation as a purely immanent process or as a purely transcendental process. Christian liberation is understood negatively as liberation *from* something (specifically oppression and sin) and positively as liberation *for* something (the free being of the Son of God). Christian liberty calls for the formation of the universal human being as well as for a new earth. "The liberator God, who transcends history, has been made present in history in a signifying way by a human, and now a human proclaims and affirms in history something that goes beyond history."[47]

If Christians do not work actively for the coming of God and the creation of the new human being, then the world cannot believe them. The church is here to be the sign of the gospel's credibility in history, to be a universal sacrament of liberation that addresses its concrete historical reality, especially the world of the poor. The people of God are characterized by a preferential option for the liberation of the poor because of God's special attentiveness to the oppressed and marginalized. By following Jesus and serving God's reign, the church realizes its vocation to make present the reign of God in history. As historical sacrament of liberation the church must become the historical body of Christ by following his life, by being a church of the poor, and by serving as a historical sacrament of liberation.[48] Ellacuría emphasizes the action of Christ's body, the praxis of God's Reign as fulfilment of the sacramental vocation of the church. The church needs to dedicate itself to liberation from injustice in this world because of its sign character as well as because it is an essential aspect of its mission and its service to the world. "If the church is to be credible to the world to which it has been sent, it needs only be in fact what it is supposed to be in nature. . . . At each and every moment in history it must look for the sign-bearing role that will serve it adequately in fleshing out its true being in history and that will enable the world to recognize its true character."[49] The signs it has to look for are intrinsically connected with its mission and must be intrinsically credible as well as credible to a concrete world. Since it cannot be denied that the church has contributed to the unjust oppression of human beings, it is necessary to recognize this contribution for becoming an effective sign of the gospel message. It not only has to undergo a painful conversion and do penance, but it also has to take positive action in the struggle against injustice. "Its

---

[47] Ibid., 108, trans. emended; see also 237.

[48] See Ignacio Ellacuría, "Pobres," *Escritos teológicos*, 188–192; idem, "Iglesia como pueblo de Dios," *Escritos teológicos,* 2:317–342; idem, "La Iglesia de los pobres, sacramento histórico de liberación," *Escritos teológicos*, 2:453–85, trans. M. Wilde as "The Church of the Poor: Historical Sacrament of Liberation," in Lee, *Ignacio llacuría*, 227–53.

[49] Ellacuría, *Freedom Made Flesh*, 110; see also 160ff.

specific contribution lies in fighting injustice insofar as injustice is sin."[50] The vocation of the church is to denounce injustice as a sin, to announce and proclaim a radical personal conversion and structural change as the only way to pass from sin to resurrection, and to support the struggle of the oppressed. The identification of the church with the oppressed will lead to its rejection by the world, but this rejection will be an irrefutable sign of its dedication to the establishment of justice and its Christian character and thus of God the Creator and Redeemer. In considering redemptive liberation and the fight against injustice, it is important not to forget the central place of Christian love.

In the central mystery of the incarnation the two basic dimensions of love, God's love for humankind and humankind's love for God, meet and interact. "The love which Christianity proclaims, the love whereby Christians will be recognized as such and will make known the divinity of Jesus, must conform itself to the love which Jesus proclaimed and lived in his own life."[51] That includes a radical power of transformation without which it would not be able to serve as a sign of salvation. The objectification of love in history has to be centered on the union of divine love and human love, and it has to struggle to eliminate sin. Faith and hope build the framework for the objectification of love in history and specify its possibilities. "Christian hope impels the church to engage in the active construction of the world, in a process that will really signify and lead towards the kingdom of God."[52]

Because the church as a whole must be a sign of Jesus the Savior, it is obliged to do what it really and truly signifies. It must not rest content with being a mere sign but move toward being more than just a sign. "The church will be able to carry out its mission of signifying and fleshing out the salvation of Jesus Christ only insofar as the church is preserved from the world and carries on the gospel message—in short, only insofar as it is the holy Church."[53]

Conclusion

The different aspects of a theology of sign explained with the examples of Christ as the sign of God and the church as the sign of God's reign, and especially its praxis-oriented character, are clearly summarized by Ellacuría:

---

[50] Ibid., 114.
[51] Ibid., 119.
[52] Ibid., 123.
[53] Ibid., 125.

The sign leads us beyond itself, but without the sign there is no beyond for us. The sign both is and is not what it signifies. And in our present context the sign cannot be something arbitrary or whimsical. By its very nature it should lead us towards that which it claims to signify, as is evident from the historical example of Christ himself. The sign enables and obliges us to transform the worldly realm because it is only in this realm that we can find the sign at all. It obliges us to look for that sign which will truly call our attention to that which God has revealed in Jesus Christ. It obliges us not to rest content within the sign itself; for if it truly is the sign established by Christ in his historical revelation, it will drive us beyond itself.[54]

Both the signs of the times, on the one hand, and also Christ and the church, on the other, owe their sign character to the prior, primary, and systematic unity of reality and the openness of real things since this unity and openness are the ground not only for the focus on historical reality but first and foremost of the close connection, the "coextensivity," between salvation history and world history. Salvation history as salvation in and of history directs the attention to the worldly realm in which the signs can be found and that has to be transformed according to God's will. This ethical and praxis-oriented character of interpreting signs and their enabling and obligating us to transform historical reality is further corroborated by the triple dimension of human apprehension of reality. According to Vatican II the signs of the times manifest the non-contradiction between the temporal and the eternal, provide a glimpse at the broad developments in humanitarianism and inhumanitarianism, and represent that which is significant for the actual historical reality. Jesus, as the sign of God's universal salvific will, signifies the possibility of transforming historical reality according to this will (and the cost of this dedication), thus calling the church and all Christians to follow him on the path of an operative faith. Doing this, proclaiming and making present the reign of God in history, renders the church a credible, visible, and verifiable sign of God's reign, fulfilling its vocation as universal sacrament of liberation and salvation.

---

[54] Ellacuría, *Freedom Made Flesh*, 140.

7

Ignacio Ellacuría and Enrique Dussel

On the Contributions of Phenomenology to Liberation Theology

ANDREW PREVOT

Ignacio Ellacuría's philosophical acumen is one of the most distinctive marks of his approach to liberation theology and one of the features that makes his thought especially valuable in contemporary conversations about the directions that liberation theology should take in the twenty-first century. The same points can be made about Enrique Dussel. Yet few commentators have put these philosophically minded liberation theologians into dialogue.[1] Moreover, although there has been much recent discussion concerning the relationship between phenomenology and theology in Europe and the United States, this conversation has tended to ignore the particular forms that this relationship takes in liberation theorists such as Ellacuría and Dussel.[2] This chapter seeks to address these two lacunae by incorporating the insights of Ellacuría and Dussel into a brief reflection on the contributions that phenomenology may make to liberation theology.

One question that this essay needs to consider is whether and, if so, in what sense Ellacuría and Dussel think phenomenologically. Those who are cognizant of Ellacuría's and Dussel's dependence on the realist philosophy of Xavier Zubiri might object that they are more strictly engaged in what he calls metaphysics [*metafísica*]. Granted, if phenomenology is taken to

---

[1] Mayra Rivera does draw a few connections between Ellacuría and Dussel in *The Touch of Transcendence: A Postcolonial Theology of God* (Louisville, KY: Westminster John Knox, 2007), 41 and 76, but does not provide any lengthy exposition of their relation.

[2] See Dominique Janicaud et al., *Phenomenology and the "Theological Turn": The French Debate* (New York: Fordham University Press, 2000); Bruce Ellis Benson and Norman Wirzba, eds., *Words of Life: New Theological Turns in French Phenomenology* (New York: Fordham University Press, 2010).

imply some sort of post-Cartesian idealism and metaphysics an adamantly post-idealist realism, a usage sometimes supported by Zubiri, then Ellacuría and Dussel are more closely aligned with the latter. However, the relation between these terms is more complicated than this sort of idealist-realist contrast suggests. The realist philosophy that Zubiri presents as a very particular kind of metaphysics owes a great deal to the principles and classical sources of phenomenology; its content comes from the phenomenal domain of sentient intelligence; and it resists the idealizing tendencies that Zubiri believes characterize the bulk of the metaphysical tradition. When Zubiri claims to surpass phenomenology, he presupposes a delimited Husserlian sense of the term that is concerned with the noetic-noematic correlates of consciousness. Conversely, when he endorses metaphysics, his endorsement extends only to his own phenomenologically inflected mode of it.[3]

To appreciate the innovations of Ellacuría and Dussel, along with those of Zubiri, we need to situate their projects within the twentieth-century tradition of critically revised or expanded phenomenology, a tradition that also includes thinkers such as Martin Heidegger, Maurice Merleau-Ponty, Emmanuel Levinas, Paul Ricoeur, and Jean-Luc Marion, to mention but a few. In different ways each of the representatives of this tradition seeks to overcome the limitations of earlier versions of phenomenology through more radical exposures to the things themselves or to the mysteries that they shelter. Reading Ellacuría and Dussel in connection with this tradition allows one to recognize their ability to approximate the deep levels of experiential awareness that phenomenology fundamentally desires.

The decision to locate Ellacuría and Dussel in a revisionist phenomenological tradition may do little to appease those phenomenologists who remain committed to the letter of Edmund Husserl or to some only slightly modified repetition of his phenomenological method. Ellacuría and Dussel could be accused of making an invalid theological, or theo-political, turn that would appear to disregard Husserl's prescribed suspension of transcendence.[4] But whether they differ from Husserl and whether their phenomenological insights are valid are arguably two distinct questions. Could that which is essential to phenomenology still be found even in some discourses that dare to test its preconceived limits? In any case, liberation theologians

---

[3] See Xavier Zubiri, *Nature, History, God*, trans. Thomas B. Fowler (Washington, DC: University Press of America, 1981), viii–xiv; Diego Gracia, *Voluntad de Verdad: Para leer a Zubiri* (Barcelona: Editorial Labor, 1986), 33–94; and Jesús Conill, "Phenomenology in Ortega and in Zubiri," in *Phenomenology World-Wide: Foundations—Expanding Dynamics—Life Engagements*, ed. Anna-Teresa Tymieniecka, 402–9 (Dordrecht: Kluwer Academic, 2002).

[4] Edmund Husserl, *Ideas: General Introduction to Pure Phenomenology*, trans. W. R. Boyce Gibson (London: Routledge, 2012), sec. 58, p. 112.

may have their own reasons for turning to phenomenology, which could significantly change the debate about its validating criteria.

Another question that this essay must address—arguably the more important question—is whether and, if so, in what respects phenomenology has anything to contribute to liberation theology. There are at least two reasons to doubt it. First, phenomenology could be perceived as an obstacle to the particular kinds of critical reflection and practical engagement that liberation theology demands. It could be construed as a Eurocentric, ideologically complacent, or egologically absorbed discourse, which is largely indifferent to the immense sufferings and injustices of the world and the concrete actions that are required to resist them. Second, phenomenology could be perceived as an obstacle to the development of a genuinely Christian theology. If the most crucial source of this sort of theology is the self-disclosure of God that occurs in scripture and tradition (that is, revelation), then phenomenology could seem only to supply a competing set of sources, derived from the immanent frames of human experience, which could interfere with the clear transmission of such revelation. In short, phenomenology could make theology more dependent on general anthropological conditions than on an unambiguously Christian exposition of the gospel.

The first of these doubts resonates with the Marxian conviction that the point of thinking is not simply to contemplate the world but to change it. The second doubt exhibits a Barthian or Balthasarian preoccupation with the authenticity of Christian witness. In many of its definitive expressions liberation theology combines these two emphases. Gustavo Gutiérrez, Leonardo Boff, Jon Sobrino, and many other liberation theologians, including Ellacuría and Dussel, have insisted that the Christian gospel is a gospel preferentially directed toward the poor and oppressed. It expresses the good news of their historical and eschatological liberation, through which alone the whole world may hope to be saved. The biblical revelation of God and the Christian witness that preserves it require active confrontations with the sinful structures that destroy the lives of the most vulnerable. Hence, there is no contradiction between being faithful to revelation and hearing and responding decisively to the cries of those who suffer unjustly. On the contrary, there is a profound and necessary connection between the two.[5]

---

[5] See Ignacio Ellacuría, *Freedom Made Flesh: The Mission of Christ and His Church*, trans. John Drury (Maryknoll, NY: Orbis Books, 1976), 32–41; Enrique Dussel, *Ethics and Community*, trans. Robert R. Barr (Eugene, OR: Wipf and Stock, 1988), 37–46; Gustavo Gutiérrez, *The God of Life*, trans. Matthew J. O'Connell (Maryknoll, NY: Orbis Books, 1991), 1–19; Jon Sobrino, *Christ the Liberator: A View from the Victims*, trans. Paul Burns (Maryknoll, NY: Orbis Books, 2001), 78–95 and 209–20; and Leonardo Boff, *Jesus Christ Liberator: A Critical Christology for Our Time*, trans. Patrick Hughes (Maryknoll, NY: Orbis Books, 1978), 292–94.

From this unified perspective phenomenology could seem doubly suspect for the reasons mentioned above. In fact, liberation theologians could have some interest in claiming, against Marxian critics, that it is not Christianity which refuses to develop serious responses to the unjust sufferings of the world but rather various kinds of supposedly disinterested or apolitical theory, such as phenomenology, which remain largely indifferent to this grave situation. Conversely, liberation theologians could contend, against Barthian critics, that the secularizing horizons of modern immanence are much more characteristic of various kinds of post-Enlightenment philosophy, such as phenomenology, than they are of their own clearly theological and kerygmatic orientation. Hence, liberation theologians could incorporate the concerns of Marx and Barth, to speak heuristically here, and repel the main objections coming from these two quarters precisely by distinguishing their own projects sharply from an undesirable image of a non-liberative and non-evangelized phenomenology.[6]

But this path of separation does not seem to be the most auspicious route to take, since phenomenology, in a richer sense of the term, may have something extraordinarily valuable to offer liberation theology and vice versa. Indeed, there is evidence to support this contention. Dussel and Ellacuría demonstrate, in distinct but related ways, that a certain kind of phenomenology can elucidate and support transformative interactions between humanity and the liberating God of revelation, precisely insofar as the human side of these interactions depends on an experientially rigorous awareness of reality, of the flesh, of history, and of the other (four themes that we contemplate below). Moreover, Ellacuría's and Dussel's treatments of these themes clarify how the tradition of phenomenology needs to be developed in order to cultivate this sort of awareness. That is, these thinkers show that phenomenology can make the most adequate contributions to liberation theology only if it undergoes significant metamorphoses in response to the particular divine, human, and worldly appearances and dynamics that justifiably and necessarily occupy the attention of liberation theologians.

Hence, although the preceding doubts—from the perspectives of Zubirian metaphysics, Husserlian method, Marxian critical praxis, and Barthian or Balthasarian witness—are warranted, they do not appear decisive. The nature of phenomenology and of a kind of liberation theology that would become its benefactor and beneficiary are matters that remain open to further consideration. Perhaps the future identities of these movements will be intertwined. There are implications for phenomenology in this

---

[6] For one version of the Marxian critique, see Alistair Kee, *Marx and the Failure of Liberation Theology* (Philadelphia: Trinity Press, 1990). For one version of the Barthian and Balthasarian critique, see John Milbank, *Theology and Social Theory: Beyond Secular Reason*, 2d ed. (Malden, MA: Blackwell, 2006), 206–56.

relationship. But the more pressing implications here have to do with the kind of liberation theology that might emerge. A kind of liberation theology that has internalized certain kinds of phenomenological lucidity will be more prepared to receive, understand, and enact the concrete forms of liberation that are promised and necessitated by the gospel.

Phenomenology, Its History, and Its Desire

To begin, we need to consider the meaning of phenomenology and ask in what general sense the works of Ellacuría and Dussel may belong to it. To address these questions, we must first recognize that phenomenology is constituted through a highly diverse, uncertain, and open-ended history. The diversity has resulted in some disagreements regarding fundamental issues, such as the meaning of phenomenology itself.[7] The uncertainty has troubled both internal and external critics of phenomenology, and the efforts that have been made to overcome this uncertainty through various—still dubitable—methods have perhaps only proven its inevitability.[8] Finally, the history of phenomenology is open-ended in at least three ways: with respect to its origins, which must be traced back before Husserl (even though he does found it in a new way), at least as far as the eighteenth century emergence of the term *phenomenology,* but also arguably much farther back into the rich ancestry of humanity's reflective engagement with the world; with respect to its future, which remains unforeseen; and with respect to its regional coordinates, which one should not be too quick to equate with the borders of a secular European or Euro-American philosophy. The phenomenology of the ages to come may outstrip many previous expectations, precisely in order to retrieve and discover its own best intuitions.[9]

---

[7] The aforementioned revisions of post-Husserlian phenomenology, which move in many different directions, illustrate this point.

[8] Jean-Luc Marion's "Phenomenology of Givenness and First Philosophy," in *In Excess: Studies of Saturated Phenomena,* trans. Robyn Horner and Vincent Berraud, 1–29 (New York: Fordham University Press, 2002), is indicative of the constant search for certifying principles and methods, which will perhaps never be wholly adequate.

[9] Although the introduction to Dermot Moran and Timothy Mooney's *The Phenomenology Reader* (New York: Routledge, 2002) gives some sense of the pre-Husserlian history of phenomenology, including the first appearance of the word in Johann Heinrich Lambert (1728–77), this introduction does little to mark the potentially immense, transmodern scope of phenomenology. By contrast, one might consider the wide range of approaches to phenomenology found in Emmanuel Falque, *Saint Bonaventure et l'entrée de Dieu en théologie* (France: Librarie Philosophique J. VRIN, 2000); Lewis Gordon, *Existentia Africana: Understanding Africana Existential Thought* (New York: Routledge, 2000); and Bret W. Davis, Brian Schroeder, and Jason M. Wirth, eds., *Japanese and Continental*

If there is any unity in phenomenology as a way of thinking, a unity that would give some continued purpose to its multifarious history and make its application to the works of Ellacuría and Dussel meaningful, it may be this: *the desire to offer a radical and conceptually precise understanding of experience.*[10] This is a desire that is widely shared among those thinkers who consider themselves phenomenologists, who have been heavily influenced by this tradition, or who might be otherwise closely associated with it. "Radical" here implies two things: an understanding that is rooted in experience and an understanding that wants to reach the roots (that is, the most original or essential characteristics) of experience.[11] This double rooting of phenomenology is indicated by doublings in phenomenological parlance: one seeks to describe not only phenomena but the phenomenality of phenomena, not only intentions but the intentionality of intentions. One wants to discover not only the things themselves but that which makes a thing appear most deeply and truly as a thing.[12]

Lest this desire for a doubly radical immersion in experience should completely diminish phenomenology's hope for intelligibility by plunging its consciousness into the perhaps unthinkable depths of pure tactility, temporality, or materiality, another tendency has also developed in the phenomenological tradition that keeps it invested in the mediation of *logos*.[13] It seems that the radical must be given the clarity of a concept in order even to begin to satisfy the phenomenologist's desire. The goal typically is not to make any sort of extrinsically linguistic imposition on some supposedly prelinguistic phenomenal field but rather to use words to convey as adeptly as possible the things that have been given, while recognizing that words

---

Philosophy: Conversations with the Kyoto School (Bloomington: Indiana University Press, 2011).

[10] The definition of *experience* cannot be taken for granted here but is precisely what must be put in question by phenomenology; the term is, therefore, a placeholder.

[11] Joseph Kockelmans associates radicality with apodicticity in *A First Introduction to Husserl's Phenomenology* (Pittsburgh: Duquesne University Press, 1967), 62–76. An insight that reaches the very roots of experience would, on this account, have attained a certain foundation for indisputable knowledge. Although this epistemological connection is evident in Husserl, it is not equally determinative of every phenomenological discussion of radicality, such as, for example, the "anarchic" one provided by Levinas in *Otherwise Than Being, or Beyond Essence*, trans. Alphonso Lingis (Pittsburgh: Duquesne University Press, 2004), 99–102.

[12] An important text on this question is Heidegger's "The Thing," in *Poetry, Language, Thought*, trans. Albert Hofstadter, 161–84 (New York: HarperCollins, 2001).

[13] This mediation of the *logos* is operative even in the paradoxical case of Michel Henry. See his *Material Phenomenology*, trans. Scott Davidson (New York: Fordham University Press, 208), 96–98.

(and, therefore, the events and structures of language) are a crucial part of the way in which things are usually given.[14]

The different sorts of philosophy that Ellacuría and Dussel develop can be comprehended, to some extent, according to this broad sense of phenomenology. Nevertheless, it would make little sense to insist that their philosophical writings are exclusively phenomenological, even in this rather broad sense. In the first place, other philosophical traditions, including certain critical theories of society belonging to the effective histories of Hegel and Marx, have greatly influenced their thinking. Moreover, as noted above, there is a way in which their dependence on Zubiri may bring them into the space of a certain kind of realist metaphysics that despite considerable debts to phenomenology, is perhaps not wholly reducible to it. In these two ways (and arguably more) Ellacuría and Dussel could be perceived as indicating the insufficiency of a phenomenological method of philosophy.

Still, there is something appreciably phenomenological about the way they treat both the complex problems of modern society and certain classical questions about the formal structures of reality and human existence. They approach these matters with a desire to understand how they enter into experience and form it at its very roots. They are assisted in this endeavor by numerous phenomenological thinkers (such as Zubiri, Heidegger, Ricoeur, and Levinas), and they can be brought into dialogue with others. In short, their philosophical aspirations are never far from the desires and *desiderata* of phenomenology. Their works are part of its unfinished history. And their contributions must, therefore, be taken into account.

Phenomenological Themes in Ellacuría and Dussel

In order to confirm and deepen this claim, I now discuss the specific avenues into phenomenology that Dussel and Ellacuría make available. The main pathways are these: reality in excess of ontology; the flesh as the sentient structure of corporeal life; history as the constitutive source of concrete givens, devastating crises, and new possibilities; and the other as the prius of ethics and society. Many of these themes have been addressed in one manner or another by other phenomenologists, but Ellacuría and Dussel take them up in their own particular ways, which are significantly coordinated with the concerns of liberation theology. I consider this coordination

---

[14] Hans-Georg Gadamer gives clear expression to this now widely accepted approach in *Truth and Method*, translation revised by Joel Weinsheimer and Donald G. Marshall (New York: Continuum, 2004), 436–52.

more closely in the next section. Here the goal is merely to see what sorts of phenomenological insight Ellacuría and Dussel offer.

The first of these themes owes a great deal to Zubiri. He insists that reality is not equivalent to being. On the contrary, he argues that we should understand being as a derivative mode of reality. Being would be the secondary actualization or manifestation of something prior, something strictly from itself [de suyo]. This something is "real" in the deepest sense. As Zubiri interprets them, being and reality are not two different things but rather two different ways of approaching the same phenomenality. But the approach of reality is more radical—hence, phenomenologically adequate—and more disconcerting for any kind of idealizing consciousness that one might find in the metaphysical tradition. Zubiri's doctrine of reality builds on and radicalizes Heidegger's break with Husserl. Prior to the operations of intentionality, and even prior to the disclosive presence of being in the world, there is the irreducible "from itself" of each thing that arises in its own right. Zubiri believes that it is only on the insurmountable basis of its own reality that anything is capable of ontological actualization in the world and some degree of conceptual actualization for intelligence.[15]

This is a lesson in phenomenological (or phenomenologically metaphysical) realism that both Dussel and Ellacuría learn from Zubiri. Still, of the two, Ellacuría does the most to explain this lesson. Ellacuría argues that Heidegger's meditations on the eventful difference between being and beings enable him to overcome the perennial philosophical danger that Zubiri calls the "entification of reality," while evincing a quite similar, problem: the "ontologization of reality." Being and its unveiling for *Dasein* would seem, like the structures of the ontic sciences, to limit phenomenological inquiry before it reaches its most radical roots in the realness of things.[16] Could not the procedure that Zubiri employs to distance himself from Heidegger's ontology also be turned against his "realogy" and repeated ad infinitum? Could not any term, even *reality,* be treated as the symbol for something secondary? It seems difficult to rule out this sort of endless reduction but also to propose any term that evokes a greater sense of radicality than *reality* or its formal equivalent, *de suyo.* Where would the search for the primordial

---

[15] Zubiri, *The Dynamic Structure of Reality*, trans. Nelson R. Orringer (Urbana: University of Illinois Press, 2003), 14–20.

[16] Ignacio Ellacuría, "La superación del reduccionismo idealista en Zubiri," in *Escritos filosóficos*, vol. 3 (San Salvador: UCA Editores, 2001), 410–12; Robert Lassalle-Klein, "Ignacio Ellacuría's Debt to Xavier Zubiri" and Antonio González, "Assessing the Philosophical Achievement of Ignacio Ellacuría," in *Love That Produces Hope: The Thought of Ignacio Ellacuría*, ed. Kevin Burke and Robert Lassalle-Klein, 73–127 (Collegeville, MN: Liturgical Press, 2005); and Enrique Dussel, *Philosophy of Liberation*, trans. Aquilina Martinez and Christine Morkovsky (Eugene, OR: Wipf and Stock, 1985), 41.

sources of experience find rest if not precisely in that which comes "from itself"?

In any case, the words *being* and *reality* matter less than the specific interpretations that have been given to them. These interpretations tend to revolve around various claims about how we access being and reality. Although Heidegger does not entirely neglect the senses (such as those of sight and hearing),[17] Zubiri and his students can arguably find greater intellectual rapport with a figure such as Merleau-Ponty, who, like Zubiri, moves phenomenology very decisively in the direction of our bodily perceptions. What Zubiri means by *reality* diverges from what Heidegger means by *being*, not only because Zubiri claims that the former is more radical than the latter, but also because Zubiri more emphatically connects the notion of reality with the sentient intelligence that recognizes and receives it. Thus, from a Zubirian perspective, Merleau-Ponty's description of the flesh—which discloses the sensory, corporeal, and reciprocal existence of beings and selves in a shared, palpable world—would bring us much closer to the reality of things than Heidegger's somewhat fleshless construal of *Dasein* ever could.[18]

Some of the differences between Zubiri and Merleau-Ponty are significant, and at least two bear mentioning here. First, Merleau-Ponty remains, even in his later writings, much closer to a Cartesian problematic than Zubiri ever wishes to be. This point can be verified by considering Merleau-Ponty's category of "perceptual faith," a category that draws attention to the possibility of doubting the reality of our perceptions. In Zubiri's work (and this may be considered a strength or a weakness), there is very little consideration of dubitability and, in fact, a strong desire to resist any gravitational pull in this direction, which, according to Zubiri's way of thinking, would likely be a pull away from the straightforward acknowledgment of the real *qua* real.[19] Another difference, and one that is emphasized in Ellacuría's proposed theological method, has to do with Zubiri's focus on the biological bases of sentient intelligence. The flesh that experiences and understands is also the flesh of a living organism, of an animal struggling to persist in a community of other animals, with all of the physical conditions that this implies. Merleau-Ponty does not disregard this fundamental biological level

---

[17] Heidegger, *Being and Time*, trans. Joan Stambaugh (Albany: State University of New York Press, 1996), 138 and 153.

[18] Ignacio Ellacuría, "Aproximación a la obra completa de Xavier Zubiri," in *Escritos filosóficos*, 3:384–87; and Maurice Merleau-Ponty, *The Visible and the Invisible*, ed. Claude Lefort and trans. Alphonso Lingis (Evanston, IL: Northwestern University Press, 1968), 48 and 146.

[19] Xavier Zubiri, *Inteligencia sentiente: Inteligencia y realidad* (Madrid: Alianza Editorial, 1991), 232, and Merleau-Ponty, *The Visible and the Invisible*, 3–14.

of bodily experience, but he does not express it with the same forcefulness that one finds in Zubiri and Ellacuría.[20]

Whereas Zubiri and Ellacuría approximate some of the insights of Merleau-Ponty, Dussel explicitly appropriates them, first in order to resist certain dualistic anthropological currents in the Hellenistic and Christian traditions, and later, with help from other theorists, in order to highlight the conditions of corporeal vulnerability in which the victims of the world find themselves.[21] Ultimately, for Ellacuría and Dussel, the flesh is not only the sentient locus of any true knowledge but also the inescapable situation of exposure in which all human beings and other earthly creatures must live and struggle to survive. The incarnation of phenomenology that these thinkers attempt, therefore, has more than epistemological significance. It reconnects one with the precarious and ethically binding determinations of real life.

Reality and the flesh are constitutively historical. Zubiri affirms this point, and Ellacuría expands upon it.[22] Ellacuría's method of "historicization" can be understood, in one sense, as a phenomenological reduction that recognizes the radically historical character of any given phenomenon. However, to make this interpretation of Ellacuría is not to imply that he is merely interested in producing an account of historicity, that is, an exposition of the virtually exceptionless claim that things appear and exist historically. Although he offers such an account, and even treats it as the most suitable path toward a profoundly integrative philosophy of the whole,[23] his writings also indicate that he is greatly perturbed by and responsive to the very particular historical conditions of Latin America in the late twentieth century. He analyzes the ways in which these conditions have shaped the development of liberation theology and, moreover, established the necessities and possibilities for a liberating historical praxis. His reasons for emphasizing

---

[20] Ignacio Ellacuría, "Hacia una fundamentación del método teológico latinoamericano," in *Escritos teológicos*, vol. 1 (San Salvador: UCA Editores, 2000), 206; in English "Toward a Latin American Theological Method," in *Ignacio Ellacuría, Essays on History, Liberation, and Salvation*, ed. Michael E. Lee, 59-87 (Maryknoll, NY: Orbis Books, 2013); and Ignacio Ellacuría, "Fundamentación biológica de la ética," in *Escritos filosóficos*, 3:251–69; and Maurice Merleau-Ponty, *Sense and Non-Sense*, trans. Hubert L. Dreyfus and Patricia Allen Dreyfus (Evanston, IL: Northwestern University Press, 1964), 84.

[21] Enrique Dussel, *El dualismo en la antropologia de la Cristiandad: Desde el origen del cristianismo hasta antes de la conquista de América* (Buenos Aires: Editorial Guadalupe, 1974), 285–86; and Enrique Dussel, *Ethics of Liberation: In the Age of Globalization and Exclusion*, trans. Eduardo Mendieta et al. (Durham, NC: Duke University Press, 2013), 67 and 215.

[22] Zubiri, *The Dynamic Structure of Reality*, 204–15; and Ignacio Ellacuría, *Filosofía de la realidad histórica* (San Salvador: UCA Editores, 1990).

[23] Ellacuría, *Filosofía de la realidad histórica*, 30–46.

history in general stem significantly from the weighty demands of *this* history, which had become his own. This immediate context gives rise to a more vital sense of "historicization" in Ellacuría's works: the transformative putting-into-praxis of concrete hopes and possibilities.[24]

In relation to Ellacuría, Dussel is certainly the more accomplished historian, that is, scholar of the historical past. This is a very distinct area of his academic output, which informs his reflections on the historical present.[25] Still, he seems to compose many of his historiographical arguments phenomenologically, that is, with a desire to think the deepest conditions of experience. He does not seek an essence through imaginative variations (as Husserl recommends) but rather contemplates actual experiences transmitted by the mediating forms of artifacts, documents, symbols, and narratives. In this work Dussel is undoubtedly inspired by the hermeneutical phenomenology of Ricoeur, even though his analyses are decidedly his own. *The Invention of the Americas* is a remarkable example of his post-Ricoeurian technique. Here Dussel presents a phenomenological description, not only of the "I conquer" (as he says explicitly), but also of the related experiences of invention, discovery, and colonization. Most crucially of all, he seeks to recover the life-worlds of certain indigenous populations, whose passivities and intentionalities have been almost completely excluded from dominant historico-philosophical articulations of the advent of modernity.[26] Dussel is not merely interested in recording facts. On the contrary, he seeks both to uncover the histories that lie at the roots of contemporary experience, whether we recognize it or not, and to retrieve the structures of experience that were constitutive of these histories.

Dussel is known for saying "the Other." He says this frequently and usually (but not always) with a somewhat particular referent in mind: the poor, the victims, the conquered and colonized, the ones who cry out "Help me!" or "I am hungry!" These are "the Other" of a totality. He theorizes this totality as an exclusionary structure of power that is manifest in Eurocentric theory and praxis; in the fetishization of capital; in the ontology, epistemology,

---

[24] Ignacio Ellacuría, "Historización del bien común y de los derechos humanos en una sociedad dividida," in *Escritos filosóficos*, 3:207–26; idem, "Teología de la liberación frente al cambio socio-histórico en América Latina," in *Escritos teológicos*, 1:313–52; and idem, "The Historicity of Christian Salvation," in *Mysterium Liberationis: Fundamental Concepts of Liberation Theology*, ed. Ignacio Ellacuría and Jon Sobrino, 251–89 (Maryknoll, NY: Orbis Books, 1993).

[25] See, for example, Enrique Dussel, *A History of the Church in Latin America: Colonialism to Liberation (1492–1979)*, trans. Alan Neely (Grand Rapids, MI: Eerdmans, 1981).

[26] Enrique Dussel, *The Invention of the Americas: Eclipse of "the Other" and the Myth of Modernity*, trans. Michael D. Barber (New York: Continuum, 1995), 27–57, 84–88, and 183n1 (from Part 3).

and ethics of Western modernity; in the culture of machismo; and in nearly any conceivable case of domination.[27] But there are moments when he says "the Other" and means by this those who arrive, suddenly, as victimizers, as conquerors, as sources of death.[28] It seems that this is a visage of alterity that must be resisted through a positive expression of one's own (or one's people's) being, thought, language, and history. In short, therefore, if Dussel recognizes a need for a Levinasian disruption of the pseudo-*parousia* of the "I," in its illusory mastery over the world, he also sees a need for a Heideggerianism or Ricoeurianism from below: an existential-and-hermeneutical analytic of threatened existences. Dussel moves phenomenology in both of these directions at once—and the same must also be said, in a certain sense, of Levinas, at least if one takes seriously his expositions of Jewish life.[29] Both Levinas and Dussel find, at the roots of experience, the other and its ethically obligating face; both believe that this is an originary moment of humanity, which, though binding on all, especially needs to be revived as a correction to certain dangerously totalizing philosophical traditions; and both recognize that the primacy of otherness does not eliminate the value, and in certain tragic cases, the urgency of a self- and community-affirming phenomenological discourse.

Dussel's proximity to Levinas makes the importance of the other unmistakable in Dussel's work. But one should not conclude, therefore, that the meaning of this sort of consideration is lost on Ellacuría. On the contrary, he too has a meditation on alterity. Moreover, like Dussel, he reveres it as the font of any genuinely human society. According to Ellacuría, the process of maturation that enables one to recognize the other *as other* is also that which enables one to appreciate the radical constitution of existence, not merely as living [*vivencia*], but as living-with [*convivencia*].[30] In a related vein Ellacuría opposes the substantivization of the social that he perceives in the dialectical theories of Hegel and Marx in order to make room for the intervention of the human person, the one with a singular life and biography, who can arguably be described as the other of such Hegelian or Marxian totalities. Ellacuría acknowledges a degree of "impersonality" in society (which might be comparable to Levinas's "third"), but this insight does not

---

[27] Dussel, *Philosophy of Liberation*, 16–66, and *Ethics of Liberation*, 209.

[28] Dussel, *The Invention of the Americas*, 41.

[29] Dussel, *Ethics of Liberation*, 299, and Levinas, *Difficult Freedom: Essays on Judaism*, trans. Seán Hand (London: Athlone, 1990), 13, 26, and 49–53. This argument may address some of the concerns regarding a certain disparity between Levinas and Dussel that Nelson Maldonado-Torres raises in *Against War: Views from the Underside of Modernity* (Durham, NC: Duke University Press, 2008), 179–86.

[30] See the section "La constitución de la alteridad social," in Ellacuría, *Filosofía de la realidad histórica*, 218–20.

prevent Ellacuría from approaching the primordially convivial person as a relative absolute and as the culmination of reality's openness to the infinite (the absolutely absolute that exceeds manifestation).[31]

The Relationship Between Phenomenology and Liberation Theology

This brief overview of the phenomenological contributions of Ellacuría and Dussel puts us in a better position to assess the significance of phenomenology for liberation theology. As we suggested at the outset, liberation theology generally affirms and sees no conflict between two aspirations: on the one hand, the desire to develop a critical theory and praxis that can respond in liberating ways to the sufferings of humanity; on the other hand, the search for a greater fidelity to the life-giving God of revelation who brings justice, freedom, and love to all creatures (that is, the gospel). We also noted that phenomenology can seem to work against both of these aspirations insofar as it concentrates on a sheltered region of egological consciousness in which neither the cries of the victims nor the glorious words and deeds of God can be received. This narrow picture of phenomenology was the basis for the roughly Marxian and Barthian doubts that seemed to make the very idea of a phenomenological contribution to liberation theology questionable from the start. But where does the matter stand now?

First, we should recognize that the lines of influence between phenomenology and liberation theology are, in both Ellacuría's and Dussel's work, somewhat reciprocal. On the one hand, it seems possible to interpret their meditations on reality, the flesh, history, and the other as a kind of *preparatio evangelii*, that is, as an anterior stage of thought that anticipates, supports, but does not yet constitute the greater understanding and concrete realization of the gospel that liberation theology demands. On the other hand, it seems just as reasonable to trace particular aspects of Dussel's and Ellacuría's phenomenological descriptions back to certain prior internalizations of the significance of the gospel that their phenomenological descriptions would secondarily, abstractly, and partially reflect. Any absolute choice in favor of either one of these views of phenomenology's relation to liberation theology (whether as preparatory or abstractive) would be artificial, since the dialectics in Ellacuría's and Dussel's intellectual and personal histories are bound to be more complex than any such rigid methodological model would allow.

Second, we should observe that the connections that Ellacuría and Dussel disclose between phenomenology and liberation theology are not only reciprocal but also non-exhaustive: there is more determinate content in both

---

[31] Ellacuría, "Persona y comunidad," in *Escritos filosóficos*, 3:93–94, 3:101, and 3:112.

phenomenology and liberation theology than that which either discursive endeavor receives from their mutual relation. Dussel's and Ellacuría's distinctive modifications of phenomenology may prepare for and show traces of liberation theology, but it does not follow that phenomenology is for these thinkers merely an imperfect image of liberation theology or that liberation theology is for them only a derivative continuation or amplification of phenomenology. On the contrary, both Dussel and Ellacuría preserve the distance and non-substitutability of phenomenology and liberation theology.

Nevertheless, in contrast to Dussel, Ellacuría does more to demonstrate the importance of a positively Christian conception of liberation theology, that is, one that is fundamentally oriented by the gift of integral liberation that comes from the triune God of revelation. Whereas both Dussel and Ellacuría move phenomenology in the direction of a critical theory and praxis of liberation, in such a way that they would be able to address a more or less Marxian set of concerns, Ellacuría also manages—especially through his biblically and traditionally rooted considerations of Christology, soteriology, ecclesiology, and spirituality—to locate the human struggle for liberation, which may include certain kinds of phenomenological illumination, quite decisively in the context of God's victoriously compassionate actions toward us. In short, Ellacuría's approach seems more capable than Dussel's of speaking to certain roughly Barthian-and-Balthasarian preoccupations. Dussel has some valuable points to offer in this regard, but his expositions of revelation are mainly limited to ethical considerations. By contrast, Ellacuría's liberation discourse clearly wishes to be not only ethical, but also theological and indeed *theologal*, that is, infused with divine presence and activity.[32]

The central question of this chapter, however, is not whether Dussel or Ellacuría is the more convincing theologian but rather whether phenomenology can contribute something to liberation theology. For this question both Dussel's and Ellacuría's reflections are highly significant. Perhaps already influenced by the gospel, their phenomenological meditations on reality, the flesh, history, and the other also promise to make the gospel more intelligible and actionable. These meditations clarify certain aspects of the constitution of experience through which the good news of liberation can appear and become effective in our lives. If one were to ask where God actively works and where we are called to work in order to manifest the

---

[32] See Ellacuría, *Freedom Made Flesh*, 13–14, 23–78, and 233–46; Ignacio Ellacuría, *Escritos teológicos*, vol. 4 (San Salvador: UCA Editores, 2002); Enrique Dussel, "The Kingdom of God and the Poor," in *Beyond Philosophy: Ethics, History, Marxism, and Liberation Theology*, ed. Eduardo Mendieta (Lanham, MD: Rowman and Littlefield, 2003), 85–102; and Enrique Dussel, *Ethics and Community*, trans. Robert R. Barr (Maryknoll, NY: Orbis Books, 1988; Eugene, OR: Wipf and Stock, 2008), 7–26.

fullness of freedom that is meant for creation, Dussel and Ellacuría would suggest the following response: precisely there amid the reality of things, which arise from themselves; there in the sentient cognitions and biological movements of our fragile bodies, which connect us to the world; there in the determinate catastrophes and opportunities of history, which disclose to us what must be contradicted and what must be put into praxis; and, finally, there in the inescapable and weighty moments of conviviality with others, which remind us of our highest obligations.

Could liberation reach deep into these four structures of phenomenality and preserve their content while making them anew? Could liberation thereby find a way of coming-to-presence on this earth and in this very age? Could the manifold constitution of experience studied by Dussel and Ellacuría be vivified and transfigured by liberating words and actions that are not only our own but also, in their deepest source, divine, that is, filled with the sanctifying graces of Christ and the Holy Spirit? Could there, then, be a phenomenology that has become radically receptive to the genuinely liberative and genuinely theological aspirations of liberation theology? Could the countless victims find their realities respected, their flesh cared for, their histories remembered, and their irreducible mysteries welcomed, not only by a secular society, but also and perhaps even more outstandingly by a faithful Christian community that lives and breathes in communion with the triune God? Ellacuría's and Dussel's phenomenological reflections make these questions conceivable and compelling, as perhaps very few other theoretical efforts have.

All in all, Ellacuría and Dussel show that phenomenology contributes a particular way of thinking that may increase our awareness of the experiential conditions that partly enable any simultaneously divine-and-human events of liberation to occur. Their works have the potential to prevent liberation theology from becoming so thoroughly invested in the analysis of sociopolitical forces and doctrinal statements that it would lose all contact with the real, fleshly, historical, and alterity-saturated experiences that constitute actual life and point most vividly toward its promised freedom. Phenomenologists have much to learn from Ellacuría and Dussel, not least about the critical questions that must be asked of any phenomenological project that might be attempted in this world of immense suffering and death. But liberation theology also has something to learn from phenomenology, in short, how to describe the—if possible, then radically experiential—manifestations of liberation that any true Christian love must endlessly desire. Dussel and Ellacuría have opened but by no means closed this line of inquiry.

8

Twelve Theses Regarding a New Method of Theology in the School of Thought of Ignacio Ellacuría

José Sols Lucia

In the course of twelve theses we will open a path through Christian theology in this twenty-first century, convinced that the contribution of Ignacio Ellacuría to fundamental theology will be valuable. Of course, we will avoid the naive assumption that a new century per se requires a new method in theology. Nonetheless, we think that the unity of Ignacio Ellacuría's contribution to hermeneutical theology within the present context of cultural pluralism and diversity, key characteristics of globalization, will open a path to a new way of conceiving the theological task within the framework of the Christian faith.

First Thesis: *Christian theology rationalizes the experience of faith many people have in the Father-God revealed by Jesus, an experience given through the Spirit. This experience, with its accompanying reflection, invites one to participate actively in the lives of human beings of every time and culture,*

I presented these twelve theses to the International Colloquium on the Thought of Ignacio Ellacuría, the first meeting of Ellacuría scholars, which took place at the Jesuit School of Theology in Berkeley, California, July 25–28, 2009. Unable to develop them in the years to follow, I took advantage of the most recent meeting of the Colloquium (held in San Salvador, El Salvador, in August 2013) to do so. I formulate these reflections in recognition of the twenty-fifth anniversary of the death of Ignacio Ellacuría (November 16, 2014).

which means embracing the sciences that study humankind (the social sciences) and our surrounding nature (the natural sciences). Therefore, theology must be in dialogue with the sciences.

When we study the scriptures, we see repeatedly that the text—whether in the Old or New Testament, whether a citation from the Law, a poem, or an epistle—gathers the human wisdom of that epoch and through it contributes a radically new message: A God who is one, personal, and the liberator of Israel; the Father-God of Jesus, whose gift we receive in the Spirit. The novelty resides in the content [*contenido*] of the text, not in the text as container [*continente*]. The sacred texts gather the scientific, social, and literary knowledge from their historical and cultural contexts, and through these transmit faith, a message that characteristically breaks through the inhumanity of historical systems. Throughout the history of the church Christian theology has shown itself to be fruitful when it has accepted the need to be culturally and historically open. It has been unfruitful when it has tried to build its own autonomous world apart from the historical world in which it tries to develop. Christian theology is only truly itself when it is expressed in culturally contextualized categories, when it incorporates scientific, historical, literary, and human knowledge in terms of which it seeks to transmit the good news to humanity in a way that makes sense.

Second Thesis: *It is a mistake to think of theology only as a discipline with its own language. It is also a discipline that needs to dialogue constantly with other disciplines (first thesis). As such, it should constantly incorporate the languages of these other disciplines, giving theological language a necessarily historical character.*

There is no doubt that theology, like any other discipline, possesses its own language, without which it could not exist. Nonetheless, taking into consideration what is affirmed in the first thesis, theology needs to incorporate the language of other disciplines, and it needs to do so constantly, unceasingly, given that it always is incorporating, in one way or another, what is affirmed in other disciplines, each with its own language. Consequently, theological language is intrinsically dynamic, because it incessantly has recourse to the historicity of human knowledge. This gives all Christian theology the paradoxical character of being perennially provisional. It is always provisional and precisely in this resides its perennial nature, like a plant that day after day absorbs the light of the sun through photosynthesis. This fact creates a crisis for the idea of theological language. Any language is theological if it communicates theological truths adequately in a given cultural and historical context. As a matter of fact, studying the history of Jewish and Christian theologies, we can confirm that many concepts that are now normal in theology were beforehand simply civil concepts: *people, community, father, brother, neighbor, church, liberation, salvation.*

Contemporary human knowledge finds its forms of expression primarily in the social, natural, and formal sciences, as well as through the humanities and the arts that are, to some extent, older disciplines. Because of this, twenty-first-century Christian theology needs to get used to finding common ground for discourse with the sciences, aiming to coincide precisely with the cutting edge of reason, indispensable for any discipline, but at the same time avoiding pastoral opaqueness, something that, unfortunately, has occurred quite frequently.

Third Thesis: *In non-Western cultures knowledge has been transmitted by means other than those of the modern sciences. What is affirmed in the first and second theses concerning the sciences should be also affirmed regarding other modes of knowledge, Western and Eastern, which differ from the sciences but possess epistemological and moral value of enormous importance.*

Little by little, churches born outside of Europe and the Mediterranean region—concretely, the churches of Latin America, Asia and Africa—have been incorporating distinctly non-Western cultures into the expression of the faith.. Liberation theology still has a very strong Western accent, in line with the Enlightenment, above all in its social branch dealing with economic and social rights. It is the sister of political theology, and it remains clearly European. On the other hand, in recent years new modes of Christian theological expression have risen in the midst of the Asian cultures, the indigenous American cultures, and to a somewhat lesser degree, in the African cultures. What is common to all these is their contextualized character. They attempt to express Christian faith in categories that are not predominantly modern, Western, European, or Mediterranean. These new modes of expression can appear to be disconcerting for a spirit accustomed to formulating faith in these older categories; but without the intent to criticize those who suffer this generally comprehensible discomfort, we need to say that Christian theology has always engaged in this process of absorbing languages initially foreign to it. We reiterate that what today are consecrated as theological concepts were once only civil concepts (second thesis).

It is impossible to predict a priori how the Christian faith will be formulated using the languages of other cultures, but we need to realize that we are on the threshold of something very new, given that a language is not an exterior coat of paint on the wall of religious truth; rather, language constitutes the steel inserted in the cement of that wall. There will not only be translation. There will be new modes of comprehending faith.

Fourth Thesis: *Salvation offered by God to humanity through the people of Israel and in Jesus Christ takes place in the history of humankind as a whole and within every given people. This bestows on theology a hermeneutical function consistent with the theological interpretation of those processes of salvation that arise through historical praxis.*

In all moments of history and in all cultures human beings have been living important processes of salvation. Salvation means removing a person or a group from a situation that endangers its well-being or life. It does so through the mediation of free action. Such historical processes of salvation have in common a dynamic that moves from emptiness to human fulfill- · ment, from the negation of the human to its affirmation. The salvation offered by God to humanity through the people of Israel and Jesus Christ is no stranger to these processes. Rather, it is intrinsic to them. God saves through the historical processes of salvation, which always involves a free action on the human being's part. Therefore, the salvation of God is not something other, something added on, that represents a distinct, exterior mode of help. Rather, it is the final content of any human salvation, of any support of life, of human dignity. Therefore, we can affirm that theology has the function of contributing a theological interpretation to those processes. Theology makes transparent God's salvation in the various historical processes of salvation. Hence, the theological endeavor is eminently hermeneutical. It contributes the interpretive key for understanding the meaning of the real.

Fifth Thesis: *The conviction that God's salvation occurs in history and the historical-hermeneutical function of theology (fourth thesis) leads to implications for Christians in politics and socioeconomics on the levels of praxis and theory. In this way, theology—the intellectual moment of Christians in the world—ought to participate in political and economic reflection regarding current events [actualidad histórica].*

Christians cannot stand outside of the historical processes of salvation, because the salvation offered by God in Israel and in Jesus Christ is interior to those processes. This hermeneutical affirmation leads to a moral imperative: the requirement that Christians be implicated in those historical processes both through praxis and theory. We speak of a *moral imperative*: we say *moral* because it has to do with human responsibility concerning the appropriate exercise of freedom; we say *imperative* because we are engaging the *deontological order* insofar as the Christian cannot avoid historical self-implication, although each person and community addresses this demand in distinct and particular ways. Theology is not and cannot be foreign to those historical processes of transformation, since it serves as the intellectual moment of theoretical and interpretive reflection on the salvific historical praxis of Christians. This leads us to contextualized theologies, not only in language (second thesis) but also in regard to theology's historical-*praxical* implications. A theologian is an agent of historical change.

Sixth Thesis: *The historical character of all theology not only bestows its particular value but also its universal value, since the totality of salvation is given in each fragment of human history, an affirmation we uphold through the experience of the total self-giving of God in the particular histories of Israel, Jesus Christ, and Jesus' disciples. In this way each person and each people, enlightened by revelation, at one and the same time, become a light for others—individual people and whole peoples—in a way analogous to how, during the night, the moon enlightens the earth with the light of the sun it reflects.*

We speak, therefore, of contextualized theologies, theologies that contribute to the meaning of human life in the interior of a particular historical process. Could this, perhaps, lead to a loss of universalism and Catholicism? Are we facing a contribution whose meaning regards a particular value only? Of course not! The whole is in the fragment, as Hans Urs von Balthasar prays in his famous study, *Das Ganze im Fragment*. The whole salvation of God is mysteriously contained in each fragment of history of human liberation, for every contextualized theology that sheds the light of God's salvation on a fragment of history is universal, catholic theology. The truth of contextualized theology is valid not only *within* this context, but also universally *from* this context. Similarly, all Christian theology is enlightened by the light of revelation that it receives, reflected off of each contextualized theology.

Seventh Thesis: *The first six theses suggest that theological plurality is not simply one possibility among others, but an intrinsic characteristic of Christian theology. The proof of this is the fact—irrefutable in the interior of faith—that the revelation of God in Israel and in Jesus Christ was not given once and for all (for example, in the Ten Commandments received by Moses) but was repeated throughout history, through multiple and distinct human lives and through multiple and distinct texts. That is why there are four Gospels, not just one.*

The constant attempts of Christian theology throughout its history to determine universally and definitively the truths of faith are surprising, when what was intended in such formulating was to welcome the revelation that is supposed to have taken place throughout history. It would be absurd and even comical to affirm that God didn't know how to find a fixed, unique, and definitive way to give Godself to us, to humanity, that God only knew how to do it through the history of Israel, Jesus, and the first Christian communities, a time in which the Old and New Testaments were written. God wished to reveal Godself progressively, throughout an entire history of about a thousand years or more, and did it through multiple fragments of history, as observed in the enormous variety of Old and New Testament writings. Why did God do it this way? Perhaps because the human person is essentially a historical being, whose experience of salvation can only be given in human history and whose language about this salvation must likewise be historical.

In this way theological plurality is not one possibility among others, but an essential trait of Christian theology as such. Although noble in cause, attempts to construct one unique Christian theology, as happened many times throughout the centuries, have been in vain. *Plurality* does not imply that we can affirm just anything about God, as some fear. Absolutely not. *Plurality* means that the fragments of self-communication and reception of God's revelation in the history of Israel, in Jesus, in the early Christian communities, and throughout the history of the church are many and diverse. We repeat: this plurality is essential to Christian theology.

Eighth Thesis: *Theo-logy, by definition, needs a logos to speak of God. However, Western theology erred when it insisted that logos must always be rational. Logos is not just reason. It is also any word that expresses something human. Consequently, it is legitimate and, in some cultural and historical contexts, necessary to find other logoi for theology, such as a historical logos, a narrative logos, a deeply felt logos, or an aesthetic logos.*

The word *theology* is confusing. It is not a concept found in scripture. It is a term first used by Plato, and later by Aristotle, and still later came to Saint Augustine through Marcus Terentius Varro. It was not systematized until the medieval-Scholastic era. It does not appear in any biblical text and hardly appears among the Patristic sources. *Theo-logy* means words and discourse about God. The confusion appears because a good number of modern sciences utilize the same root suffix, *logy* (philology, geology, biology, physiology, anthropology, dermatology, and so on—although not all do, for example, physics, chemistry, mathematics, politics). These sciences attempt a systematic knowledge of reality, definitive and universal. Without a doubt the knowledge is acquired bit by bit, with the passage of time and as the fruit of the scientific method, but it is always formulated with the supposed claim of universality. A German physicist does not do physics for Germany but for all of humanity. An American oncologist does not investigate American cancer but cancer. When speaking of theology, it can seem that the French theologian is not making theology for France but for the whole of humanity, but this is not entirely true. Of course, the faith of a French Catholic is the same as the Filipino Catholic, but since French culture, being European, is not identical to Filipino culture, there are significant differences in their theological formulations.

Perhaps the key is in understanding that the *logos* of theology isn't necessarily a rational *logos*, common to modern science, but that there are different types of *logoi* that effectively give a reason for one's hope. Such might be found in the historical *logos* (a discourse that gathers up human temporality), the narrative *logos* (a story about a lived experience), a deeply felt *logos* (for example, that found in the *Canticle of Canticles*), or an aesthetic *logos* (for example, a painting, a sculpture, architecture, music, dance). Nothing is new under the sun. One only has to read the Bible to realize that the revelation of God in Israel and in Jesus Christ covered almost all the *logoi* known in that era, including, for example, the books of history, law, psalms, poetry, wisdom, epistles, apocalyptic, and narratives, among others. It would make no sense to deny theology access to these other *logoi* when theology is born from them.

This openness to other *logoi* includes those that are typical to other cultures. Christian theology formulated in Mexican or Guatemalan indigenous communities will probably contribute new and extremely interesting elements.

Ninth Thesis: *Theology is not just a theoretical matter, but the theoretical moment of the historical praxis of faith. Praxis is not subordinate to theology. Rather, the latter is subordinate to the former. In each historical context theology must choose those logoi that help Christians understand and express their own faith.*

The experience of faith situates itself in the order of meaning and in the order of praxis. In the order of meaning, faith permits one to see all things with a new light, to understand the whole of reality and of human life, not in its natural or phenomenological functioning, but in its comprehension. And in the order of praxis, the individual who has the experience of faith feels called to transform reality, to change the situation of humanity for a world in accord with the reign of God. Theology is the theoretical moment of Christian praxis, a praxis that is pastoral, yes, but also social, economic, political. Briefly, in one word, it is historical. Because of this, just as in the Middle Ages, some asked for humility in philosophy, considering it a servant to theology [*ancilla theologiae*], now we should ask for humility in theology for being a *servant to praxis* [*ancilla praxis*], although in the final analysis both theory and praxis adhere to the experience of faith. Christian praxis takes multiple and diverse forms because the human situations in which God's salvation is needed and welcomed are multiple and diverse. If theology is the theoretical moment of these multiple forms of praxis, theology necessarily must be plural. Its *logos* should adapt itself to different forms of praxis.

Tenth Thesis: *The Bultmannian conception of the hermeneutical circle, extended by Ellacuría to the historical present—beyond the existential situation of the individual and into the terrain of politics—does not develop the peripheral relation that the different contemporary circles might have among themselves. Each circle—whether individual-existential, historical-collective, or cultural—places not only the individual, the society, or the culture in relationship with the Bible, but at the same time all are intertwined with other similarly contemporaneous circles in such a way that, together, they constitute a great circle of circles connected in some way with the one Bible, which remains in the center of the system. Bultmann and Ellacuría developed the diachronic hermeneutical circle but neglected the synchronic.*

There is no doubt that the hermeneutical circle of Rudolf Bultmann was one of the great contributions to theology in the twentieth century. He formulated the brilliant insight that the biblical text does not contain the truth in itself, as if it were a question of an objective truth, but that, in the line of a hermeneutics of Jewish origin, it contains truth in the measure that it awakens an experience of faith in the reader who encounters the word. Moreover, this happens in such a way that the reader understands his or her own existential experiences from the reading of the Bible and understands the Bible from his or her own existential experience. Now then, Bultmann remained in the order of the individual, something typically central-European. Ellacuría, for his part, sought to correct him on this point, noting that the individual reader of the Bible is the whole people, for the hermeneutical circle does not occur only between the biblical text and the individual reader but between the biblical text and the historical present of the faithful (that is, the people). The two worlds that come in contact are the world of the author of the text—Israel in its different historical eras—and the world of the reader, in the case of Ignacio Ellacuría, Latin America with its postcolonial economic structure. However, both Bultmann and Ellacuría neglected the fact that the readers of the Bible are multiple at the same time—many distinct individuals, in the Bultmannian perspective, and the many different peoples in the Ellacurian perspective. The reflection concerning the hermeneutical circle should be necessarily accompanied by reflection concerning its synchronic plurality of hermeneutical circles and in regard to the peripheral relationship between the two. Is the relationship between two close but distinct circles also hermeneutical? Probably not, because one circle does not understand itself in the light of the other, but there is no doubt that in the moment they become aware that they share the same world, dialogue among them becomes indispensable. We are at the doors of a formidable pluralism, not only ecumenical, which itself is not negligible, but even intra-ecclesial.

Eleventh Thesis: *Theology is the reflection about faith as the light of salvation offered to all human beings. Light can only illuminate the darkness. As such, the place of theology is human darkness, where what is human is denied in one way or another. Ellacuría, in the context of Latin America and the Third World in the 1960s, 1970s, and 1980s, spoke of the poor as a theological place [lugar teológico]. Beyond the problem of poverty, which is important and at the same time particular, in general the theological place is human darkness in its various forms: poverty; violence; dictatorship; the violation of human rights; the damage to the environment; linguistic, cultural, racial, sexual, and social discrimination; pedophilia; prostitution; abortion; certain genetic investigations; and more. Therefore, the theologian will not only study the light of theology, but at the same time the darkness of the human, and the way in which that light can enlighten this darkness in the historical present.*

Faith is light. It enlightens, allows one to see, permits us to understand where we are, where we come from, who we are. Theology is the reflection about this faith that is light. Now, light can only illuminate darkness. Faith can only give light where in humanity there is something being denied (although without a doubt, in heaven there will be no need for darkness to believe, and we have living rays to prove it). For this reason the adequate place for theology is there where humanity lives in darkness, where human life is at risk. Ellacuría affirmed that the poor are a *theological place* in the church, given that within the socioeconomic structures of his time—and in many ways, still within our time—the poor were those who were systematically denied their right to a life with dignity. Nonetheless, entering the twenty-first century and still aware of the enormous global problem of economic inequality, we cannot consider the poor as the only place of theology. A theological place is any place where human life is being denied in one way or another. To give importance to one place does not legitimize ignoring others. Theology is called to be formulated in all realities of human denial, in these places of darkness, in order to become light.

Twelfth Thesis: *Too many times throughout history, theology has made of itself a god [se ha autoendiosado]. It has considered itself as the supreme theology. That a particular theology be the most adequate for a historical context does not in any way legitimize the disregard (by those who formulate it) of other theological expressions given in other contexts. To disregard one is to be inconsistent with the principle of contextualization that legitimizes this theology. Self-respect implies respect for all the rest. Liberation theology and political theology have failed on this point.*

We have come to the "Achilles' heel" of contextualized theologies. Each one of them has the tendency to believe that its context is *the* context, its place *the* place, its truth *the* truth. It is something profoundly human. Perceiving the radical truth of something, we find it hard to accept that there can be a different truth. Liberation theology was highly critical of the dogmatism of Scholastic theology. Nevertheless, no few theologians of liberation have adopted the same dogmatic attitude in the defense of their truth, which they view as *the* truth. He who writes these lines listened in person to a famous liberation theologian disregard in a public conference the value of so-called Christian martyrs imprisoned for life in gulags. The validity of the Latin-American context as a theological place kept that renowned theologian from recognizing the validity of the Soviet prison system as a theological place, as a source, perhaps, for another theology.

Every contextualized theology has the tendency to make itself a god, to believe that it has found the theology par excellence: the poor, women, the indigenous cultures, the dialogue with the sciences, interreligious dialogue, the environment, and so on. However, while each context is *a* context, none is *the* context. Because of this, all Christian theology should not be just contextualized but should be humble with respect to theologies distinct— including the most distinct—from itself.

Although European political theology and Latin American liberation theology have contributed to Christian theology, they have not come to understand our twelfth thesis.

—Translated by Teresa Malave, VDMF, and Kevin F. Burke, SJ

PART III

THE PUBLICS OF CHURCH AND ACADEMY IN THE THEOLOGY OF ELLACURÍA

9

The Church of the Crucified People

The Eschatology of Ignacio Ellacuría

RODOLFO CARDENAL, SJ

The ecclesiology of Ignacio Ellacuría is spread over several of his essays, the majority of which were written between 1978 and 1984 and are collected in volume 2 of *Escritos Teológicos*.[1] My purpose in these pages is modest: to systematize the ecclesiology of Ellacuría dispersed over these documents.

Ellacuría's ecclesiology is not a finished product, since it always developed in obedience to historical and ecclesial realities, namely, Vatican II, Medellín (1968), Puebla (1980), and his experiences of Monseñor Romero, among others. His ecclesiology takes its starting point from his experience of base Christian communities, which he took to be a fundamental theological event and a new way of being church. Thus, Ellacuría does not begin with books as traditional theologies do but with a theology that springs from life itself. That is why he understands the church to be the people of God, a people fundamentally constituted by the poor and, for that reason, a church of the poor. This approach has been elaborated by various liberation theologians, but no one has done it the way Ellacuría did, analyzing, in light of the crucifixion of Jesus and of the people, the soteriological dimensions of the reality of the poor and of poverty.

The two keys to his ecclesiology are his understanding of (1) the irrevocable decision of God to save humanity, and (2) historical reality, where this salvation occurs and by virtue of which history comes to be to the history of salvation. What is new about this ecclesiology is that it springs from the historicization of these concepts. However, Ellacuría's theology does not stop with theory, but speaks to the pastoral implications of any given

---

[1] All of Ellacuría's essays in ecclesiology cited by the author can be found in the select bibliography at the end of this chapter. Citations to these writings are found in the text by date of authorship/original publication as these appear in the bibliography.—*Eds.*

theory. What is more, the effectiveness of the pastoral work is fundamental for verifying the truth of the concept of the church of the poor.

The Church as the Poor People of God

Ellacuría understands the church as the people of God, which inverts the traditional perspective, reorienting its "from above to below" approach. In this way the identity of the church is related to humanity. That is why he does not speak about God *in se*, but in relation to the people. With this understanding of a God who is revealed as a God of the people, Ellacuría emphasizes the ecclesial meaning more than the theologal.

Speaking historically, the relation between God and the people is a close one, since every people regards its god to be a constitutive element of its character as a people. Speaking theologically, the God of Israel repeatedly declares, "I shall be your God and you shall be my people" (1987). According to revelation, there exists a people of God because there is a God of the people, in contrast to a God of the cosmos or a God of nature. God's being is understood and experienced in God's free relationship to the people, because God is that which exists in the gift and manifestation of God that is found in what happens to the people. On the other hand, the people gains reality, full self-awareness, and freedom by being God's people and by opening itself to God.

Israel arrives at this conception through the historical mediation of an experience of oppression and the struggle for a people to liberate itself and to constitute itself as a free people. There is no getting around this mediation for Ellacuría because oppression prevents the establishment of a true people, a necessary condition for them to be a people of God and for God to be fully revealed and made historically present in them. Therefore, there can only be a true people in the measure that it comes to be a people of God. But just as there cannot be a people without one who reigns, or a reigning without a people, the people of God refers one directly to the reigning of God.[2] Logically it makes more sense that the reign has a people than that it have a church. Theologically, the people of God is prior to the church in revelation (1981).

The reigning of God brings salvation to the people, but this is historically mediated by a project that seeks to liberate it from the injustice and the sin of the world. Even if liberation is a utopian and eschatological goal, it does not launch the reign into a future without a present. If this were the case,

---

[2] The author, following Ellacuría, deliberately speaks here of the *reigning of God* [*reinado de Diós*] instead of the more familiar *reign of God* [*reino de Diós*], in order to bring out the *active* or *dynamic* character of God's historical presence in the world.—*Trans.*

salvation wouldn't mean anything. Salvation is not outside of history but retained within it. The connection between the eschatological utopia and current reality is given by the historical mediation that forms salvation into social structures. Now, even if these structures bear a resemblance to the reigning and to the people of God, the historical project does not exhaust salvation, because salvation, although promised to a people and within a people, does not limit itself to a specific people (1978c, 1983, 1987).

In any event, the church needs an institutional mediation that will form it as a social force so that it can fulfill its mission of struggling against the sin of the world. This sin must be eradicated because it negates the presence and revelation of God in history and because it structures history on the basis of this negation, and on that basis, the lives of individuals, and impresses a meaning and direction on their actions in such a way that positively annul the love of God. The structural dimension does not nullify or overshadow personal sin, however, because sin happens, in one way or another, through the will of the individual. But sin also takes, in one way or another, an objective form that is not only the fruit of personal sin but of objectified sin. As a consequence of all this, to the extent that the church enables humanity to be more human, it brings humanity closer to its fullness and carries out the "final judgment," since it acts from the reign.

This means that the church's center is found in humanity, that is, outside its institutional borders. Therefore, it cannot announce itself but rather the reign already announced by Jesus, not excluding its prophetic dimension. Nor can it hide behind the excuse that the reign of God will arrive with the Second Coming, because it must contribute actively to preparing for "the breaking forth of the glory of God." Neither can it renounce making what it announces real, because, without detracting from its own identity, it needs to manifest the salvific effectiveness of God in humanity. The church will only be able to consider its mission complete when it is able to affirm with complete precision what the true people of God is in its totality (1978c).

Despite what was just said, and without them coinciding completely, Ellacuría does attribute to the people of God an ecclesial dimension in the strict sense, because it falls to the church to hand on to that people the fullness of God's work. Therefore, the church is no more than an "exceptional instrument" for establishing the reign of God, and the most adequate mediation to accomplish this is liberation, justice, and love, three moments of a single historical process. In virtue of the reign the church has to liberate from injustice in order to live out love, the sign par excellence of God, the savior of the world, and the sign par excellence of the credibility of the church. That is why every ecclesial proclamation and action must make this salvation visible, and, in this sense, ought to be a sign that is intrinsically historical. Discernment shows the church what the sin of the world is in each historical moment. This is so because starting from this the church can interpret the other sins and get rid of them and also interpret what the hope of the world is, so that it can respond to the urgent question that humanity poses about the meaning of life, both future and present, and in their mutual relationship, responding without any limits other than what comes from its liberative mission. Therefore, there is no sense in asking whether the church, by liberating, is getting involved in politics. The only question that we can ask, and that we should want to ask, is whether the church is faithful to its mission (1978c, 1984).

Ellacuría is absolutely convinced that God is actively present in history and history is present in God in the proximity and the incipient (but definitive) presence of the reign. Therefore, only a church that makes salvation in history possible can discover and speak about the God of history—the God historically given. If people are scandalized by this, Ellacuría reminds them that this historicization of God is just as scandalous as God's incarnation and the deification of history. God is God-with-us (1978c, 1984).

Marks of the Church of the Poor

Ellacuría assigns to the church of the poor four marks [notas]: the preferential option for the poor, the incarnation in the struggle for justice, the presence of the Spirit in that struggle, and persecution. These marks, whose relevance and novelty lie in their historicization, specify the church of the poor. These are historical characteristics of an essentially historical reality and, because of that, they are necessary to make mystery credible and effective in history (1981, 1987).

The Preferential Option for the Poor

The people of God is the historical people of the poor. *The poor* is not an abstract concept for Ellacuría but rather those who are dispossessed and excluded by the rich and the powerful. The dialectic rich–poor avoids evading reality. It is also the poor who contribute to destroying the unjust order that produces them. Neither is this a profane concept, but rather one that puts its roots down deeply into the essence of the faith. Simply by being powerless, weak, and the victim of injustice at the hands of the powerful, the poor person is preferred by God, by virtue of God's mercy and justice. In a world of sin God expresses God's love for humanity as justice. Not only has God expressed a preference for the poor, but God has called them to reign in God's kingdom. By virtue of this election God has given them strength capable of bringing down the powerful. The preference of God constitutes them as the true social place [lugar] of the church, since starting from them the totality of the evangelical message can be embraced most fully and most concretely. Consequently, the church should opt for the poor and has to interpret, judge, and organize itself from this option (1980–81, 1982, 1983).

The truth of the church of the poor is justified, according to Ellacuría, on the basis of its radical sacramentality. The church is not simply a sacrament of salvation, but a *historical* sacrament of salvation through which it reclaims the fullness of meaning of the terms *sacrament* and *salvation*. The foundation of this sacramentality lies in a prior reality, that of corporality. Jesus having disappeared, the Resurrected One "takes on a body" [*toma cuerpo*] in the church and in this way acquires a historical corporality in order to continue "embodying himself" [*incorporándose*] in history. By taking on a body in the other, Jesus Christ becomes the church, but without ceasing to be who he was. It is through being embodied in the other that Jesus Christ *becomes* in the church while still retaining who he was. This "taking on a body" is necessary because, for his followers, only a corporeal presence (understood as the actual presence of the person) is really a presence. Theologically, "taking on a body" corresponds to the Word's "becoming flesh" [*hacerse carne*] so that the Word can intervene in a fully historical way in the actions of humanity. In "taking on a body" in order to "embody" himself, Jesus Christ concretely commits himself in a specific way to the historical salvation of humanity (1981).

Consequently, the church needs to "embody" Jesus Christ in that history, and do so concretely in the poor, his true historical body, where God becomes present in a way that is invisible for the world but visible for faith. This does not mean that the church stops being the mystical body, since its embodiment is not exhausted in history, but opens up to a "more" that goes beyond all possibility of being captured and represented. In this way, the church is "more" than what is visible in it, but the "more" is given, and must be given, in what is visible (1981, 1982).

The church's preferential option for the poor has, for Ellacuría, two serious practical consequences. The first is that faith needs to signify something real and verifiable in our lives. Given the historical structure of reality, the church is obligated to take away the sin of the world and to make present the incarnate life of God. Therefore, its mission consists in saving both ends of the rich–poor dialectic, which is knotted together by sin. When this dialectic is broken, there is salvation, which is always salvation "of" someone and, in that someone, salvation "from" something. In this way effective faith is constituted as the principle of universal salvation. The other consequence is that the poor are the primary subject and the structuring principle of the church. The union of God with humanity in Jesus Christ is, historically, the union of a God who has emptied himself, in the first place, into the world of the poor. Corresponding to this emptying, the church has to incarnate itself in them, dedicating its life to them, and dying for them. In this complete and total dedication the church establishes itself as an efficacious sign of salvation for humanity. It is not, then, a church that, being rich, looks after the poor, or one that generously helps the poor from afar. Rather, the poor are the body of Christ, the historical place of his presence and the "base" of the community gathered around Jesus. In this sense, base ecclesial communities institutionalize the preferential option for the poor (1977b).

Ellacuría does not reduce ecclesial action to sociopolitical force that exhausts itself in an ideological struggle against unjust structures. Rather, he affirms the primacy of the gift and the action of God. In particular, the creative and liberating Spirit takes precedence over human effort. However, the existence of urgent human needs denies this gift, which then takes flesh in the suffering of humanity. According to revelation, it is "divinity crucified in humanity," and according to Christology, it is the cry of "Jesus, who takes on a body historically in the needs and the suffering" of oppressed humanity. It is not just the future of humanity that is settled in the universal cry of peoples, classes, and individuals to be liberated, but the question of God in history (1977b, 1981).

Incarnation in the Struggle for Justice

The church of the poor cannot ignore historical struggles for justice. Rather, in fidelity to its mission and identity, it has to participate in those struggles, since justice and freedom are necessary in order for humanity to become the people of God. Starting from the exteriority[3] of reality, justice and freedom designate the path from history toward transcendence and vice-versa. Starting from the interiority of faith, there are characteristics so universal that with all requisite nuances, they are valid for all times, peoples, and societies. In this way, the liberating and justifying action of God converges with actions of justice and liberation on the part of the people (1978c, 1981).

The church does not intend to introduce a political order. It does not have the capacity to do so and, even more important, Jesus did not try to do this. Rather, Jesus dedicated himself to the realization of the reign of God and, insofar as he did this, to save this or that political system. From this, Ellacuría derives several important practical consequences. First, although the realization of the liberating project demands the use of power, this power

---

[3] The author, following Ellacuría, makes made use of Zubiri's understanding of "exteriority" of the world as a formal ontological structure of the human subject, not as something in opposition to or added to the subject. "The being of the subject consists formally in lying open to things" (Xavier Zubiri, *Nature, History, God*, trans. Thomas Fowler [Washington, DC: Catholic University Press of America, 1980], 320–21).—*Trans.*

has to be sought in order to put it at the service of those "without power," not of the leaders. Second, in this regard leaders should only serve as mediators in service of the reign and of the people, since they can never replace the one king of God's people. Third, the church does not need to be more than a leaven in the dough, in the realization of the historically liberative project, and consequently it must limit itself to pointing out the direction and indispensable values for bringing that project closer to the utopia of the reign. Fourth, it must be remembered that there is no "one size fits all" project, and that no project matches this utopia perfectly, even when justice is being put into practice. In short, utopia is the surest way to come closer to the transformation of social structures.

Notwithstanding the aforementioned points, the struggle for justice has been rejected for allegedly being supported by Marxism, for resorting to violence, and for using historical mediations. In the first place, Ellacuría responds that if we are scandalized by class struggle, we should likewise be scandalized by the existence of those classes and by the struggles within and between nations. Classes do not exist because there is a struggle; rather, the struggle exists because there are classes. In the second place, Marxist class struggle is not asserted out of some kind of subjective passion but a socially objective reality and a scientific question that falls outside the realm of theological speculation. Third, Ellacuría recognizes the influence of Marxism, but in a secondary way and as a second moment, when it is necessary to clarify social reality theoretically. In particular, it is useful for unmasking the interpretations driven by vested interests, for naming those who are sociopolitically poor and identifying the reasons for their poverty, and for promoting solutions that situate the church of the poor in its "authentic place." So then, its influence is positive and Christian, since it triggers the preferential option for the poor (1982).

On the other hand, to invoke pacifism in order to discredit the struggle for justice is not only mistaken but usually lacks sincerity, because it hides the exploitation of the oppressor. Ellacuría reminds anyone who lodges this objection that violence is often found in the Old Testament and in Christianity, although not in the New Testament. In any case, not all struggles for justice are violent, nor are they all class struggles either. And if they were, the people of God would have to participate in them in order to guarantee justice and unmask the false peace. Although it does not fall to the people of God to initiate armed conflict, because it goes against its nature and because it is not prepared for such struggle, it should participate in it and contribute to the revolutionary victory, but with its own proper weapons, which, without being warlike, are not for that reason less effective. In any particular case, the fundamental criterion is to opt for the best for the people (1978c, 1981).

Contrary to what its detractors say, the preferential option for the poor does not arise out of a primary hatred toward the rich over and against the exploited and oppressed but out of love for them. The point of departure is not hatred toward one of the extremes but love for the other. The ultimate goal is the conversion of the oppressor and the restitution of his or her character as a child of God. Theologically, it is a redemptive process for persons and societies dominated by the cross. For this reason love should not only inform the means utilized in the struggle for justice, even when that love demands difficult conditions, but it also should place certain limits on the people of God: respecting the existence of laws that condition the solutions, independent of personal will, sticking with the technical solutions, and taking up those that are put forth to eradicate sin (1981).

The Spirit and the Struggle for Justice

Misfortunes and sufferings, in themselves, do not save—not even the people of God—without further ado. Salvation comes from the presence and the orienting action of the Spirit of Christ. Ellacuría distinguishes between the people as a political entity struggling for liberation using formally political means and the people of God as the community of the followers of Jesus, inspired and guided by his Spirit in their fight for the liberation and salvation of the people. This is an important distinction, because Ellacuría thinks that the struggle for justice only delivers on its promise through the ferment of the Spirit. Therefore, the singular, indispensable, and irreplaceable mission of the church of the poor consists in spiritualizing poverty and raising awareness of that reality as oppression and as principle of liberation (1981, 1979).

The Spirit of Jesus gives birth to the true people of God in order to continue and extend the transformation of history. The Spirit does not leave them alone in fulfilling this command but guides and accompanies them. The presence of the Spirit is real and creative, the proof that Jesus continues living in history, realizing in it the task that he began in his historical life until it is ultimately achieved. Therefore, the great challenge consists in incarnating or historicizing the spirit of the poor and in spiritualizing the real flesh. The spiritualized People is the proper representative of the presence of the Spirit in the world and, thus becomes the ecclesial "remnant" par excellence. By "the spirituality of poverty" Ellacuría is not aiming at spiritualizing the people in exclusively mystical terms; rather, he has in mind a realization made full by the Spirit of Jesus (1981, 1979).

Historically, God has chosen to realize the fullness of humanity through poverty. This is why, Ellacuría points out, the first Beatitude invites one to become poor as long as there are poor. The logic is different from that of the other Beatitudes. To be sure, the hungry are promised satiety, and those who weep, joy. But the poor are not promised wealth but rather God's reign, which cannot be described in terms of historical wealth. There will be abundance there for all, "but no one will be able to be considered rich in contrast with the poor and in opposition to them!" The nucleus of the church of the poor is not constituted by the poor, but by those who are "poor in spirit," that is to say, those who live completely from the Spirit of Jesus. Theologically, the poor in spirit are the "poor with Spirit," that is, the poor who take up their real poverty from the perspective of the reign, in its human and Christian partiality (1979).

Ellacuría emphasizes that the poverty that is blessed is not one accepted with resignation and passivity, but one that is actively overcome, despite being a gift, to the extent that the reign is built. As a consequence of this the spirit of the Beatitudes necessarily raises the contradiction (already expressed in the counter-balancing of the blessings and the curses) that opposes the rich, the well-fed, and the ones who laugh, to the poor, the hungry, the ones who weep, and those who are despised. God is on the side of the latter and against the others (1979).

The spirituality of the people of God is marked by the faith that opens them to the manifestation of the reign of God, by the hope that encourages them to await its coming in transformative action, in which it is already present, but not in its fullness, and by their love that moves them to struggle against injustice and sin, because they know that they are the preferred of God. In short, the love of God is transformed into the love of his sons and daughters in the task of constituting a single people (1981, 1979).

Even though the contrary might seem to be the case, the presence and action of the Spirit of Christ in the people does not detract from the radicality or universality of historical liberation. The spirit of poverty is the most radical option of all, because it not only attends to the economic roots of oppression, but also strives to eradicate its social, political, and individual causes. Likewise, it is the most universal, because it is not limited to the liberation of one people but seeks the liberation of all humanity (1981).

Persecution for the Cause of God's Reign

Inexorably, the church of the poor suffers persecution from the world. Persecution is a direct consequence of confronting the two principal contraries: the rich and the poor, and sin and grace. The church can avoid persecution if it identifies itself with the rich and the powerful. But then it makes itself worldly. Persecution ensues when it identifies itself with the poor. Then it finds holiness. Persecution is a sign of fidelity to the gospel and a verification of its authenticity. So, theologically, persecution does not present any difficulties at all. The criterion of authenticity is Jesus, that is, announcing the reign to the poor and doing good to them. In sum, the church is called to be a sign of contradiction.

Persecution of the poor and of those who actively choose to help them begins as the structural violence that creates and even impoverishes the oppressed majorities more and more, while at the same time making the rich minorities even richer. Then oppression takes the form of violent repression in order to curb the action taken by the majorities who seek to liberate themselves. Therefore, according to Ellacuría, the continual and systematic action against the movement for liberation is persecution for the cause of God's reign in the strictest sense, because it is directed against the poorest, because the persecutors are those responsible for the unjust system and structures of sin, and because through persecution they aim to halt the march toward the reign.

In this view persecution because of the reign has a political and theologal character. It is political because Christ and his church are signs of contradiction, and it is theologal because it is unleashed against the people of God. However, in practice it is not easy to distinguish these spheres. The political conflict of an organized people with other organizations is not, in the strictest sense, theologal persecution for the cause of the reign (no matter how just the struggle may be) but is directly political persecution. Now, insofar as it works in favor of the reign, it can be indirectly and implicitly theologal. However, when it is directed against the people of God who seek to liberate themselves, it is directly and explicitly theologal. But insofar as it represents a threat to secular exploitation, it is indirectly and implicitly political. This distinction is very useful for resolving certain controversies, such as whether Monseñor Romero was assassinated for political reasons or was a martyr for justice. Politically, a leader is killed to restrain both a popular movement and the support of the church. Theologically, persecution brutalizes the shepherd and the prophet—leaders of the people of God who announce God's reign with historical words and who impel the popular movement—in order to scatter the flock (1973, 1981, 1984).

The Crucified People

Ellacuría's ecclesiology culminates in his formulation of the church as a crucified people. In his search for where and how the salvific action of Jesus continues in history he discovers the historical reality of the people crucified today by the sin of the world. The leading thread of his search is the historical character of the salvation of Jesus and the salvific character of the history of crucified humanity. Convinced that the implausibility that the passion of Jesus could be salvific illuminates the same implausibility regarding the crucifixion of the people, he explores how Jesus and the crucified people can be put in dialogue one with the other for the sake of the full realization of salvation (1978a).

The focus is more soteriological than ontological, since it does not emphasize the identity of Jesus and the people but instead emphasizes what both represent for the salvation of humanity. In fact, this is historical soteriology, because it accents the dual historical character of the reality of salvation in the one history of humanity and of the active participation of humanity in that history. The fundamental question regards, on the one hand, the meaning of the apparent failure represented by the death and crucifixion of the people, because there is played out both the failure of God and of humanity against the sin of the world and the presence of evil in history, and on the other hand, the meaning of history for the immense majority of humanity (1978a).

It is not easy to recognize the soteriological nature of poverty and of the poor, that is, that they are the first and most fully evangelized, and they are also those who evangelize. It is not immediately obvious how they can be both. One could accept, although with reservations, that they have been called preferentially to be evangelized and to be first in God's reign. But one cannot admit that, in virtue of that call, they are also those chosen by God to be the saviors of humanity. They have definitely been promised the reign, and for this they are called blessed, but it is not clear how they can save others when not even they have been saved. Ellacuría finds the answer to this paradox in Jesus, who, like the poor, ends up on the cross, broken by persecution. Both have brought—and bring—salvation into history, in the same way and despite their situation of abasement, but we can only see this when we recover the scandal and the madness of the cross (1978a).

Both the deaths of Jesus and of the people have historical—not natural—causes. Both deaths are produced by a historical "necessity" with causes that necessitated it. Even though the crucifixion of the people does not occur always and in every place in the same form or as a result of the same specific causes, the most important cause is the sin of the world, whose very existence makes the cross necessary in order to arrive at the resurrection. The Gospels refer to this sin in proclaiming the death of Christ "for our sins." The confrontation between the reign of God and the reign of sin makes resistance and struggle, persecution and death inevitable. Therefore the necessity does not answer to sacrificial expiatory considerations but to historical ones (1978a).

Jesus' death is a consequence of his life. It puts an end to the way that he lived but not to the meaning of his life, because that has to be reproduced and followed in new lives with the hope of resurrection and exaltation. That is why his life gives meaning to his death and why the latter is nothing more than a consequence of the former. The resurrection necessarily refers back to the passion and the passion to the life of Jesus as the one who announces the reign. Therefore, the life, death, and resurrection of Jesus not only continue on in heaven, but also occur in human history by a kind of "historical displacement" on the part of his body that is still in pilgrimage in it (1978a).

Jesus Christ has, then, not only a sacramental and mystical continuity, but also a historical one. In virtue of this, the uniqueness of Jesus lies not in what separates him from humanity but in the definitive character of his person and in the saving omnipotence that is proper to him. In other words, the *totum* of the presence of this continuity is not the cult, and not even the Eucharist, but the historical continuity continuing to realize what he realized and in just the way he realized it. Therefore, the historical dimension of salvation as well as its reality and meaning are assured in their continuity with history. Eternal life only has meaning in continuity with the present and the future of the history of humanity (1978a).

The continuity–discontinuity of Jesus displays his exemplarity for the crucified peoples. Thanks to this, the historical consequences of the resurrection are a hope and a future for those who still find themselves in "the days of passion." But this is a mystery that Ellacuría tries to approach starting from the metaphor of the Suffering Servant of Second Isaiah, in continuity with the tradition that saw Jesus' passion foretold in the servant (1978a).

The servant is sent to implement the law and universal justice, that is to say, he will do justice for the oppressed people and legislate for the equitable distribution of the goods of creation in order that all may enjoy them. This is contrary to the interests of the rich, and for this reason they despise the servant. Ellacuría reminds anyone who might object that this is a political mission, and that it is God himself who chooses, sends, and supports the servant. Likewise, the servant calls for the internalization of the love of justice in order to create a new human being. The third song emphasizes the importance of suffering during the people's liberative journey, in order to keep the lengthy experience of abasement from causing despair. The Lord not only endorses the suffering of the servant, but also will give him victory, despite the fact of his apparent defeat for having carried the sins of others, being himself innocent. The death of the suffering servant is an act of absolute and scandalizing injustice. But his sorrow is not in vain, for God is encountered behind it. Nor is his hope empty, because he will touch it with his hands and transform his life. Accepting his destiny to save through suffering those who cause it, God cannot do less than attribute the full salvific value to his sacrifice. In this way, the prophet opens a great hope for the afflicted and the persecuted. However, Ellacuría cautions that only a difficult act of faith can discover the salvation that is hidden from human eyes (1978a).

Just like the crucified people, the suffering servant is accepted by God and his passion is objectively related to the realization of God's reign. Therefore, the suffering servant of Yahweh is anyone who carries out the mission described by the Songs. In the strictest sense the suffering servant will be everyone unjustly crucified for the sins of humanity, since all the crucified constitute a single reality in the unity of expiation. Therefore, the crucified people is the historical continuation of the suffering servant, without completely matching up with the servant (1978a).

In virtue of its election, the crucified people is set up as "*the* sign of the times" through which God is made present to humanity. The peoples, social classes, and individuals who cry out for their liberation constitute "the crucified divinity in humanity" whose cry is the very cry of Jesus, who "became embodied in the flesh, in the needs and the suffering" of the oppressed people. All the other signs should be discerned and interpreted in the light of this principal sign.

Despite the emphasis on suffering and apparent failure, the hope of triumph always stands out; it also has a public and historical character, and it relates to the implementation of the law and justice. In this way the crucified people is not only the victim of the sin of the world but also contributes to its salvation. However, given the collective dimension of the figure of the servant, resurrection does not happen outside the boudaries of the crucified people (1978a).

Ellacuría stops here, with the crucifixion, and does not develop how those who are crucified bring about, through their resurrection, the salvation of the world. This is a necessary reality, because there is no salvation by virtue of the mere fact of crucifixion and death. The church of the poor, as the continuer of the work of Jesus and as the sacrament of salvation, should understand itself as a church of the crucified people.

—Translated by Jeanette "Lil Milagro" Henriquez-Cornejo,
Kevin F. Burke, SJ, and J. Matthew Ashley

Selected Bibliography:
Ignacio Ellacuría's Writings in Ecclesiology

The essays cited in this chapter are listed below with the original date of composition and/or publication. We have supplied English language citations for those entries that have been translated and published in English. For a complete publication history for these writings, please consult the bibliography in *Love That Produces Hope: The Writings of Ignacio Ellacuría*, ed. K. Burke and R. Lassalle-Klein (Collegeville, MN: Liturgical Press, 2004).—*Eds.*

Ignacio Ellacuría. 1973. "La Iglesia, signo de contradicción." In *Escritos Teológicos*, vol. 2, 397–416 (San Salvador: UCA Editores, 2000).

———. 1977a. "Liberación: misión y carisma de la Iglesia Latinoamericana." In English: "Liberation: Mission and Charism of the Latin American Church," in *Freedom Made Flesh: The Mission of Christ and His Church*, trans. John Drury, 127–63 (Maryknoll, NY: Orbis Books, 1976).

———. 1977b. "Iglesia de los pobres, sacramento histórico de liberación." In English: "The Church of the Poor, Historical Sacrament of Liberation," in *Ignacio Ellacuría: Essays on History, Liberation, and Salvation*, ed. Michael E. Lee, 227–53 (Maryknoll, NY: Orbis Books, 2013).

———. 1978a. "El pueblo crucificado. Ensayo de soteriología histórica." In English: "The Crucified People," in Lee, *Ignacio Ellacuría*, 195–224.

———. 1978b. "La Iglesia que nace del pueblo por el Espíritu." In *Escritos Teológicos*, 2:343–55.

———. 1978c. "Recuperar el reino de Dios, des-mundanización e historización de la Iglesia." In *Escritos Teológicos*, 2:307–16.

———. 1979. "Las Bienaventuranzas, carta fundacional de la Iglesia de los pobres." In *Escritos Teológicos*, 2:417–37.

———. 1980–81. "Opción preferencial por los pobres. Discernir 'el signo' de los tiempos." In *Escritos Teológicos*, 2:133–35.

———. 1981. "El verdadero pueblo de Dios, según Monseñor Romero." In *Escritos Teológicos*, 2:357–96.

———. 1982. "El auténtico lugar social de la Iglesia." In English: "The True Social Place of the Church," in *Towards a Society that Serves Its People: The Intellectual Contribution of El Salvador's Murdered Jesuits*, ed. J. Hasset and H. Lacey, trans. Phillip Berryman, 283–92 (Washington, DC: Georgetown University Press, 1991).

———. 1983. "Pobres." In *Escritos Teológicos*, 2:171–92.

10

A Different Kind of University Within the University

Ellacuría's Model in the Context of the United States

DAVID IGNATIUS GANDOLFO

In 1975, ten years after the founding of the Universidad Centroamericana José Simeón Cañas (UCA) in San Salvador, Ignacio Ellacuría penned an anniversary tribute titled "Is a Different Kind of University Possible?"[1] The essay functioned as much more than an anniversary tribute. It was an important programmatic statement about the mission and identity of the UCA, and it remains one of Ellacuría's most striking contributions to a much-needed conversation on the meaning and purpose of any university in this postmodern, post-universal age. Twenty-five years after his brutal assassination—along with five other Jesuit priests, a seminary cook, and her daughter—this chapter revisits his vision of "a different kind of university" as part of another important anniversary celebration.

Ignacio Ellacuría was a major contributor to philosophical and theological reflection on liberation, bodies of thought that nuance our understanding of the theory/practice relationship and that have strong implications for personal *and* institutional conduct. For twenty-two years, until his death in 1989, he made decisive contributions to the creation and leadership of a university built upon the insights taken from liberation theology

---

[1] Ignacio Ellacuría, "¿Diez años después: es posible una Universidad distinta?" *Estudios Centroamericanos*, no. 3224–25 (1975): 605–28. In English: "Is a Different Kind of University Possible?" in *Toward a Society That Serves Its People: The Intellectual Contribution of El Salvador's Murdered Jesuits*, trans. Phillip Berryman, ed. J. Hassett and H. Lacey, 177–207 (Washington, DC: Georgetown University Press, 1991).

and philosophy.[2] The UCA has become a model for universities that take seriously their responsibility to make their indispensable contributions to the forging of a more just world. Ellacuría's vision for a university acting in the service of human need is rich and complex. My aim here is modest: to highlight key aspects of his model and explore the ways in which this model, created in a context of extreme and violent polarization, might be useful to a contemporary conversation about the nature of the university in general, with special attention to the particular context of universities in the United States.

Ellacuría's Model: Placing the Focus on Reality

What is the fundamental purpose or mission of the university? This question puts us squarely in the conversation with the UCA model that Ellacuría helped to fashion and implement. For Ellacuría, the mission of the university must shift the focus from a passive model of transferring knowledge to an active emphasis on socio-historical change in favor of the equality and justice required for overcoming oppression and moving toward a fuller realization of human dignity. A different kind of university is one that "by its very structure and proper role as a university is *actually committed to opposing an unjust society and building a new one*" (emphasis added).[3] The "ultimate significance" of a university, and "what it is in reality," is "its impact on the historical reality in which it exists and which it serves."[4] Ellacuría insisted that the poor, the marginalized, the oppressed must be the horizon of the university's activity.[5] Everything the university does must be done within an awareness of and as response to the fact that the majority of humankind

---

² See Ignacio Ellacuría, *Escritos Universitarios* (San Salvador: UCA Editores, 1999); in English, see Hassett and Lacey, *Toward a Society That Serves Its People*, the following three articles: "The Challenge of the Poor Majority," 171–76; "Is a Different Kind of University Possible?" 177–207; "The University, Human Rights, and the Poor Majority," 208–19. For further reading see Teresa Whitfield, *Paying the Price: Ignacio Ellacuría and the Murdered Jesuits of El Salvador* (Philadelphia: Temple University Press, 1995), esp. chap. 8; see also Dean Brackley, "Higher Standards for Higher Education: The Christian University and Solidarity (1999), http://onlineministries.creighton.edu/CollaborativeMinistry/brackley.html; idem, *The University and Its Martyrs: Hope from Central America* (San Salvador: Centro Monseñor Romero, 2004); David Gandolfo, "A Role for the Privileged? Solidarity and the University in the Work of Ignacio Ellacuría and Paolo Freire," *The Journal for Peace and Justice Studies* 17, no. 1 (2008): 9–33; Robert Lassalle-Klein, *Blood and Ink: Ignacio Ellacuría, Jon Sobrino, and the Jesuit Martyrs of the University of Central America* (Maryknoll, NY: Orbis Books, 2014).

³ Ellacuría, "Is a Different Kind of University Possible?" 177.

⁴ Ibid., 178, trans. emended.

⁵ Ibid., 180.

is dehumanized by conditions of poverty, marginalization, and oppression. What does the university have to say when it comes face to face with reality, with the concrete wounds caused by these dehumanizing conditions?

Ellacuría identifies the specific kind of impact the university ought to have on historical reality when he asserts bluntly that the "the university should not only devote itself formally and explicitly to having the fundamental rights of the poor majorities respected as much as possible, but it should even have the liberation and development of those majorities as the theoretical and practical horizon for its strictly university activities, and it should do so preferentially."[6] The goal of a university should be to solve the complicated problem of "attainment by the poor majority both of living standards sufficient for meeting their basic needs in a decent manner and of the highest degree of participation in the decisions that affect their own fate and that of society as a whole."[7] In other words, in addition to empowering the poor in their search for a decent standard of living, the goal of university activity must be to re-empower their agency as *effective* participants in society, "assuring them their proper place in the political and economic process."[8]

Thus, the different kind of university that Ellacuría sought to create is one with a real and substantial commitment to the poor and oppressed, people who constitute the vast majority of humanity. How can this be justified? Ellacuría argues for his model not primarily on moral grounds, as one might expect, but on ontological grounds. He argues that the university must be focused on the poor and oppressed *if it is to remain true to its role as a university*.

The Foundational Disposition of the University

Ellacuría calls the foundational disposition of the university "social projection" [*proyección social*]. Social projection moves in two directions at once: (a) the university's recognition of its need and responsibility to insert itself (its knowledge, its research, its teaching) *effectively* into society; and (b) the university's recognition of its need and responsibility to allow the needs of society to penetrate and permeate the university, determining its curriculum and research agendas. In a nutshell, social projection makes explicit the university's commitment to respond to the real needs of the social-historical location within which it exists.

---

[6] Ellacuría, "The University, Human Rights, and the Poor Majority," 209.
[7] Ibid., 211–12.
[8] Ibid., 214.

Ellacuría usually presents social projection as one of the three areas of activity appropriate to the university, along with teaching and research, but it is clearly first among equals:

> A university works out its political nature [*politicidad*] in a manner appropriate to a university when, from among its various functions— teaching, research and social projection—it gives priority to social projection such that the latter determines the others although it is, in turn, also determined by them. . . .
> This social projection . . . is not something apart from the other two fundamental functions of the university. It presupposes teaching as its basis of support; likewise, it presupposes research as the fundamental illuminator of its task. But it becomes the regulator of these.[9]

Social projection is not simply one among many of the university's activities but the heart of its mission and identity. The university's foundational disposition is no longer conceived primarily in terms of the handing on of knowledge (teaching) and pushing back the frontiers of the known (research). The fundamental disposition is now conceived in terms of encountering and affecting reality. Naturally, this does not remove the need for teaching and research, but it does mean that the relationship between social projection and the canonical university activities of research and teaching is not a simple one. For example, social projection is dependent upon research to determine the real needs of society, but this in turn requires that the research be focused on determining the real needs of society and solutions to those needs:

> It must be emphasized that knowledge and know-how that do not respond to what a society is, here and now in its entirety, especially when this society suffers fundamental deficiencies, are not [the kind of] knowledge appropriate to a university.[10]

The theoretical and practical knowledge developed and housed at a university is not for its own sake but for the good of society, for the common good. This is even clearer in a consideration of the goal of social projection which, as the cornerstone of the whole university edifice, "prioritizes radical transformation of the established disorder and of structural injustice."[11]

---

[9] Ellacuría, "Universidad y Politica," 186, 189.
[10] Ibid., 184.
[11] Ibid., 186.

The Nature of a University: Three Cardinal Points

Upon this foundational disposition Ellacuría's vision takes shape around three cardinal points related to the nature of a university. First, the university is inextricably part of society. Second, within the societal division of labor, the university's particular tasks are the search for and the propagation of truth. These tasks are carried out in the university's canonical activities of teaching and research. Finally, under the present conditions of society, which are known to the university by way of its research, the search for truth leads inevitably and appropriately to a preferential option for the marginalized. Let us examine these essential dimensions of the university and their interrelationships in more detail.

First, the university is part of society. More technically, the university is part of socio-historical reality, that is, the part of reality that humans have created. The human part of reality is thoroughly social, thoroughly historical, because it is formed by temporally bound social beings. All human institutions are conditioned by this provenance and are thus, inextricably, social and historical. Similarly, they are all political because they, unavoidably and by their nature as social entities, affect and are affected by the organization of society in general and the distribution of power in society in particular:

> The political [*politicidad*] is a fact and also a necessity. By "the political aspect of the university" we mean, provisionally, the fact and the necessity to be shaped . . . by the socio-political reality in which it exists, and the fact and the necessity to shape . . . this socio-political reality.[12]

In other words, it is not possible for the university (or any other institution) *not* to be political. The important thing is that it be *appropriately* political, political in a way that is faithful to its identity as a university.[13]

The second cardinal point that orients Ellacuría's vision of the university is this: the essential purpose of the university within human society is the pursuit and propagation of truth. As we have just seen, the university is unavoidably implicated in processes of social organization and change. The question, Ellacuría contends, is not whether the university should become involved in sociopolitical pursuits, but how it should and should not do so given its specific identity as a university. The university must be interested in uncovering the truth about reality, making the truth known to society, and in holding all, especially the powerful, accountable to the truth.

---

[12] Ibid., 171.
[13] Ellacuría, "Is a Different Kind of University Possible?" 178–79.

Therefore, the university must be political "universitarily" [*universitariamente*], that is, in the manner of a university and not some other entity. The university is not political in the same way government agencies, political parties, or other secular institutions like media outlets are political. It is political by doing what universities do—teaching, research, the work of institutes and publications, and so on. But it undertakes these activities with an expressed and overt awareness of and responsibility for the way they do or do not actually impact their historical context. That is, a university's activities all have political implications. The point, for Ellacuría, is to recognize this and allow this recognition to shape the very identity of the university as such. For Ellacuría—living as he did in a situation of extreme crisis and civil unrest—that meant paying attention to the lived reality of the majority of Salvadorans. It meant recognizing that their impoverishment stemmed directly from unjust social, economic, and judicial structures. The results of research focused on the real needs of society show that the status quo is unjust, and the university's teaching, research, and social projection takes place within the horizon of this knowledge.

In this vision the university's responsibility vis-à-vis the truth about reality is not one of discovery and dissemination alone. It also involves confrontation with institutionalized lies and biases and, following Ellacuría's theory of intelligence, the pursuit and propagation of truth must be properly oriented toward action for the transformation of reality. The purpose of our intelligence is to grasp reality, including the possibilities latent within it; to evaluate the possible futures that could be brought about by various actions; to decide which of those possibilities we should work to realize; and to figure out the best ways to realize the future we have chosen. In this way human beings work with and within reality to bring forth new reality. Hence, Ellacuría is able to claim that we are the part of reality responsible for the further development of reality; we are what he, following Zubiri, calls "the reality animal." The goal of the reality animal, as we shoulder our responsibility for the future, is the further humanization of reality.[14]

Ellacuría does not deny that the university must maintain itself as a "place of freedom." However, neither does he focus primary attention on the important academic value of freedom of inquiry. He focuses on something even more important: a "prior [and more] fundamental freedom which is won by continually striving for liberation from the existing

---

[14] By this, Ellacuría does not intend a strong anthropocentrism that privileges humans against other species but rather a weak anthropocentrism that recognizes the centrality of human action in achieving a better world. That such a world needs to be run in a way that respects the complexity of a sustainable future, and not in the sole interest of human beings, is something that human intelligence is learning and must learn.

social structure."[15] The university cannot be faithful to its essence if it is only training people to take up positions in the existing social structures. It must also maintain the space for critiquing those structures, holding them up for critical scrutiny, and envisioning new structures that would answer the problems revealed in such inquiries and would move the world in the direction of greater justice. The emphasis on envisioning new, just, non-oppressive, life-affirming social structures is a vital part of the university's activity.

> Criticism and tearing apart are not enough; a constructive criticism that offers a real alternative is also necessary. . . . Not only must we unmask the ideological trap in this tidal wave of ideology. We must also produce models which in a fruitful interchange between theory and practice may really generate ideals intended to stimulate . . . the task of building history."[16]

Finally, the third cardinal point orienting Ellacuría's vision of the university is that its role as a university leads it toward a preferential option for the marginalized. In Ellacuría's vision the poor and oppressed are *the horizon of university activity* that grounds all other aspects of the university's mission. Everything the university does takes place within an awareness of the manifest injustice of the world as currently structured. The "ultimate standpoint and deepest purpose" of the university is the reality in which it exists. That reality is social and historical. Hence, the university should study and engage society, as currently structured, and the history that brought it to its present structure. What are the causes of this reality? What is its moral significance? What are the possibilities latent within it? Which of those possibilities should be realized? What are the obstacles to the realization of those possibilities? The university, given its mission as the pursuit of truth, is in a unique position to examine the strengths and weaknesses of the possible answers to these questions. The results of such investigations show society to be fundamentally divided with the various sides having clashing interests. In such a situation the university must take sides. And while this may appear to be a betrayal of the university's mission to pursue truth, it is not. In the first place, in a divided situation in which power differentials are part of the division, it is not possible not to take sides; not to take sides is automatically to side with the dominant side. In such a situation the university has only two options: to work for a future that continues the oppression or for a future that ends it. There is no middle ground between maintaining the

---

[15] Ellacuría, "The University, Human Rights, and the Poor Majority," 216.
[16] Ellacuría, "The Challenge of the Poor Majority," 173–74.

current structures and transforming them.[17] The university, in its pursuit of truth must be free and objective, "but objectivity and freedom may demand taking sides. [The UCA is] freely on the side of the popular majority because they are unjustly oppressed and because the truth of the situation lies within them."[18] Being objective means being true to the object under study. The object of study with which the university is concerned is reality. Being faithful to our task of humanizing reality, especially when the study of reality shows it to be oppressive, means working to end that oppression.

Ellacuría's Model Today:
Challenges and Possibilities for US Universities

Is Ellacuría's "different kind of university" relevant today? Might it speak to the various forms universities take in the United States today? His model was developed in the Salvadoran context, where vastly unequal distribution of wealth and violent repression of the poor and their allies maintained an unjust status quo. Confronted with this reality Ellacuría and his colleagues organized the UCA such that its activity would take place within the horizon of this knowledge. Today, the reality in which US universities are located, locally and globally, while very different than El Salvador in the 1980s, is similarly unbalanced and unjust, despite massive efforts to hide the injustices in the system. The possible relevance of Ellacuría's model does not hinge on the similarity or dissimilarity existing between the different contexts of Ellacuría's UCA and universities in the United States today. Rather, it depends on the prior option to make actual context—historical reality—the horizon of all of a given university's operations. From there, individual universities would need to take up the task of detecting where reality is fundamentally just or unjust—a constitutive component of Ellacuría's model—and then respond accordingly. Even if a university makes what Ellacuría understood as "an option for historical reality"—an option rooted in its own version of social projection—discerning what to do and how to go about doing it, although not impossible, will be extraordinarily difficult. And as Ellacuría's own life witnesses, such choices might well entail very serious consequences.

The recognition that the context within which a given university finds itself is unjust cannot be drawn from research alone. Research can objectively show that the distribution of resources, wealth, opportunity, and power is unequal, and that the level of inequality is growing to unprecedented

---

[17] In this statement I focus on outcomes. Taking process into account there *is* a middle ground, the place of discernment, which emerges in answer to the question, *how* do we best transform those structures?

[18] Ellacuría, "The Challenge of the Poor Majority," 175.

levels. But the further, normative claim that this inequality is unjust needs a theory of justice and, ultimately, a conception of human dignity to ground it. Under the extreme conditions that existed at the UCA in the 1970s and 1980s, agreement that the status quo was unjust was easier to obtain, if only because faculty members didn't have the luxury of endless debate. The severe repression touched the UCA's professors directly, not because they were inherently vulnerable, but because they chose to conduct their scholarship from within the horizon of the marginalized. At US universities today it is considerably harder to come to provisional conclusions that can stand long enough to orient decisions as important and contested as the content of the curriculum and the focus of faculty research. US universities fancy themselves as molding those who will shape the future. Yet the universities are very reluctant to engage the normative questions pertaining to the optimal perspectives for perceiving reality and the ways in which reality ought to be molded. Overcoming this reluctance would involve facing and overcoming several important challenges.

First, even the objective facts about economic inequality, including the history that has brought us to the current distribution of wealth and power in the world, are not well known. There is much work to be done to achieve this crucial, indispensable first level in the service of the truth about historical reality. Learning about reality is clearly *a* legitimate pursuit of the university. But that it should be the *primary* pursuit of the university needs further support. Here, the insights of standpoint epistemology are helpful.[19] As college students are coming to an understanding of reality, their place in it and their responsibilities toward it, knowledge that will show what needs to be done in the construction of a more just, more humane world is appropriate. The knowledge available on the margins is precisely that knowledge. From the margins we can see things difficult to see from the center, difficult for many reasons, chief among them being that the powerful who constitute the center do not want these things to be seen and, therefore, actively try to hide them. The interest of those at the center is to preserve the status quo. To the extent that the status quo is seen to be legitimate, its preservation is made easier. The mere existence of large numbers of marginalized people calls into question that legitimacy, making questionable the supposedly unquestionable superiority of the status quo; hence, the center will try to

---

[19] See Nancy Hartstock, "The Feminist Standpoint: Developing the Ground for a Specifically Feminist Historical Materialism," in *Discovering Reality*, ed. Sandra Harding and Merrill B. Hintikka, 283–310 (Dordrecht: Kluwer Academic Publishers, 1983); Sandra Harding, "Rethinking Standpoint Epistemology: What Is 'Strong Objectivity'?" in *Feminist Epistemologies*, ed. Linda Alcoff and Elizabeth Potter, 49–82 (New York: Routledge, 1993); and Sandra Harding, ed., *The Feminist Standpoint Theory Reader: Intellectual and Political Controversies* (New York: Routledge, 2004).

hide the marginalized. But for anyone who desires to build a better, more just, more human and humanizing future, it is precisely the awareness that oppression exists that is needed; if we are to create a world with less oppression, we must focus on the oppressed. The view from the margins is precisely what is needed for the knowledge of what needs to be done to build a better future. So, while the powerful want to hide this view, the just must actively seek it. We have, thus, not just an awareness of the importance of the marginal perspective, but a mandate to seek it preferentially.

Second, evaluating historical realities necessarily involves normative claims, something that is almost anathema to the postmodern academy. One cannot define a better world as "one with less oppression" unless one believes humans ought not to be oppressed, and such a belief further requires a commitment to the idea of human dignity, which means embracing some version of the following fundamental ethical principles. (1) Each and every person has inherent and inalienable dignity. (2) Society should be structured such that all people have the opportunity to achieve the fullness of their humanity. (3) The fullness of one's humanity consists in achieving robust agency and in recognizing a responsibility both to know what is going on and to contribute to making the future more just.

However, these ethical claims, woven into the very fabric of Ellacuría's vision for the university, are not arbitrarily asserted. They are grounded in a basic epistemological assertion: one has to become aware of one's responsibility to be responsible and to know what is the case. For the matter does not merely hinge on a fundamental ethical stance. If one accepts that humans *qua* "reality animals" need to know as much as possible about their context in order to fulfill their responsibility in deciding the future direction of reality, then those parts of the situation that have been covered up by powerful vested interests should receive special attention.

Third, a difficulty arises around the connection between one's normative commitments and one's conclusions about the state of the world. Upon an expansive awareness of the vast inequality that exists, universities could be doing much more in the exploration of how various theories of justice and various approaches to human dignity would judge the status quo. Knowing reality, studying the differing interests of the various groups who constitute the status quo (especially vis-à-vis the maintenance of the status quo), knowing the possibilities for change latent in the status quo, evaluating these possible futures according to the criteria of various visions of human dignity—these are legitimate university pursuits. But how do we initiate a discussion regarding what would constitute a just society and what would be required to build it? These issues also encroach onto normative terrain, making claims about what constitutes human responsibility. But perhaps these claims are not outlandish.

Ellacuría's argument that "a different kind of university" is possible focuses the commitment to social justice in the concern for truth. As such, while different, such a university would not be completely new. Indeed, it would preserve the very heart of the long tradition of the university. It would be a university grounded in a conception of human dignity that sees humans as necessarily agents of their own destinies and demands that this conception applies to all humans. This is a defensible, reasonable position, but not one that will be accepted by all. There will be those who object, in a social-Darwinist fashion, that not all humans are suited for agency, or that the agency of many people is only suited for small, personal decisions, not for the larger political decisions about the direction in which reality should be taken. But as a US university addresses this controversy in the classroom, it can insist, for solid pedagogical reasons, that its students get to know the historical realities and the particular peoples about whom they are forming conclusions. When the students know the stories of some of the marginalized they can begin to appreciate and decide for themselves the possibility that unjust structures unfairly limited the opportunities for success, and that the marginalized might therefore not be ontologically unsuited for robust agency but only opportunistically disadvantaged.

We should not underestimate the commitment required of academics who want to realize a different kind of university. The religious metaphor of conversion is applicable here: if we aren't able to persuade ourselves with our conclusions, who else should be persuaded? The UCA model was put together, to a great extent, by vowed religious, which has many implications, both profound and practical. They sought motivation, insight, and guidance for their efforts through, among other things, spiritual exercises.[20] Their work in forging and enacting the UCA model was the enactment of their vocation. They were "all in," completely committed, bending their lives according to the demands of their vocation. The UCA was, for each of them, their life's work. Those of us who want to continue their work will need to be prepared also to live vocationally, to allow the conclusions of our research to direct our entire lives (not just the papers we publish in academic journals), and to evangelize others into the need to also live vocationally. An academic evangelization is needed to proclaim to our colleagues the need for and necessity of the different kind of university.

Finally, the people who put the UCA model together held all of the key positions of leadership in the university, from the board to senior administrators to chairs of key departments to directors of key institutes. As such, in animating the rest of the university they could draw on a century of Catholic

---

[20] The *Spiritual Exercises* of Saint Ignatius Loyola anchors the spirituality that formed the habits and hearts of the UCA Jesuits and many of their colleagues.

social teaching, the momentum of Vatican II, and the rededication of the Society of Jesus to a faith that does justice. With these kinds of institutional support they could devote their energies to creating curricula and research agenda rather than to endless self-justification and assessment projects to "prove" the worthiness of the new direction. This set of circumstances is not likely to be repeated at contemporary US universities, and this reality suggests a significant amendment to Ellacuría's model. Perhaps it is unreasonable, at least for now and at most universities, to aim for the transformation of the entire university. But what is fully achievable today at most of these institutions is the creation of robust programs within the university that *do* focus scholarship from the standpoint of the marginalized. This amended model might be termed a "different kind of university within the university." And this different university, these programs, can gain focus and legitimacy from Ellacuría's model. Anchored in their historical reality, recognizing their responsibility for social projection, they can focus their teaching and research on the work of creating a more just world.

Ellacuría insisted that the university does not live for itself but for the people[21] and, by extension, for the common good. There is a lot of pressure on academics at US universities to care about their own interests or their institutions' interests.[22] As we create and adapt programs along the Ellacurian model we will be reorienting our universities to institutions that serve the common good.

---

[21] "The UCA exists neither for itself nor for its faculty and students. Its emphasis is not within itself, nor in its students or professors or leadership. It is for the Salvadoran people who must be the center and ultimate goal of its activities." Ignacio Ellacuría, "Funciones fundamentales de la universidad y su operativización," in *Escritos Universitarios*, 108; written in 1978 and first published in 1989, this document summarizes the conclusions of a university-wide consultation process on the role of the UCA.

[22] The hyper-precarious, hyper-competitive academic job market and the organization of that model around national searches combine to produce intellectuals who are forced to engage in endless self-promotion for at least the first decade of their professional lives (from the last years of graduate school to the tenure decision), and who, at the same time, have little connection to or knowledge of the communities where they teach and do research. The resulting self-promoting vagabond intellectual *cum* independent contractor must be overcome. (Indeed, more-senior faculty who are sensitive to the soul-debasing effects of this process should institute a post-tenure cleansing process that would aim to move the now-stable scholars beyond themselves, to plug them into the community, to urge them to refocus on the needs of the community.) This is a huge structural impediment to forging an academy that is engaged in and relevant to the problems of oppressed people; it raises another difficult question, beyond the scope of the present essay: should being anchored in the historical reality in which one conducts one's professional life be some part of the criteria used at the different university for hiring, tenure, and promotion?

I I

The Christian University
for a Globalized World

*Ignacio Ellacuría's Vatican II Advance on
Cardinal Newman's Classic Statement*

ROBERT LASSALLE-KLEIN

Ignacio Ellacuría's vision of the Christian university integrates and advances beyond John Henry Cardinal Newman's seminal 1852 "Idea of a University" by implementing the Latin American bishops' interpretation of the role of the church in the modern world outlined at Vatican II (1962–65). In making this argument I first assert that Newman's insistence that Catholic education must engage the intellectual and cultural achievements of secular culture anticipates and is extended to the entire church by Vatican II. Second, I argue that Ellacuría's model of the university operationalizes both the central mandate of the council's *Pastoral Constitution on the Church in the Modern World* (1965) and its "historicization"[1] in the preferential option for the poor by the Latin American bishops at Medellín (1968). And third, I suggest that Ellacuría's vision of the university, with its emphasis on the agency of the poor majorities of the planet, both complements recent breakthroughs in

---

[1] For Ellacuría's definition of this concept, see Ignacio Ellacuría, *Filosofía de la realidad histórica* (San Salvador: UCA Editores, 1990), 169, 491–598. See also idem, "La historización del concepto de propiedad como principio de desideologización," *Estudios Centroamericanos* 31, no. 335–36 (1976): 425–50; in English: "The Historicization of the Concept of Property," in *Toward a Society That Serves Its People: The Intellectual Contribution of El Salvador's Murdered Jesuits*, trans. Phillip Berryman, ed. J. Hassett and H. Lacey, 177–207 (Washington, DC: Georgetown University Press, 1991), 109. See also Lassalle-Klein, *Blood and Ink: Ignacio Ellacuría, Jon Sobrino, and the Jesuit Martyrs of the University of Central America* (Maryknoll, NY: Orbis Books, 2014), 223–24.

cognitive neuroscience and serves as a model for twenty-first-century Jesuit university education around the globe.

Newman's Idea of the University

John Henry Cardinal Newman's classic treatise "The Idea of a University"[2] exercises tremendous influence on the self-understanding of twenty-first-century Catholic universities today. Speaking as rector of the newly established Catholic University of Ireland, Newman rejects the utilitarian views of education espoused, on the one hand, by the secular allies of Jeremy Bentham, and on the other, by ecclesiastical authorities preoccupied with passing on the faith and vocational training for Irish Catholics. He argues instead that the primary end of the Catholic university is neither the acquisition of trades, technical skills, and useful information, nor simply knowledge of the faith, but rather the cultivation of the mind and the development of critical thinking among its students.

Newman clearly understands the practical implications of a university education for Irish youth when he states:

> Robbed, oppressed, and thrust aside, Catholics in these islands have not been in a condition for centuries to attempt the sort of education which is necessary for the man of the world, the statesman, the landholder, or the opulent gentleman. Their legitimate stations, duties, employments, have been taken from them, and the qualifications withal, social and intellectual, which are necessary both for reversing the forfeiture and for availing themselves of the reversal. (xv–xvi)

Newman nonetheless boldly insists that the primary goal of the Catholic university must be to develop "the culture of the intellect" (xv) among its students through the study of science and other types of "universal knowledge," including theology (IU, ix). The role of the church is simply to assist the university in maintaining its "integrity" (ix) while fulfilling the essential "office of intellectual education" (ix) producing graduates with "the force, the steadiness, the comprehensiveness and the versatility of intellect, the command over our own powers, [and] the . . . just estimate of things as they pass before us, which . . . is not gained without much effort and the exercise of years" (xvi).

---

[2] John Henry Cardinal Newman, "Idea of a University," *Newman Reader* (The National Institute for Newman Studies, 2007), available on the newmanreader.org website. In-text page references following are to this document.

This vision of the Catholic university as a humanistic enterprise dedicated to "teaching universal knowledge" (ix) through the study of society's intellectual achievements helped to neutralize the utilitarian *geist* of Newman's age by situating critical thinking at the core of the mission of Catholic higher education. And this ideal continues to exert profound influence today. On December 15, 1961, however, speaking in the aftermath of two world wars and US atomic attacks on civilian populations, John XXIII broadened the focus of Catholic institutions worldwide from the service of the faithful *to a dynamic concern for the world in which they live*, announcing an ecumenical council intended to open the "windows of the church" to the hopes, anxieties, accomplishments, and sufferings of the modern world.[3]

In many respects Newman's idea that the Catholic university should "embrace all departments and exercises of the intellect" (456) anticipates the council's conviction that the church must fully engage the modern world. In Newman's view the Catholic university studies the various forms of "universal knowledge" produced by the world because this is the best way to develop the intellectual capacities of its students and deepen their appreciation for truth. But Newman's somewhat narrow focus on "the diffusion and extension of knowledge" (ix) among the university's students, "rather than the advancement" (ix) of knowledge in service to the larger world, reflects the provincializing conviction of Pius IX and many of the cardinals at Vatican I that the church was under siege from modernity.

This stance was dramatically reversed at Vatican II, as seen in its *Pastoral Constitution on the Church in the Modern World (Gaudium et spes).* This constitution describes the church as a faithful community *entrusted with a dynamic message of salvation and a mission of service to the larger world*, which it operationalizes in a universal mandate to the church and its leadership "of reading the signs of the times and of interpreting them in light of the Gospel" (*Gaudium et spes*, no. 4). The document calls for civic engagement and advocacy on issues like migration, population, family life, economic justice, and war and peace. This dynamic vision soon found expression in a new idea of the Catholic university.

Ellacuría's Latin American Idea of the Christian University

There is no doubt that Vatican II's dynamic vision of *the church in service to the world* initiated a renewal touching virtually every area of Catholic life and practice, including Catholic education. Jon Sobrino, SJ, argues that the

---

[3] Giuseppe Alberigo and Joseph A. Komonchak, eds., *History of Vatican II*, vol. 1, *Announcing and Preparing Vatican Council II: Toward a New Era in Catholicism* (Maryknoll, NY: Orbis Books, 1995), 168.

idea of the university developed by Ignacio Ellacuría and his colleagues at the University of Central America (UCA) after the council constitutes "a new idea of a Christian university . . . comparable in importance to that of John Henry Newman a century ago."[4] In this section I suggest that Ellacuría's proposal integrates and advances beyond Newman's understanding of the Catholic university precisely by following the lead of Vatican II and the Latin American bishops.

Vatican II, Medellín, and the Central American Jesuits

In 1968 the Second General Conference of Latin American Bishops took up the council's mandate at Medellín, Colombia, declaring, "A deafening cry pours from the throats of millions of men and women asking their pastors for a liberation that reaches them from nowhere else." In response to this cry the bishops committed themselves to becoming a church that "gives preference to the poorest and most needy," to "solidarity with the poor" and to "make ours their problems and their struggles."[5] Forty years later the bishops would say that Medellín's "preferential option for the poor" had become "one of the distinguishing features" of the Latin American church after Vatican II and an "essential task of evangelization" for the universal church.[6]

Building on the work of Pope Paul VI in *Populorum progressio*, which uses the term "integral development" to critique developmentalist strategies that change little and legitimate an oppressive status quo, Medellín asserts, "If development is the new name for peace, Latin American underdevelopment, with its own characteristics in the different countries, is an unjust situation which promotes tensions that conspire against peace."[7] This criticism is emblemized in Medellín's use of the word *liberation*[8] to highlight and clarify

---

[4] Jon Sobrino, SJ, *Companions of Jesus: The Jesuit Martyrs of El Salvador* (Maryknoll, NY: Orbis Books, 1990), 38.

[5] Second General Conference of Latin American Bishops, "Poverty of the Church," nos. 2, 9, 10, in *The Church in the Present-Day Transformation of Latin America in the Light of the Council*, vol. 2, *Conclusions*, 2nd ed. (Washington, DC: Secretariat for Latin America, National Converence of Catholic Bishops, 1973).

[6] Fifth General Conference of Latin American and Caribbean Bishops, "Concluding Document," nos. 391, 146, *Disciples and Missionaries of Jesus Christ, So That Our Peoples May Have Life in Him* (Aparecida, Brazil). Available on the usccb.org website.

[7] Fifth General Conference of Latin American and Caribbean Bishops, "Document on Peace," no. 1, *Disciples and Missionaries of Jesus Christ, So That Our Peoples May Have Life in Him,* citing *Populorum progressio* (no. 87).

[8] For example, see Second General Conference of Latin American Bishops, 1:3–4; 4:2, 9; 5:15; 8:6; 10:2, 9, 13; 14:2, 7.

its claim that fundamental social and structural "change will be essential in order to liberate the authentic process of Latin American development and integration."[9] Thus, the bishops' discernment that God was calling the Latin American church to a preferential option for the poor was understood to imply church support for demands emerging in civil society for real social, political, and economic change.

A little more than a year after Medellín the Jesuits of Central America gathered from December 24 to December 31, 1969, at the diocesan Seminary for a province retreat to discern prayerfully how the Jesuit order should respond to Medellín's prophetic interpretation of Vatican II. The team, which included Ellacuría, used the long-neglected tradition of group discernment described in the *Deliberatio primorum Patrum (Deliberation of the First Fathers)*,[10] the official account of the 1539[11] discernment by Ignatius of Loyola and his companions to found the Jesuits. "Following the parameters of the Spiritual Exercises of St. Ignatius,"[12] Ellacuría's team sought to achieve prayerful consensus on the fundamental principles for how to renew the Jesuits of Central America by constituting them as a single subject united "in communal reflection and prayer."[13] The retreat concluded with the recommendation that the province develop an apostolic plan to implement the preferential option for the poor in its internal life, its apostolic works, and Central America as a whole. Father Juan Hernandez Pico, SJ, suggests that it was here that "the Jesuits committed themselves to . . . attend to the cries that were coming from the unjustly impoverished and oppressed majorities of Central America, putting aside disordered affections for established works and lifestyles [in order to promote] . . . efficacious action on behalf of the poor."[14]

---

⁹ Second General Conference of Latin American Bishops, "Justice" (no. 11).

¹⁰ *Constitutiones societatis Iesu* I, 1–7, in *Monumenta Historica Societatis Jesus, Monumenta Ignatiana*, Series 3. See Jules J. Toner, SJ, "The Deliberation That Started the Jesuits: A Commentario on the *Deliberatio primorum Patrum*, Newly Translated with a Historical Introduction," *Studies in the Spirituality of the Jesuits* 6, no. 4 (June 1974).

¹¹ Ignatius and his early companions deliberated for several months during 1539 on whether to constitute themselves formally as a religious order. This decision was confirmed during communion of a mass celebrated for the group by Pierre Favre on April 15, 1539.

¹² "Presentación," in "Reunión-Ejercicios de la Viceprovincia Jesuítica de Centroamérica, Diciembre 1969," *Reflexión teológico-espiritual de la Compañia de Jesús en Centroamérica*, vol. 2 (San Salvador: Archives of the Society of Jesus, Central American Province, Survey S.J. de Centroamerica), 2.

¹³ Ignacio Ellacuría, "Finalidad y sentido de la reunión," in "Reunión-Ejercicios de la Viceprovincia Jesuítica de Centroamérica, Diciembre 1969," 2.

¹⁴ Juan Hernández Pico, *História reciente de la Provincia de Centroamérica (1976–1986)* (San Salvador: Ediciones Cardoner, 1991), 8, 9.

Important changes quickly followed. Father Miguel Estrada, SJ, called a September 1970 meeting of delegates representing the various "works and nations" of the province to address "apostolic programming." A twelve-volume "sociological survey" of the region was completed and after much debate it was decided that all Jesuit works would be reoriented to "foment attitudes of commitment to the social liberation of our peoples . . . as an integral part of the redemptive liberation of Jesus Christ."[15] Father Pedro Arrupe, SJ, superior general of the Society of Jesus in Rome, approved the document and the UCA Jesuits began to see the preferential option for the poor as a defining aspect of the university's Christian identity. In 1975 the option for the poor became normative for all Jesuits when the 32nd General Congregation stated that "service of faith and the promotion of justice" would be the defining marks of what it means to be a Jesuit today.[16]

A Vatican II Model

Building on these efforts, beginning in 1970 Ellacuría and his colleagues began formulating a Vatican II vision for the UCA as a Christian university with its windows and doors open to the sufferings, hopes, systems, diverse cultures, and religious experiences of the modern world. By May 1979 the university had developed a clear formulation of its new self-understanding, as seen in the following statement representing a broad consensus of faculty, staff, and administration:

> The UCA seeks to be an institutional university response to the historical reality of the country, considered from an ethical perspective as an unjust and irrational reality which should be transformed. This is rooted . . . in a purpose: that of *contributing to social change* in the country. It does this *in a university manner* and . . . *with a Christian inspiration* (emphasis added).[17]

This statement concretizes Medellín's call to promote "integral liberation"[18] through the UCA's commitment to work in a specifically "university manner"

---

[15] Ibid., 10.

[16] 32nd General Congregation of the Society of Jesus, "Our Mission Today: The Service of Faith and the Promotion of Justice," Decree 4, 2, no. 48, *Documents of the 31st and 32nd General Congregations of the Society of Jesus* (St. Louis: Institute of Jesuit Sources, 1977), 411.

[17] Universidad Centraoamericana José Simeón Cañas, "Las funciones fundamentales de la universidad y su operativización," in *Planteamiento universitario 1989*, 37–121 (San Salvador: Universidad Centroamericana José Simeón Cañas, 1989), 47.

[18] Second General Conference of Latin American Bishops, "Justice," (no. 4).

to transform the "historical reality of the country" guided by the "Christian inspiration" of the Gospels and Catholic social teaching.

> The document draws several implications from this model. First, the UCA does not exist for itself, or for its members. Its center is not within itself, nor in its students, nor in its professors, nor in its authorities. It exists for the Salvadoran people . . . for the majority of our people who suffer inhuman conditions . . . This means the work of the UCA is decidedly oriented by social outreach.[19]

Second, the UCA must always do its work precisely "as a university," teaching classes, writing books, giving talks, analyzing the causes of oppression, and developing ideas and theoretical models that will help to "humanize" society.[20] Third, the UCA's Christian inspiration demands that it promote values consonant with Christian faith, embracing human achievement and history as a medium of God's self-revelation while actively resisting the effects of sin embodied in oppressive structures. Thus, the university works for the salvation of the whole person and all of humanity, especially that part (the majority) of humanity that suffers most. As a result,

> the most explicit testimony of the Christian inspiration of the UCA will be putting itself really at the service of the people in such a way that . . . it allows itself to be oriented by oppressed people themselves. This will help it see and denounce what there is of sin in our reality; it will impel it to create models that correspond better historically to the Reign of God; and it will help it develop typically Christian attitudes, such as operational hope, the passion for justice, the generous self-giving to others, the rejection of violence, etc.[21]

In this way, then, the model of the Christian university developed by Ellacuría and his colleagues operationalizes the engagement of the church with the modern world mandated by Vatican II and its historicization in Medellín's call to a preferential option for the poor.[22]

---

[19] Ibid., 49.

[20] Ibid., 49, 50.

[21] Ibid., 53.

[22] For more on this see Lassalle-Klein, *Blood and Ink*; Charles Beirne, *Jesuit Education and Social Change in El Salvador* (New York: Garland, 1996), 47–62, 84–87; and Teresa Whitfield, *Paying the Price: Ignacio Ellacuría and the Murdered Jesuits of El Salvador* (Philadelphia: Temple University Press, 1994).

Historicizing the Model

Vision is one thing and implementation another, however, and the UCA's efforts to historicize its new self-understanding were largely mediated during the 1970s through the agency of the country's elites. This would not change until the end of Archbishop Oscar Romero's three-year leadership of the archdiocese and the twin failures of the October 1979 military-civilian reformist coup and the 1981 FMLN "final offensive" against the government. Only then would Ellacuría and the UCA find the practical means to focus the resources of the university on the agency of the poor and their emerging role in Salvadoran civil society.

In 1985 Ellacuría insisted, while presenting a posthumous doctorate to Archbishop Romero, that while the UCA offered consultation to Romero,

> no one doubted who was the teacher and who was the assistant, who was the pastor setting the direction and who was the implementer, who was the prophet revealing the mystery and who was the follower, who was the one who encouraged and who was the one encouraged, who was the voice and who was the echo.[23]

Further, Jon Sobrino suggests that the UCA learned how to fulfill its mission as a university by watching Archbishop Romero run the archdiocese from the perspective of a preferential option for the poor.[24] Above all, Sobrino adds, the UCA learned from Romero how "to do in our university way what he did in his pastoral way." Less than a year after Romero's assassination on March 24, 1980, Ellacuría spelled out in more detail what the UCA learned from its martyred archbishop. First, the university learned how "to historicize the power of the Gospel" in the Salvadoran context. Second, the university learned that Romero "led the poor to historicize their own salvation" and to give "historical flesh to the eternally new word of God." Third, he showed the university that its initial conversion to God's preferential option for the poor implied letting the crucified people be "the guiding light" of its apostolic ministry.[25] And fourth, the archbishop taught the university to look to the common Salvadoran people themselves in order to find the salvation preached by their mentor. Thus, Archbishop Romero helped the UCA understand how its work as a Christian university could

---

[23] Ignacio Ellacuría, "La UCA ante el doctorado concedido a Monseñor Romero," *Escritos Teológicos*, vol. 3 (San Salvador: UCA Editores, 2002), 104; reprinted from *Estudios Centroamericanos*, no. 437 (1985), 168.

[24] Jon Sobrino, interview by Robert Lassalle-Klein, May 8, 1994.

[25] Ellacuría, "La UCA ante el doctorado concedido a Monseñor Romero," 102, 94, 96, 98.

be historicized in programs designed to empower the "poor majorities of El Salvador" to become active participants in shaping their future.[26] The university had been working for "social change," "in a university manner," guided by a "Christian inspiration" for over a decade, but it was only just beginning to understand how to make its preferential option for the poor into an effective historical force.[27]

Two initiatives from the 1980s embodied this development in the UCA's self-understanding of its role in Salvadoran society. First, after Ellacuría became university president in 1979, the UCA repositioned and/or initiated a variety of university programs to more directly serve Salvadoran civil society and what Ellacuría called its "poor majorities."[28] For example, in May 1980 the university reorganized its documentation center as the Center for Information, Documentation and Research Support, whose weekly publication, *Proceso*, soon became the most important source of independent documentation and analysis of current events in the country. In 1984 Ellacuría created the Chair for the National Reality at the UCA, which provided a national forum for public debate on virtually every major proposal on the future of El Salvador during the 1980s. In 1985 Ellacuría's colleague and fellow martyr, Father Segundo Montes, SJ, created the Human Rights Institute, which began publishing annual studies focusing international attention on the needs and hopes of Salvadoran refugees, who made up 20–25 percent of the population of the country. The following year, another colleague and fellow martyr, Father Ignacio Martín-Baró, SJ, opened the university Institute for Public Opinion, which, as the only credible opinion-polling agency in the country, provided a "social mirror" to average (mostly poor) Salvadorans. This legitimated their growing opposition to the ongoing civil war. And in 1988 Romero's successor, Archbishop Arturo Rivera Damas, invited a broad cross section of groups from Salvadoran civil society to the UCA for a national debate on the future of the country, creating a turning

[26] Ignacio Ellacuría, "Monseñor Romero, un enviado de Dios para salvar a su pueblo," *Escritos teológicos*, vol. 3 (San Salvador: UCA Editores, 2002), 99.

[27] Universidad Centraoamericana José Simeón Cañas ,"Las funciones fundamentales de la universidad y su operativización," 47.

[28] Ignacio Ellacuría, "Función liberadora de la filosofía," *Estudios Centroamericanos* 40, no. 435 (1985): 46; see also idem, "Historización del bien común y de los derechos humanos en una sociedad dividida," in *Capitalismo: violencia y anti-vida*, vol. 2, ed. E. Tamez and S. Trinidad, 81–94 (San José: Editorial Universitária Centroamericana, 1978); in English, "Human Rights in a Divided Society," in A. Hennelly and J. Langan, eds., *Human Rights in the Americas: The Struggle for Consensus* (Washington, DC: Georgetown University Press, 1982), 52–65; idem, *Teología Política* (San Salvador: Ediciones del Secretariado Social Interdiocesano, 1973); in English, *Freedom Made Flesh: The Mission of Christ and His Church*, trans. John Drury (Maryknoll, NY: Orbis Books, 1976), 7–11, 127–63.

point in the emergence of a clear national majority in favor of a negotiated peace. In all of these cases the intellectual, moral, institutional, and human resources of the UCA were redirected to support and enhance the agency of Salvadoran civil society and its disenfranchised majorities.

A second major 1980s initiative began with Ellacuría's April 27, 1981, proposal to the university's board of directors that "the social outreach of the UCA should now ground itself in the perspective of a political solution and . . . a process of mediation" for the civil war.[29] Ellacuría insisted that this initiative be carried out in a thoroughly "university manner" through the activities of the president; the university's communications center (including its press, *UCA Editores*, and key journals; its Center for Information, Documentation, and Research Support, and its flagship journal, *Estudios Centroamericanos*; as well as through the extensive community service provided by UCA students. Ellacuría envisioned public events like "round tables, conferences, congresses, etc.," ongoing contacts with leading "politicians, economists, religious, military figures, etc.," and the addition of a university radio station and weekly newspaper, all designed to stimulate the "national collective consciousness" of Salvadoran civil society through reflection on current events.[30] He stressed the need to be in dialogue with non-elite social groups, including professional organizations, small businesses, other universities, labor unions, political and military personnel, the FMLN-FDR, and student organizations. This led to the creation of a new social outreach council, of which Jon Sobrino was appointed interim director on May 15, 1981. On September 6, 1982, the board formally established the position of vice-president for social outreach, to which Ellacuría was appointed in addition to his role as president.

Ellacuría and his companions eventually died for their efforts to make the UCA "a critical and creative conscience" for Salvadoran society.[31] Their vision carried the UCA beyond Newman's focus on the need to know and understand the world, insisting that in addition the university has a responsibility to help change the world. Ironically, the Salvadoran government's brutal attempt to silence the voice of the university in favor of negotiations helped to bring about the very outcome the assassinations were designed to prevent: the collapse of US Congressional support for

---

[29] Ignacio Ellacuría, "La Proyección Social de la UCA Hoy," appendix to the minutes of the board of directors of the University of Central America (San Salvador: Archives of the University of Central America, José Simeón Cañas, April 27, 1981), 3. Cited in Beirne, *Jesuit Education and Social Change in El Salvador*, 174.

[30] Ellacuría, "La Proyección Social de la UCA Hoy," 5, 1–3.

[31] Ignacio Ellacuría and Román Mayorga (ghost writers), "Discurso de la Universidad Centroamericana José Simeón Cañas en la Firma del Contrato con el BID," in *Planteamiento universitario 1989*, 12.

the war and the negotiated peace long sought by UCA's Jesuit martyrs and their colleagues.

A Christian University for the Twenty-First Century

In this section I suggest that Ellacuría's Vatican II vision of the university, with its Latin American emphasis on the agency of the poor majorities of the planet, complements recent breakthroughs in cognitive neuroscience and has emerged as a model for twenty-first-century Jesuit university education around the globe.

Sentient Intelligence

Ellacuría's claim that the UCA has a responsibility to contribute in a university manner toward social change is grounded in Xavier Zubiri's theory of sentient intelligence. Building on Zubiri's model of sentient intelligence, Ellacuría developed a powerful ethical mandate from Heidegger's signature concept that human beings are the kind of being (*Dasein,* "being there," or "presence") that must take a stance on their being-in-the-world. Zubiri's model of intelligence, however, switches the object of human perception and cognition from *being* to *historical reality.* Building on this work Ellacuría argues that if perception and cognition force us to take a stance on their reality, this generates the roots of an ethical dilemma: Will we let those perceptions and cognitions be real for us by accommodating ourselves to their reality, or will we refuse to let their reality affect us? If what I perceive is historically real, what implications does that have for me? Ellacuría insists that a human being is that "reality" which must take a stance on what it perceives and knows and whose authenticity and relation to truth depends upon letting what it perceives as real, *be real for it.* Stated in another way, human cognition is inextricably tied up with the demand that we take a stance on the reality of perceptions and cognitions that arise from our interactions with the world.[32] For Ellacuría, this makes the university a privileged place where individuals and groups must debate, formulate, and finally take stances on the great issues of our day, such as access to healthcare, global climate change, poverty, and genocide. With Zubiri, Ellacuría asserts that we avoid coming to terms with the realities we perceive at our own risk. Denial brings diminishment, and dishonesty produces corruption.

What, then, is the substance of Zubiri's theory of sentient intelligence and how does it lead Ellacuría to the claim that human beings cannot avoid

---

[32] For more on this, see Lassalle-Klein, *Blood and Ink,* 278.

taking a stance on our world? Zubiri argues that intellection and sensing are two dimensions of a single act of sentient intelligence. He writes:

> It is not only that human sensing and intellection are not in opposition. Rather, their intrinsic and formal unity constitutes a single and distinct act of apprehension. As sentient, the act is an impression. As an intellection, the act is an apprehension of reality. In this way, the distinct and unified act of sentient intellection is an impression of reality. Intellection is a way of sensing. And, in human persons, sensing is a mode of intellection.[33]

Here Zubiri rejects idealism's tendency to overstate the distinction between the mind and its object, which holds that intelligence apprehends reality by thinking about the data given by the senses. He also rejects a reductionistic empiricism, which tends to reduce the apprehension of a thing to its sensible impression.[34]

In contrast, Zubiri and Ellacuría describe thinking and sensing as a structural unity. This coheres well with an emerging consensus among some neuroscientists regarding the structural unity of perception and cognition, and of the mind and the brain, which helps explain why we *see* much more (or sometimes less) than is present on the retina. Just as in a *gestalt*, or in the case of materials that obstruct or distort the passage of light on its way to the retina, the mind adds or eliminates aspects of what it concludes is lacking or extraneous in its perception of the object. A prominent neuropsychologist wonders, "How far down the perceptual stream does this constructive activity occur?" And he responds:

> It does not affect what reaches the retina, obviously (except that attention and goals direct where the retina looks)—does it affect what reaches the thalamus? Probably not. I don't know whether it affects what reaches the amygdala, however it certainly biases the strength of response there. But past that point, what reaches the cortex is probably selected and even modified by biasing systems. At the level of visual cortex, the information is already selected/biased by a task set and by an emotional set (survival value). So that by the time it reaches consciousness [or perception], when you see the object, the information has been heavily biased or edited. So if you

---

[33] Xavier Zubiri, *Inteligencia sentiente: Inteligencia y realidad*, vol. 1 (Madrid: Alianza Editorial, 1980, 2006), 13.

[34] Ibid.

see the object, you really see it—but you only see the object if your bias systems allow it.[35]

What is clear from this exchange is that while cognition may be distinguished from perception and while the activity of the mind may be distinguished from that of the brain, it makes no sense to treat cognition and the mind as dichotomous or posterior to the sensing activity of the brain (as part of the central nervous system), or as anything less than part of a profoundly integrated system. A more adequate epistemology grounded in cognitive neuroscience suggests that perception and cognition (like the brain and the mind) form a structural unity in our interactions, no matter how passing, with the persons and things that we encounter.

This fits well with the synthetic view of cognitive neuroscience presented by Tim Shallice and Richard Cooper, who describe consciousness and thinking[36] as mental processes that incorporate and transform the lower processes of the brain using relatively stable schemas or patterns of cognition and action (for example, supervisory processing, episodic memory, consciousness, and problem solving) in order to interact effectively with people and things in the environment. Thus, while the neuroscience continues to evolve, I suggest that Zubiri's theory that human sensing and cognition form a structural unity as two dimensions of a single act of sentient intelligence in social interactions anticipates important findings and trends in twenty-first-century cognitive neuroscience. And since interaction demands a response, I argue the same is true of Ellacuría's claim that sentient intelligence generates the roots of an ethical dilemma by forcing us to take a stance on the reality of the perceptions arising from our interactions with the world.

Ellacuría's understanding of the imperatives imposed by perception and cognition is consistent with the work of some of the giants of twentieth-century theories of learning and human development. It fits well, for instance, with Urie Bronfenbrenner's bio-ecological model, which addresses "the scientific study of the progressive, mutual accommodation throughout the life course, between an active, growing human being and the changing properties of the immediate setting in which the developing person lives, as the process is affected by relations between these settings, and by the larger

---

[35] Joel Nigg, director, Division of Psychology, professor of psychiatry, pediatrics, and behavioral neuroscience, Oregon Health and Science University, Portland, Oregon. Personal correspondence with Robert Lassalle-Klein, August 17, 2012. Transcript in personal files.

[36] Tim Shallice and Richard P. Cooper, *The Organization of Mind* (New York: Oxford University Press, 2011), 431, 461, 498–501.

contexts in which the settings are embedded."[37] Following Bronfenbrenner and consistent with Ellacuría and Zubiri, consciousness and thinking cannot be seen as passive, static entities, but must rather be understood as dynamic processes evolving and developing through interactions simultaneously restructuring both the subjects (including their brain) and the people and environments with whom they interact. This insight finds confirmation in now well-established evidence of neural plasticity, which shows that the brain (and perception) actually changes when the person adapts and accommodates as part of the organism's progressive, mutual accommodation with its environment.

While there is not space to develop the whole argument, I would argue, based on these and other insights, that Zubiri's theory of sentient intelligence anticipates aspects of the emerging consensus in cognitive neuroscience regarding the structural unity of cognition and perception, and of the mind and the brain. This is important for our discussion of the university because Zubiri's theory provides the cognitive basis for Ellacuría's claim that the Christian university must be vigorously engaged with the modern world and take responsibility to bring about social change in accord with its nature as a university and its commitment to the values of the gospel.

A Worldwide Model

Finally, Ellacuría's idea of the university is increasingly being taken as a model for Jesuit university education in a global context. On April 23, 2010, Father Adolfo Nicolás, SJ, superior general of the Society of Jesus, convened the first ever worldwide meeting of Jesuit universities. In his talk Father Nicolás asks, "What kind of universities, with what emphases and what directions, would we run, if we were refounding the Society of Jesus in today's world?"[38] The answer, he says, must respond to the challenge posed by the dehumanizing aspects of globalization to the most vulnerable parts of humanity. With Ellacuría he insists that Jesuit universities "bear a common responsibility for the welfare of the entire world and its development in a sustainable and life-giving way"[39] (GC 35. Decree 2, no. 20). Even more remarkable is his assertion that "every Jesuit university is striving to become what Ellacuría has called a *proyecto social*."[40] Here Father Nicolás elevates

---

[37] Urie Bronfenbrenner, *Making Human Beings Human* (Thousand Oaks, CA: Sage, 2005), 107.

[38] Adolfo Nicolás, SJ, "Depth, Diversity, and Learned Ministry: Challenges to Jesuit Higher Education Today," keynote address for Networking Jesuit Higher Education for the Globalizing World, Mexico City, April 23, 2010, 11. Available on the ajcunet.edu website.

[39] Ibid., 6.

[40] Ibid., 7.

the defining aspect of Ellacuría's advance beyond Newman into a standard for Jesuit universities around the world, stating:

> Each institution represented here, with its rich resources of intelligence, knowledge, talent, vision, and energy, moved by its commitment to the service of faith and promotion of justice, seeks to insert itself into a society, not just to train professionals, but in order to become a cultural force advocating and promoting truth, virtue, development, and peace in that society.[41]

Building on this idea, Father Nicolás offers three ways in which Jesuit universities can respond to dehumanizing impacts of globalization. First, as places of instruction he calls Jesuit universities to counter "the globalization of superficiality" through teaching that promotes "depth of thought and imagination . . . [through] a profound engagement with the real, . . . a world of suffering and need, a broken world with many broken people in need of healing." Second, as centers of service he challenges Jesuit universities to create "international networks" addressing "issues [of] . . . faith, justice, and ecology that challenge us across countries and continents." Third, as centers of research, he calls Jesuit universities to find "ways of sharing the fruits of research with the excluded" in order to overcome "the inequality of knowledge distribution." And finally in response to the rising struggle between secular modernity and fundamentalist faith he calls Jesuit universities to promote local dialogues "between faith and culture."[42]

My argument in this section, then, has been that the cognitive foundations of Ellacuría's model of the Christian university correlate well with recent breakthroughs in cognitive neuroscience and that his dynamic Vatican II vision of the UCA as a Christian university that serves its entire people, especially the poor, has emerged as a defining model for twenty-first-century Jesuit university education in a global context. We must not forget, however, that Ellacuría and his companions died for exposing the agony of El Salvador's suffering poor produced by US foreign policy and its support for that country's war against its own people. This should make us suspicious of claims that the other victims of US globalization are morally neutral "collateral damage" produced by the invisible hand of the markets and that efforts to determine responsibility for "the conditions of . . . material and moral poverty in which vast multitudes still live"[43] are misguided

---

[41] Ibid.

[42] Ibid., 2, 4, 7, 8, 10.

[43] J. Matthew Ashley, "The University as an Instrument of Consolation in the Modern World," keynote address, Santa Clara University, faculty colloquium, "The Idea of a Jesuit University," November 4, 2010, 10. Available online.

and irrelevant protests against inevitable, morally neutral structural adjustments produced by free-market forces.[44]

Like Augustine of Hippo, who confronted his age with responsibility for the evils of Rome in *City of God* and *On Free Choice of the Will*, Ellacuría insists that, with certain material and cultural constraints, we have shaped and bear responsibility for our historical reality today. In three volumes of political writings, four volumes of theological writings, three volumes of philosophical writings, and two books, he insists that markets, like all aspects of historical reality, are simply human creations. He warns that, while some worship markets as immutable idols, we avoid taking stances on the suffering they cause at the peril of our humanity and that the Christian university bears a special responsibility in this regard.

When all is said and done, then, Ellacuría sees the Christian (and Jesuit) university as an exhilarating and risky place. His idea of the university builds on the contributions of Newman, who sees the Catholic university as a place that teaches its students to think critically through serious engagement with the intellectual and cultural achievements of the world. But with Vatican II, Ellacuría came to believe that critical thinking is properly historicized at the Christian university only when it takes responsibility for itself as an intellectual community and a social force. Accordingly, such a university can only be what it is by taking stands on the crucial issues of the day guided by the gospel and an abiding concern for the hopes and aspirations of all of humanity, especially the least. This is the essence of Ignacio Ellacuría's Vatican II idea of the Christian university, which I and many others have come to see as "comparable in importance to that of John Henry Newman a century ago."[45]

---

[44] This same criticism of free-market forces is made by Pope John Paul II in *Centisimus Annus*, no. 42.

[45] Sobrino, *Companions of Jesus*, 38.

12

Toward a New, Historical Evangelization

MICHAEL E. LEE

What does it mean to proclaim the Christian gospel of salvation with fidelity to tradition and with freshness for its hearers today? As it took form during the papacies of John Paul II and Benedict XVI, much attention was given to the so-called new evangelization.[1] However, contrary to its rhetoric, the new evangelization was hardly new. Concerned primarily with the manner that the church's message is conveyed, the new evangelization focused on the sense of "communicating" the good news of salvation through technology and new media but did not advance any new understanding of salvation itself.[2] To the contrary, in the face of what it diagnosed as the primary challenges for the church, declining numbers of believers and perceived threats from secular culture, the new evangelization combined a doctrinal conservatism with an almost sectarian anti-secular rhetoric.

The change in tone introduced in the new papacy of Francis, the first Latin American and Jesuit pope, has the potential to introduce a profound shift in evangelization away from the defensive, embattled posture of his predecessors. Francis's gestures of openness and inclusivity and his call for a church that imaginatively and humbly addresses issues such as poverty and immigration as essential to the way it lives out its faith, serve to open up a space to reconsider the manner that the church carries out the work of

---

[1] The notion is first articulated by John Paul II in an address to Latin American bishops. See John Paul II, "The Task of the Latin American Bishop," *Origins* 12 (March 24, 1983): 659–62.

[2] Father Robert Barron, whose Word on Fire ministry is a veritable cottage industry of new evangelization programs, speaks of "John Paul II's call for a 'new ardor, expression and method' of evangelization." See Gretchen R. Crowe, "Film Is 'how-to' for Catholics to Share Faith," in *Our Sunday Visitor*, August 18, 2013. Available on the osv.com website.

evangelization. These gestures, however, must be complemented by theological reflection that creatively considers the content of evangelization.

This chapter draws upon the theology of Ignacio Ellacuría to reconsider the theological basis for a "new evangelization." It does so for two reasons. The first involves the animating center of Ellacuría's theology. His creative engagement with the notion of salvation is done in light of the most pressing sign of our times: the continuing misery of poverty and oppression suffered by the majority of human beings on the planet. The second reason for turning to Ellacuría lies in the particular content of his theology. Over the course of his writing, Ellacuría's soteriological orientation took two different forms: those essays explicitly focused on working out the notion of salvation, and those in which other theological topics, such as Christology or ecclesiology, are reinterpreted in light of his soteriology.[3] The subtitles attached to some of these latter essays indicate this connection; "The Crucified People" and "Utopia and Propheticism from Latin America" are described as essays in "historical soteriology."[4] Thus, these essays not only indicate the influence of soteriology, but they reveal the nature of this influence—that the soteriology is *historical*.[5]

I explicate Ellacuría's historical soteriology by examining how he treats the interconnected notions of the nature and content of salvation, the role of Jesus Christ, and the mission of the church, and how spirituality and praxis flow to and from these ideas. In doing so I highlight two central contributions of Ellacuría's thought: (1) the importance of a truly historical soteriology, and (2) the indispensable role of the poor and oppressed in any proclamation of the good news today. These provide a substantive theological basis for an evangelization demanded by the needs of our world today.

Salvation in History

Though Ellacuría explicitly referred to salvation throughout his theological writings, he was reticent to offer a simple definition. Positively, he often made the case for the intimate connection between human liberation and

---

[3] Examples of the first form include Ellacuría's "The Historicity of Christian Salvation" and "Salvation History." See *Ignacio Ellacuría: Essays on History, Liberation, and Salvation*, ed. Michael E. Lee (Maryknoll, NY: Orbis Books, 2013), 137–68 and 169–94.

[4] See Ignacio Ellacuría, "The Crucified People: An Essay in Historical Soteriology," in Lee, *Ignacio Ellacuría*, 195–224; and "Utopia and Propheticism from Latin America," chap. 2 in this volume.

[5] In addition, Ellacuría's most significant ecclesiological essay utilizes the language of history. See Ignacio Ellacuría, "Church of the Poor, Historical Sacrament of Liberation," in Lee, *Ignacio Ellacuría*, 227–54.

salvation, sometimes using the language of divinization or *theosis*.[6] Yet, and perhaps more important, Ellacuría's central concern was negative—deficient or misguided notions of salvation correspond to deficient and misguided forms of Christian life. Therefore, to understand what Ellacuría meant by salvation, one must begin with how he diagnosed problematic views of salvation.

For Ellacuría, though it gets expressed in different ways, the basic deficiency in Christian thinking regarding salvation is the "prejudice that salvation is ahistorical."[7] It involves the tendency to "spiritualize" salvation in a manner that makes human historical life and, indeed, all of history itself, ancillary to salvation if not altogether irrelevant. In this view the good news of salvation is a post- or meta-historical human destiny, and human history is essentially accidental to it. Human life provides, at best, the fodder for a juridical condemnation that is lifted by divine action that is itself ahistorical.

To understand this diagnosis properly, one must recognize Ellacuría's soteriology as a continuing trajectory of those seminal insights from the previous generation of Roman Catholic theology. Figures such as Henri de Lubac and Karl Rahner (Ellacuría's own teacher) broke against the extrinsic view of grace presented in the neo-scholastic, or "manual," treatises in theology that had been the bedrock of Catholic theology for the previous century.[8] For Ellacuría, an "otherworldly" notion of salvation supports and is supported by this extrinsic view of grace that, while perhaps placing a fitting emphasis on the primacy of God's initiative and action, empties out any significance to human historical agency and distorts a proper understanding of transcendence.

To counter the neo-scholastic dualism of natural-supernatural, Ellacuría turned to the notion of salvation history as a richer and more biblical way to express what theologians had been calling the "supernatural." The language of salvation history had become widespread in biblical scholarship at the time.[9] However, Ellacuría linked the language of salvation his-

---

[6] For example, see Ignacio Ellacuría, "Iglesia y realidad histórica," *Estudios Centroamericanas* 331 (1976): 213–20. "Theosis," or Zubiri's term, "dei-formation," is more frequent in Ellacuría's earlier work. It is beyond the scope of this essay to explore its relationship to the language of salvation history dominant in Ellacuría's later work.

[7] Ignacio Ellacuría, "Salvation History and Salvation in History," in *Freedom Made Flesh: The Mission of Christ and His Church*, trans. John Drury (Maryknoll, NY: Orbis Books, 1976), 11.

[8] For a thorough account of these issues, see Stephen J. Duffy, *The Graced Horizon: Nature and Grace in Modern Catholic Thought* (Collegeville, MN: Liturgical Press, 1992).

[9] See, for example, Oscar Cullmann (whom Ellacuría frequently cites), *Salvation in History* (New York: Harper and Row, 1967). For another Catholic theologian influenced by this biblical approach, and an under-cited influence on Ellacuría, see the work of Jesuit Joseph Moignt.

tory to the idea of "salvation in history" that he believed surpassed "the natural" in terms of describing the actual situation of human beings. He did not formulate these two concepts in parallel, lest the dualistic separation of the terms be assumed. Rather, Ellacuría makes the claim that "salvation history is a salvation in history."[10] Though at first glance this claim appears to reduce salvation, if seen within the contours of Ellacuría's philosophy of historical reality, it indicates how Ellacuría overcomes the older extrinsic and dualistic view of salvation while preserving a sense of divine transcendence.

In his essay "Salvation History," Ellacuría makes the remarkable equivalence that "to maintain the classical language, we can say that the natural is material nature, and the supernatural is history."[11] How can he make this bold assertion? How can history, the apparent domain of the finite, of the temporal, of humanity, be thought of in a cognate way to the supernatural or the divine? The answer lies in Ellacuría's dynamic understanding of historical reality. Ellacuría speaks of history as the actualization of possibilities and the exercise of freedom such that openness and dynamism toward creative fullness characterize all reality.[12] This allows Ellacuría to replace the logic that opposes nature and super-nature, human and divine, and conceive of history as the presence of the triune life of God.

For Ellacuría, historical reality is not merely the temporal stage upon which human beings have their exits and their entrances but a dynamic structure that includes life from its material and biological roots to human praxis.[13] For reality is not simply the collection of things around us. Undoubtedly, reality is material, spatial, biological, and temporal, and one cannot speak of reality without these characteristics. Yet, reality also involves a dynamism, a progression if you will, from matter to life, and ultimately to human life. Human beings, in their sentient intelligence, respond to possibilities, and by doing so, open and close a spectrum of further possibilities. In essence, they create more reality. The way that human beings transmit, or hand on, this opening and closing of possibilities constitutes history.[14]

[10] Ellacuría, "Salvation History and Salvation in History."

[11] Ellacuría, "Salvation History," 193.

[12] Héctor Samour describes his thought as an "open materialist realism." *Voluntad de liberación* (San Salvador: UCA Editores, 2002).

[13] For his definitive statement of this philosophy, see Ignacio Ellacuría, *Filosofía de la realidad histórica* (San Salvador: UCA Editores, 1990).

[14] Ellacuría describes history as a "transmisión tradente" (what David Gandolfo translates as "traditioning transmission"). See ibid., 492–514. For Gandolfo's explication of these issues, see David Gandolfo, "Human Essence, History, and Liberation: Karl Marx and Ignacio Ellacuría on Being Human," Ph.D. diss., Loyola University of Chicago, 2003.

This drive of history, as the actualization of possibilities and the "traditioning" of the actualizations, places a profound demand on human beings. As reality unfolds, human beings are responsible for this unfolding. In particular, they must seek to create the conditions that make possible the full realization of all other human beings. Indeed, given the profound interrelated nature of all reality, one can see that a view of individual historical "success" at the expense of other human beings' "failure" really indicates a structural tragedy. The liberation of all human beings, then, is the drive of historical reality and provides us clues to what Ellacuría speaks about when referring to salvation in history.

In its dynamism, reality includes what Ellacuría terms respectivity [*respectividad*]—the way in which things, as real, are all interrelated, but not a consequent interrelation (independent 'things' that are subsequently or extrinsically related). No. Ellacuría is speaking of a constitutive relation, what Zubiri calls the 'power of the real,' that formally dominates real things. Ellacuría sees in this connection a way to speak about the divine-human relation such that the relation is marked by unity, not extrinsic dualism. Rather than a view of creation as God (a thing) creating another (thing), Ellacuría speaks of the taking-form [*plasmación*] *ad extra* of trinitarian life. This is the "theologal" dimension of reality that indicates the profound presence of God. Throughout his theological work Ellacuría signals this presence of God using the language of the theologal.[15]

Thus, salvation history, the divine will for the fullness of human flourishing, is a salvation in history because the dynamism of history is toward the full, free, and liberating flourishing of all human beings. It does not mean a reduction of salvation to the merely physical or historical. On the contrary, it is an affirmation of the profoundly trans-historical nature of salvation, namely, that salvation as the ultimate destiny of human beings must occur through history, not outside of it or in spite of it. The key is to move away from an extrinsic notion of transcendence to one of depth and fullness. As Ellacuría avers:

There is a radically different way of understanding transcendence. . . . This is to see transcendence as something that transcends *in* and not as something that transcends *away from*; as something that physically impels to *more* but not by taking *out of*; something that pushes forward, but at the same time retains. . . . God is transcendent, among other reasons, not by being absent, but by being freely present.[16]

---

[15] See Ellacuría, "The Historicity of Christian Salvation," 151. For a fuller explication of the term *theologal*, see above, 60n7.

[16] Ibid., 142.

This view of transcendence demands that though human liberation might not represent the fullness of Christian salvation, one cannot speak of salvation without human liberation. Indeed, the greater the expression of human life and freedom, the greater the actualization of God's will and the triune Life. If there is a division to be found, it is not between the supernatural and natural; rather, it is the division between grace—that which makes possible and manifests the divine life—and sin—that which opposes it and kills it.

If Ellacuría's thought is a reduction, it is only in the sense of the medieval *reductio*, that is, a moving back to an essential principle. If salvation history is a salvation in history, then where is that location that reveals both the need for and the in-breaking of salvation? Here we see the importance of the poor and oppressed. Philosophically, the poor indicate the location where the opening of reality's possibilities must be generated.[17] Theologically, the struggles of the poor and oppressed are the place that makes most obvious the presence of sin and the need for grace in the world. Thus, if Christian soteriology is not historical, it either proclaims a "docetic" salvation that only appears to touch upon real human life, or it falls prey to idolatries that mask the real presence of sin, proclaiming a "news" that is ideological rather than "good." If this danger is true of the concept of salvation, it reveals itself as well when the considering the person and role of Jesus Christ in the economy of salvation.

Carrying Forward Christ's Mission

Because traditional christological doctrines involve notions like incarnation and crucifixion of Jesus as central to salvation, Christology appears to possess intrinsically a strong historical component. Yet, Ellacuría recognized how ahistorical logic jumps to metaphysical and theological meanings of these historical tropes to "naturalize" them. Jesus' life and ministry become secondary to (if not elided altogether from) dogmatic definitions, so that the scriptural witness to the life, death, and resurrection of Jesus serves merely as proof text to doctrines rather than a primary way that Christians understand how to live in a Christlike manner.[18]

Ellacuría does not necessarily argue against the process by which the proclaimer became the proclaimed in Christian theology. However, he does maintain that the shift from focusing on Jesus' ministry and preaching to his person cannot represent a rupture. It is that ministry and preaching, along

---

[17] As Gandolfo puts it, "The struggles of the oppressed represent the leading edge of reality's further development." David Gandolfo, "Ignacio Ellacuría," Internet Encyclopedia of Philosophy.

[18] On this logic, see Ellacuría, "Salvation History."

with the biblical understanding of them, that provides norms for how the person of Jesus is to be understood and how the proclamation of his good news is to be carried out.

Ellacuría distills this problem of ahistorical Christology by distinguishing between two questions and their importance. The questions "Why did Jesus die?" and "Why was Jesus killed?" indicate two very different approaches to the biblical portrayal of Jesus' passion.[19] While Ellacuría acknowledges the first question as important, for it clearly has a soteriological thrust, it is the second question that must receive priority of consideration. Only when one answers the question about why Jesus was killed, when one enters into the drama of Jesus' ministry as portrayed in the Gospels and accounts for all of the social, political relationships there, can one begin to answer the former question about the meaning of his death. This is what it means to historicize the memory of Jesus Christ.

Recall that, for Ellacuría, *historical* does not merely denote "in time." To historicize the memory of Jesus does not mean to restrict consideration of Jesus to the historical Jesus of biblical studies or reduce the significance of Jesus Christ to that of a good model to be imitated. Ellacuría's historical soteriology insists that what is salvific about Jesus Christ cannot be separated from what is historical; it must be seen as a transcendence "in" to the fullness of history. This holds important consequences for Christian theology and life.

At one level, one cannot consider themes such as the redemptive death of Jesus or the relationship between Jesus' person and the reign of God apart from the testimony to Jesus' historical ministry. More important, however, historicizing these themes means inquiring epistemologically about how these concepts are employed ideologically, and in terms of Christian praxis, how they are realized by believers and the larger ecclesial body in action.[20] The consideration of Jesus' death, particularly as necessary, provides a good example of the historical dynamism of Ellacuría's Christology.

In his magisterial essay "The Crucified People" Ellacuría identifies the problem of making "natural" the necessity of Jesus' death. It is a view of redemption that, because it understands the death of Jesus in an abstract economy of transaction, elides Jesus' ministry. In sum, Jesus came to die. To Ellacuría, making Jesus' death necessary in this way "would entail eliminating the responsibility of those who kill prophets and those who crucify humankind, thereby veiling the aspect of sin in historical evil."[21]

---

[19] See Ignacio Ellacuría, "¿Por qué muere Jesús y por qué le matan?" *Escritos Teológicos,* vol. 2 (San Salvador: UCA Editores, 2000), 67–88.

[20] On this dual thrust of historicization, see Kevin F. Burke, *The Ground Beneath the Cross* (Washington, DC: Georgetown Universtiy Press, 2000), 123–24.

[21] Ellacuría, "The Crucified People," 204.

In contrast, Ellacuría speaks of the historical necessity of Jesus' death—a necessity that comes not from abstract logic or juridical formulas, but from the reality of sin's domination over human affairs. Jesus' preaching of God's reign, and the actions that manifested that reign, countered the domination of sin. Historically, resistance to this domination means death, but the good news is that this death is not the final story. The historicized death of Jesus is connected to a historicized resurrection that means the divine validation of his entire life—a life that then provides a norm for the Christian disciple. As Ellacuría relates, "Jesus' death is not the end of the meaning of his life, but the end of that pattern that must be repeated and followed in new lives with the hope of resurrection and thereby the seal of exaltation."[22]

In the end a historical understanding of Jesus' role serves to overcome a false dichotomization of the Chalcedonian doctrine. Jesus' full divinity and full humanity are not in inverse proportion. The fullness of Jesus' humanity does not detract from Jesus' divinity—it actualizes it and underscores the profound divine revelation found in the person of Jesus. In the Synoptic Gospels the good news that Jesus preached focuses on the reign of God.[23] The preaching and manifestation of the reign in Jesus' ministry is depicted as *for* those who were poor and marginalized and *against* those whose exercise of power violated God's covenantal justice *(sedeq)*. Even in the Johannine realized eschatology of Jesus' own person, the focus is on the liberative words and acts of Jesus. The "I AM" of John's Gospel is the one who washes his disciples' feet, forgives the woman caught in adultery, and confronts those who oppose the will of God. A historical focus on Jesus does not detract from his divinity but demands that the believer pay attention to the salvific will of God for humanity. As Ellacuría makes clear, "Historical soteriology is a matter of seeking where and how the saving action of Jesus was carried out in order to continue it in history."[24]

Repeatedly, Ellacuría underscores that Christians are called not just to follow [*seguir*] Jesus, but to carry forward [*proseguir*] Jesus' mission. How

---

[22] Ibid., 207.

[23] Scripture scholars increasingly prefer "reign" over "kingdom" as the translation of the Greek *basileou*. On the one hand, "reign of God" more accurately captures the sense of "God actively reigning in history." On the other, "kingdom of God" is not only disfiguring for its patriarchal overtones, but it also tends to call up images of a physical place (like the Kingdom of France, the Kingdom of Bhutan, and so forth), images that feed an overly literal, otherworldly-centered imagination. Jesus wasn't focused on some otherworldly place; he was focused on this world and on God's active involvement in this world. Regarding the problems of patriarchy associated with the male term *kingdom*, see the creative use of *kin-dom* as an alternative translation coined by Ada María Isasi-Díaz. *La Lucha Continues: Mujerista Theology* (Maryknoll, NY: Orbis Books, 2004), 243–51.

[24] Ellacuría, "The Crucified People," 207.

can they discern this? While each person must discern how to go about historicizing the example of Jesus in the circumstances of his or her own life, the fuller sense of historical reality and its unity dictates that that discernment must take into account the social, institutional, and structural realities of the planet. How are these known? Perhaps the most well-known phrase in Ellacuría's theological lexicon is *the crucified people*, which he defines as "that collective body that, being the majority of humanity, owes its situation of crucifixion to a social order organized and maintained by a minority that exercises its dominion through a series of factors, which, taken together and given their concrete impact within history, must be regarded as sin."[25]

To the uninitiated it might seem as though Ellacuría's approach might usurp the salvific work of Jesus, that somehow, "the crucified people" might replace Jesus Christ as the definitive source of salvation. This objection fails to understand the historical connection that Ellacuría establishes between Jesus, the Crucified One, and those who are "crucified" today. If history is, in part, a traditioning transmission, the dynamic handing on of the opening and closing of possibilities of previous generations, then the historical and theologal dimensions of Jesus' saving ministry-death-resurrection persist today. The redemptive possibilities of bearing the weight of sin identified in the Hebrew Bible's suffering servant songs, those possibilities that early Christians saw fulfilled in the person of Jesus, continue today. Repeatedly, Ellacuría affirms the definitive role of Jesus Christ in the economy of salvation, as indeed do those involved with the developments in interreligious dialogue in recent decades. However, the crucified people, those poor and oppressed who bear the weight of the world's sin today, represent the greatest challenge to Christian disciples called to carry forward the mission of Jesus today: making present the reign of God by taking away the sin of the world.

To be clear, the crucified people do not endure an expiatory suffering that somehow redeems those who look upon them, or worse, assuages the guilt of those who offer them charity.[26] They are a historical sign, of hope or condemnation, of the domination of sin and the hope for divine life. They are the historical, kenotic presence of Christ; by selflessly plunging into their reality, proclaiming the good news to them, taking them down from their crosses (to quote Jon Sobrino), the church carries on and fulfills the salvific mission of Jesus.

---

[25] Ibid., 208.

[26] To address the issue regarding voluntary and involuntary suffering, Jon Sobrino has distinguished between the crucified people and those he calls the "Jesuanic martyrs." See Jon Sobrino, "Jesuanic Martyrs in the Third World," in *Witnesses to the Kingdom: The Martyrs of El Salvador and the Crucified Peoples* (Maryknoll, NY: Orbis Books, 2003), 119–33.

Church as Sacrament of Salvation

Ahistorical views of the work (salvation) and the person of Jesus Christ inevitably result in ahistorical theologies of the church, approaches that avoid history by remaining unchanged or that escape history by focusing on exclusively "spiritual" concerns. Because of this, Ellacuría challenged the position that holds that the church "has been, is, and always should be the same in all times, identical in all places."[27] In his context of El Salvador this image of a "changeless" church was adopted by those nervous about the changes instituted by Vatican II, by those suspicious of the pastoral and ecclesial transformations after Medellín, and by those who did not want to see their worldly power and possessions challenged.[28]

Indeed, this viewpoint persists in theology today because of its under-lying assumptions. If nature is understood as substance, then mutation or change can only be accidental. As an a priori assumption, the church cannot change. Besides exhibiting a naivete about the actual historical development of the church, the assertion that the church must never change implies the denial of the very historical character of the church and its salvific mission. Yet, attention to history reveals that, in seeming irony, the church changes in history precisely to remain faithful to its mission and purpose. Ellacuría would invoke Zubiri's pithy phrase, "La Iglesia deberá siempre la misma, pero nunca lo mismo" (the church should always remain the same, but never unchanging) to indicate how one can acknowledge a sense of continuity in the church's nature and mission over time without asserting it as outside of history.[29] The good news of the gospel, as it is proclaimed and lived out in different contexts and periods, can be good only if it truly responds to the particular needs of those different historical contexts and periods.

---

[27] Ignacio Ellacuría, "Liberation: Mission and Charism of the Latin American Church," in Ellacuría, *Freedom Made Flesh*, 131. Ellacuría continued to insist on this theme throughout his life, returning to it in the closing paragraphs of his lapidary final essay, "Utopia and Propheticism from Latin America: "The church as institution tends to be more conservative of the past than renewing of the present and creative of the future. Certainly, there are things to preserve; but nothing vital and human, nothing historical, is preserved if it is not maintained in constant renewal" (p. 53, above).

[28] Archbishop Oscar Romero addressed these concerns, criticizing those guilty of a "nonevolving traditionalism" that saw the church's tradition as "a museum of souvenirs to be protected." See Oscar Romero, "The Church, the Body of Christ in History," Second Pastoral Letter of Archbishop Romero, August 6, 1977, in *Voice of the Voiceless: The Four Pastoral Letters and Other Statements*, trans. Michael J. Walsh (Maryknoll, NY: Orbis Books, 1985), 70.

[29] Ellacuría, "Liberation: Mission and Charism of the Latin American Church," 132.

In addition to a distorted notion of change, Ellacuría critiques either extreme of a spectrum regarding the relationship between the church and world. On one end lies that view of the church as outside the world, refusing to occupy itself with temporal things.[30] As an antidote to this view Ellacuría turned to an image of the church from Vatican II. Though one might expect that image to be that of the people of God, the most frequent image that Ellacuría employs is that of "sacrament of salvation" from Vatican II's *Lumen gentium* (no. 48). Sacramentality or signification—Ellacuría often used *sign* and *sacrament* interchangeably—offers Ellacuría a way to speak about the active mediation of divine and human in history without resorting to dualisms.[31] He reflects, "If the church, then, is capable of constituting itself historically as a historical sign of the reign of God's presence among human beings in its historical march in time [*proceder*], its apparent duality would be overcome: its theologal aspect and historical aspect, without being identified, would be unified."[32]

A historical understanding of the church does not minimize the dignity of its calling or reduce a sense of divine presence in the church. However, it sounds these notes as a serious calling and not a triumphal badge of honor. The church does not simply accept an honorific like "sacrament of salvation" as an ontological reality that it displays with pride, or worse, uses as a weapon of exclusion. The sacramentality of the church is bound intrinsically to a challenge to be the liberating presence of God in the world. As Ellacuría makes clear, "The church realizes its historical and salvific sacramentality by announcing and realizing the reign of God in history. Its fundamental *praxis* consists in the realization of the reign of God in history, in action that leads to God's reign being realized in history."[33] It is a theologal principle: just as Jesus manifested the presence of the Father, so the church manifests the presence of Jesus as it carries forward his mission.[34]

---

[30] This tendency is true of both of the dominant pre–Vatican II images of church that focus on it as belonging to a different order: the post-Tridentine ecclesiology of the *societas perfecta*, and Pius XII's *mystici corporis Christi*.

[31] Robert Lassalle-Klein demonstrates the connection between Ellacuría's theology of sign and the notion of crucified people in "Jesus of Galilee and the Crucified People: The Contextual Christology of Jon Sobrino and Ignacio Ellacuría," *Theological Studies* 70, no. 2 (Spring 2009): 347–76.

[32] Ellacuría, "Iglesia y realidad histórica," 2:505.

[33] Ignacio Ellacuría, "La Iglesia de los pobres, sacramento histórico de la liberación," in *Escritos Teológicos*, 2:461. For a slightly different translation of this text, see Ignacio Ellacuría, "The Church of the Poor, Historical Sacrament of Liberation," in Lee, *Ignacio Ellacuría*, 234.

[34] It is the principle that allows Ellacuría to claim that "Jesus was the historical body of God, the full actualization of God among humanity, and the church must be the historical body of Christ, just as Jesus was of God." See Ellacuría, "The Church of the Poor, Historical Sacrament of Liberation," 231.

While Ellacuría criticizes an abstract or "spiritualized" view of the church, he also identifies an opposite extreme, a view that reduces the church's activity only to the political sphere. The mission of the church goes beyond merely secular liberation. The church is called to be a source of light, of the life of God, and of ongoing incarnation, taking flesh among people. No political party, movement, or secular agenda can presume to represent, in itself, the definitive presence of the reign. Fighting injustice is an essential part of a twofold task of liberation from sin (negative) and the divinization of humanity (positive).[35] This twofold task corresponds to a dual theologal mission of taking away the sin of the world and incarnating the life of God. The church can fulfill this mission only by being a church of the poor.[36]

The phrase *church of the poor* is not a sociological designation of exclusion meaning that only the poor make up the church. Nor is it a descriptive task of an exclusively material work, the church reduced to social service agency or NGO. These misunderstandings come from the dualistic thinking that Ellacuría opposed. What Ellacuría means by *church of the poor* is that church that prophetically denounces the sin of the world while envisioning, proclaiming, and making present the good news of salvation, that utopic vision of the reign of God. That mission requires an incarnation, a plunging into the historical reality that, as we have seen, is revealed by the reality of the poor and oppressed.

In some sense contact with the poor can provide a way to "measure" the process of realizing the reign in history. Of course, Ellacuría refuses to identify the reign with any human project. Realizations are partial and are subject to reversals (history is the opening *and* closing of possibilities). However, he affirms that the "operative repudiation of injustice" and the "stances that oppressive powers take with respect to it" are indicative signs of the realization of the reign.[37]

Conclusion

These reflections on historical soteriology, written twenty-five years after Ellacuría's murder, arise from a reality that desperately needs to hear good news. Global poverty, environmental devastation, violent wars, and massive forced migrations are signs of our times. In the wake of a financial crisis that could have cast the mighty from their thrones, only the powerful seem to

---

[35] See, for example, Ellacuría, "Iglesia y realidad histórica," 2:501–15.

[36] For more on Ellacuría's ecclesiology, see Rodolfo Cardenal, "The Church of the Crucified People: The Eschatology of Ignacio Ellacuría," chap. 9 in this volume.

[37] Ellacuría, "Theology as the Ideological Moment of Ecclesial Praxis," in Lee, *Ignacio Ellacuría,* 269.

have recovered while the poor remain in darkness and the shadow of death. Even in the most powerful nation on earth, the gap between rich and poor widens, racial discrimination continues its insidious march, and the thrall of a consumerist-militarized imagination has its hold on the populace.

In this context some invoke the need for a new evangelization. In this frame of mind an external "culture of death" has been identified in contradistinction to a "church of life" that must combat it by aligning itself with political parties and groups that share its vision of culture. Not even the scandal of priestly sex abuse and episcopal cover-up abates the hubris of those who envision the church as the triumphant defender of faith in an evil, secular world.

This is not good news. The exigency of our times demands more.

I have explored the theology of Ignacio Ellacuría as a fruitful source for thinking about how the church might really convoke a truly new evangelization, a new proclamation and manifestation of that reign of God preached by Jesus and revealed in his ministry and person. It is an evangelization that must be "new" as well as being "good," and Ellacuría provides three key ideas for how to historicize the proclamation of the good news.

The Awareness of Sin. The awareness of sin and hell for the contemporary believer need not, and indeed should not, come from Dante Alighieri's *Inferno* or Hieronymous Bosch's hellscapes. The preacher need not, and should not, imitate Jonathan Edwards's invocation of hellfire or the unforgettable sermon in Joyce's *Portrait of the Artist as a Young Man* ("Hell is a strait and dark and foul-smelling prison"). As important as these examples are historically and artistically, if they divert believers' attention to exclusively otherworldly or interiorized visions of hell, then they occlude the hells that exist in our world: of starvation and malnutrition, of war, of violent narcotraffic, of sexual slave trade, of forced migrations, of rape with impunity, of deaths from curable diseases, of the multifarious (and structural) dimensions of the demon that is addiction, of all of those hellish conditions that constitute the reality of the majority population of Planet Earth. A new, historical evangelization must confront sin in its personal forms. However, it must also recognize what Archbishop Romero called the "crystallization of individuals' sins into permanent structures that keep sin in being, and make its force to be felt by the majority of the people."[38]

Conformity to Christ. Ellacuría realized that that there will never be changed structures without changed people. A new, historical evangelization must cultivate a following of Christ that views the carrying forward of Jesus' ministry, in all its prophetic density, as the primary mark of discipleship. This is an *imitatio Christi* that does not reduce discipleship

---

[38] Archbishop Oscar Romero, "The Church, the Body of Christ in History," 68.

to the following of the human Jesus' example, which is itself no small task. Rather, genuine Jesus-like discipleship will challenge the followers of Jesus to see the full divinity of Christ in the fullness of his humanity. Plunging into the struggles of the poor as one's own (because they are), embodying genuine mercy, denouncing injustice even at great cost, and hoping in the God who resurrects—these are the characteristics of the disciple of Jesus Christ.

The Church as a Sign. The praxis of the church, the example of the church, must serve to mediate the very hope in salvation that the church proclaims. The threat of the world is not secularization. It is what Ellacuría termed worldliness [*mundanización*], the temptation to seek wealth and to exercise power that either ignores or contributes to the suffering and marginalization of others. The church cannot pretend to be for life while accommodating itself to a civilization of wealth, a barbarous "civilization" that means death for the majority of people on earth.

If the church takes on the task of a truly historical evangelization, its embodied witness can overcome disbelief and signal a future in which God's reign can come and God's will can be done on earth as in heaven. Ellacuría's vision for a church of and for the poor constitutes a new, historical evangelization.

PART IV

ELLACURÍA AND JUSTICE IN AN UNJUST WORLD

13

The Concept of Common Evil and the Critique of a Civilization of Capital

HÉCTOR SAMOUR

In a paper given in 2012, Raúl Fornet-Betancourt lists the various terms that have been utilized in recent decades to define the fundamental character of our times. Each term reflects a different diagnosis, while aiming to present a basic sketch of the general development of our age.[1] For example, beginning with sociological typologies, attempts have been made to present the dominant features of our historical present utilizing terms such as *atomic era, scientific-technical society, consumer society, at-risk society, leisure society, information society, society of knowledge, virtual society, image-society, society of sensation,* and *liquid society,* among others. Meanwhile, deploying other terms, philosophical-theological studies prefer for their part to speak about *a secularized society, post-Christian society, pluralistic society, contingent society, society of relativism,* and so on.

All of these terms reflect the complexity of the present course of history that resists being diagnosed with a single formula. Moreover, this sparks a debate regarding which of these terms is most appropriate for describing the character of historical life in the present moment. However, my main objective in this essay is not to enter into this debate but simply to introduce it in order to propose a term that does not pretend to be exclusive, but may

---

[1] R. Fornet-Betancourt, "El mal común, o el de un posible nombre para nuestra época" (2012), unpublished. Social ethicists and moral theologians frequently use the language of the "common good" *(el bien común)*. The term "common evil" *(el mal común)* that Samour introduces in the title and body of this essay is not part of the traditional literature. Rather, it was forged by Ellacuría to present an exactly opposed diagnosis of the ethical character of our civilization.—*Eds.*

help at least to "round off" the proposed diagnoses present in the other terms. These precisely tend to begin their characterization of the present situation of humanity by privileging, above all, the implicit perception of those so-called highly developed societies. In contrast, the term that I propose attempts to accent the perception of the present state of the world

> beginning with those societies whose impoverished majorities stake a claim to the justice owed them in order to have a dignified life. In other words, I begin with the situation of those whose "discomfort in the world" represents the negation of the utopia of a just world and of a humanity that lives together or, if one prefers Christian theological language, the negation of the promise of the reigning of God.[2]

I refer to the term *common evil* [*el mal común*]. This is a concept forged by Ignacio Ellacuría that has the backing of the real situation in which the impoverished and marginalized majorities of the world presently find themselves. This perspective lends legitimacy to the characterization of the times in which we are living as the epoch of common evil.

In view of the complexity and intensity of the problem of evil, the term *common evil* centers on an aspect of this problem and confronts us with the reality of the socio-historical moral evil that is usually explained as the result of the free actions of the human being. More specifically, the term condenses the manifestation of the evil in its historical reality as common evil. Therefore, when speaking of common evil, I do not presume to present it as the only form of evil about which we can and must speak today.

Common Evil

Ignacio Ellacuría explicitly developed this concept in the schematic notes prepared for his class in 1989. Those notes, which were published twenty years after his martyrdom, deal with a concept that was central to understanding his work in all its dimensions (theological, philosophical, political, and religious), and they deal very specially with the spirit of his legacy.[3]

We are not, therefore, talking about a marginal concept but about a central concept that expresses the decisive historical contrast for Ellacuría: the contrast between the negativity of the reality that the dominant course of history makes of the world and the "expected and favored" reality judged

---

[2] Fornet-Betancourt, "El mal común, o el de un posible nombre para nuestra época."
[3] Ignacio Ellacuría, " El mal común y los derechos humanos," *Escritos Filosoficos*, vol. 3 (San Salvador: UCA Editores, 2001), 447–50.

from a horizon of complete positivity or, to say this theologically, from the reality both "expected and favored" of the will of God.

We could ask ourselves whether in the concept of common evil, we have not improperly mixed philosophy and theology. Before this, we have to insist that to understand fully the thought of Ignacio Ellacuría one would need to journey back to a previous dimension in the disciplinary differentiation of philosophy and theology. We are referring to the dimension of spirituality, of Ignatian spirituality and its specific forms of concrete discernment.[4] Jon Sobrino affirmed this sense that "one does not know fully the thought of Ellacuría without grasping his comprehension of the *Spiritual Exercises* of Saint Ignatius, the homilies of Monseñor Romero, and of course, the recounted-and-reflected-upon reality of Jesus of Nazareth."[5] In view of this, Ignacio Ellacuría—both in his life and his work—manifests in the concept of common evil a spirituality of discernment in light of the reign promised to the impoverished. This is what gives character to his theoretical work in its diverse manifestations, whether political, philosophical, or theological.

Returning to our theme, we see how this concept unfolds in the writings of Ellacuría. In the first place, in his *Filosofía de la realidad historica* [philosophy of historical reality], Ellacuría presents common evil as a historical evil, rooted in a determinate system of the possibilities of historical reality or of the social body, through which reality actualizes its power by configuring in a damaging way the lives of humans, both as individuals and as groups.[6] It has to do with a negativity incarnated in and generated by social structures that negate or block the personal humanization of the majority of humanity that has been the case from key moments onward in the process of history.

He is dealing, therefore, with a formally historical evil and not with an evil rooted in the realities of human nature or personal biography. It is an evil, Ellacuría affirmed, that "can continue acquiring concrete historical forms that affect the social body as a whole," and that have a power

that is now not merely possible but something that takes over my very life, inasmuch as it belongs to a specific historical moment: there is a historical evilness . . . that is there as something objective and that is capable of configuring the lives of everyone. It has to do not only with recognizing the existence of structural sin, as we say today, because the structural sin is in itself a social sin, something that affects society,

---

⁴ See ibid.

⁵ Jon Sobrino, "El Ellacuría olvidado: Lo que no se puede dilapidar," in *Ignacio Ellacuría 20 años más tarde: Actas del congreso internacional* (Seville: Instituto Andaluz de Administración Pública, 2010), 320.

⁶ See Ignacio Ellacuría, *Filosofía de la realidad historica*, ed. Antonio González (San Salvador: UCA Editores, 1990), 590.

structurally understood. Historical sin, in addition to being structural, alludes to the formally historical character of that sin: it is a system of possibilities through which is conveyed the real power of history.[7]

When it occurs, this historical evil, which is as such a common evil, is definitive and is not reducible in any sense to a pure negativity in the Hegelian sense. In the Ellacurían conception the evil that appears in history does not become integrated in a rational, teleological explanation, as happens in the Enlightenment conceptions of history, especially in Hegelian philosophy or in the dialectical materialism of Engels.[8] That is why the overcoming of evil does not happen automatically through the logic of a process or through the laws of history, but only by changing the system of possibilities *qua* system or, at minimum, by changing the figure before the system of possibilities available to humanity in a given moment.[9] But this can only be realized through the initiation of a historical praxis of liberation, understood as ethical actions that seek, through real possibilities, to negate in a surpassing way the historical negativities of that given moment.

In the schematic class notes alluded to earlier, Ignacio Ellacuría introduced the concept of common evil, contrasting it with the classical concept of common good. He included the following annotation at the beginning of his notes:

The classics speak of the common good. But the straightforward definition of the common good cannot adequately be accomplished if only sought formally and abstractly. This formalism and abstractness may serve as a framework and even a horizon, but they are not sufficient. They point, of course, to the good of a community that is not just an aggregate of individuals. The common good is not achieved looking at the good of each one, in the way that this good be just the sum of all individual goods. The good of each one separately is not the general good, nor is it the common good. . . . All of this is very important, but in reality, it tells us nothing about what is happening regarding the common good. Because the common good is in fact an ideal, nevertheless it should be needed also so that truly human behavior becomes possible. Yet what happens in the real world is "common evil."[10]

This affirmation gives us a glimpse of the true intention of Ignacio Ellacuría with this counter position as well as the critical-prophetic range of his

---

7 Ibid., 590.
8 See ibid., 451–60.
9 See ibid., 446.
10 Ellacuría, "El mal común y los derechos humanos," 447.

concept of common evil. The tension between the ideal (common good) and reality (common evil) is presented in the form of a contradiction. It does not simply manifest the contrast between the ideal and the real in the sense of proposing the ideal as the dimension of the "is-ought" that should be closer to the reality. Rather, it manifests said contrast with the added peculiarity of presenting the reality that exists, the common evil, as the dimension whose negativity requires the actualization of the good *qua* historically operative reality, and certainly with the same qualities or properties that have made and make of evil a common evil.

In the light of this counter position, what is needed is the what and the how this common evil happens, in terms cited earlier. It is often noted that common evil is not an evil that simply and straightforwardly affects the many, nor is it simply the evil of the many. Rather, by virtue of its own dynamics, it should also be seen as a structural reality that spreads and communicates as a power configured and organized by real, personal, social, and public processes. In this way, states Ellacuría, "common evil is that structural and dynamic evil that, because of its own structural dynamism, has the capacity of also rendering evil most of those who form a social unit."[11]

Common evil is, therefore, an actual state of the world in which the majority of people are structurally evil because of the same ordering of the conditions of life in the world. This is why common evil occurs as an order or form of organization that institutionally and functionally configures historical reality in such a way that it carries a dehumanizing dynamism which condemns the majority of those that live in the so-called situation (of the real) to *being* or living badly.

We need to point out that, for Ignacio Ellacuría, common evil entails a still deeper significance. For, as deduced from the last quotation, it has to do with a structural situation that can affect the very being of those affected, making them evil.

If we undertake a metaphysical and not merely an anthropological reflection, where history is viewed as the summit of the transcendental order, that is, the specific sphere in which the totality of reality is given and reveals itself, then common evil would not only be historical evil, but metaphysical evil, blocking and undermining from its depths the realization and revelation of reality itself. Even more could be said about what this proposal means theologically.

Ignacio Ellacuría concludes his class notes by summarizing his explanation of common evil as a referent for thinking about the historical realization of the common good:

---

[11] Ibid., 448.

Seeing things from the perspective of real common evil, which is the evil that effects the majorities, especially when this evil takes on the qualities of structural injustice—unjust structures that hardly make human life livable and that to the contrary, dehumanize the majority of those subject to them—of institutionalized injustice—the institution- alization of laws, customs, ideologies, etc.,—the problem of common good emerges as a demand to negate that structural and institutional injustice. Consequently, the common good, emerging as a negation that overcomes "common evil," must be set in contrast as good against evil, but it should have the same characteristics that make common evil something really common.[12]

This "negation that overcomes" mentioned by Ellacuría implies making a precise diagnosis of the situation at hand and of proposing a human response that functions as a negation of the negation. Otherwise there is a risk of supporting evil or of palliating its manifestations by not attacking its roots. This in turn means putting into play a process of liberation that con- tinues "creating affirmations which then should be surpassed. The dynamism of the negation of the negation is fundamentally positive and it fundamen- tally relies on an intolerance of evil and of what is negative."[13] Therefore, it is about linking itself to and accompanying a praxis of liberation so as to make possible the historical establishment of the common good. Moreover, since it has to do with negating the specific, concrete negativity of a given historical reality, the human work of liberation "can think of itself as a fundamental moment in tandem with the affirmation of the positive and the surpassing of what is positively affirmed."[14]

We must emphasize the consequence that Ellacuría extracts from all of this with respect to the question concerning human rights. His way of de- termining the "what is" and the "how it comes about" of common evil leads him to consider that the elemental demands contained in the program of human rights are, in truth, necessary to make possible the actualization of the (other) reality of the common good. A situation determined by com- mon evil and in tension with the desired common good that it provokes grounds for Ellacuría the necessity of reclaiming human rights, but as a concrete reclaiming of the necessity of making reality good or of historically achieving the common good. In line with this he writes: "A consideration of human rights from this perspective of a predominant common evil would demonstrate how the concrete common good—which should be visualized

---

[12] Ibid., 449.

[13] Ignacio Ellacuria, "Ética Fundamental," in *Cursos Universitarios* (San Salvador: UCA Editores, 2009), 255.

[14] Ibid.

as a negation that overcomes the common evil—really presents itself as in a situation where human rights are permanently and massively violated."[15]

A Critique of the Civilization of Capital

In his last writings, summing up this proposal regarding common evil, Ellacuría highlights the necessity of proposing a new general project for humanity. He proposes a radical change in our present civilization configured by common evil by means of a new project based on the Kantian idea that the order of common evil, the dominating order of the civilization of capital, cannot be made universal.

The diagnosis he made of his time—his sense that it was a conflictive epoch marked by the predominance of common evil—caused him to place a critical-utopian wager that was at the same time radically prophetic. Ellacuría called this critical-utopian and prophetic wager the civilization of poverty.

The destructive effects of the reality of the common evil—of that "malice" inherent in the dominate civilization—lead Ellacuría to propose a negation that overcomes the civilization of capital and its fundamental dynamism by constructing a new world society not controlled by the laws of capital, but instead giving primacy to the "dynamism of humanizing work."[16] The historical inauguration of the common good for all of humanity demands, in his view, that we overturn the principal sign configuring world civilization and start a new historical order founded on the promotion and liberation of human life, one that radically transforms our present age.

> The civilization of poverty . . . rejects the accumulation of capital as the engine of history and the possession and enjoyment of wealth as the principle of humanization. It makes the universal satisfaction of basic needs the principle of development and the growth of shared solidarity the foundation of humanization.
>
> The civilization of poverty is so named in contrast to the civilization of wealth, and not because it proposes universal pauperization as an ideal of life. . . . What is here meant to be emphasized is the dialectical relationship between wealth and poverty, and not poverty in itself. In a world sinfully shaped by the dynamism of capital and wealth,

---

[15] Ignacio Ellacuría, "El mal común y los derechos humanos," 449. For a detailed proposal on human rights in Ellacuría, see Juan Antonio Senent de Frutos, *Ellacuría y los derechos humanos* (Bilbao: Desclee de Brouwer, 1998).

[16] Ignacio Ellacuría, "El desafío de las mayorías pobres," *ECA* 493–94 (1989): 1077–78.

it is necessary to stir up a different dynamism that will overcome it salvifically.[17]

In the face of the common evil generated by the civilization of wealth and capital, Ellacuría proposes a civilization of poverty that is not reduced to programs of reform to alleviate the damaging consequences of the dominant order. Rather, with a clear conscience he proposes another order based on a "principial dynamism [*dinamismo principial*]"[18] radically distinct from the order of capitalism. In other words, his is a global project that really can be universalized and where there exist possibilities of survival and humanization for all. In the face of the current prevailing principle of universalization [*universalización*]—one that is characterized by being mostly an imposed principle of standardization [*uniformización*] governed by laws of the economic market—Ellacuría proposes the constitution of a

universalism . . . that does not reduce but enriches, so that the entire wealth of peoples may be respected and developed, and their differences seen as the completion of the whole and not as the clashing of the parts. In this way, all the members will complement one another, and in this complementing the whole will be enriched and the parts strengthened.[19]

Along these lines Ellacuría is specifically referring to the constitution of a stable economic order that guarantees basic necessities and facilitates a common source of personal development and possibilities for self-realization. He envisions a new social order in which it is possible that more people become the subjects of their destiny, with greater chances for creative freedom and participation. All of this supposes a new political order beyond that of liberal democracy and existing collectivist models, and a new cultural order separate from other western models.[20] The overcoming of this alienating culture should carry with it in turn the recuperation of humanity's secular cultural wealth that is presently being crushed by standardized technological and consumerist models. The reality of "overcoming negation" goes to the

---

[17] Ignacio Ellacuría, "Utopía y profetismo," *Revista Latinoamericana de Teología* 17 (1990): 170; in English, "Utopia and Propheticism from Latin America," 40–41 in this volume.

[18] Samour is quoting Ellacuría, who makes use of the archaic word *principial* to refer to God's viewpoint as the source and principle of all things. This idea is central to the thought of the great medieval mystic, Meister Eckhart.—*Eds.*

[19] Ellacuría, "Utopía y profetismo," 156; in English, "Utopia and Propheticism from Latin America," 25 in this volume.

[20] Ibid., 173–80; in English, 47–52.

heart of how Ellacuría understands the terms *revolution* and *liberation*. We conclude with his lapidary summation:

> The revolution that is needed, the necessary revolution, will be the one that intends freedom deriving from and leading to justice and justice deriving and leading to freedom. This freedom must come out of liberation and not merely out of liberalization—whether economic or political liberalization—in order to overcome in this way the dominant "common evil" and build a "common good," a common good understood in contrast to the common evil and sought from a preferential option for the mass of the people.[21]

—Translated by Teresa Malave, VDMF, and Kevin F. Burke, SJ

---

[21] Ibid., 178.

14

Socioeconomic Thoughts on Historical Mediations

Toward the "Civilization of Poverty"

Jonas Hagedorn

The ultimate vision of the concretions of the reign of God and its historical mediations culminates, according to Ignacio Ellacuría, in the "civilization of poverty," a conceptual approximation of the kingdom of God, which could also end up being intelligible for those who consider themselves distant from any kind of religious meaning.

Ellacuría's insistence on finding answers to the question of how to realize the reign of God justifies the effort of identifying historical mediations leading to a civilization of poverty from the perspective of the social sciences, methodologically leaving aside the religious-eschatological responsibility.[1]

Indicators of the Civilization of Poverty and Two Basic Rules

Ellacuría did not develop the concept of civilization of poverty systematically. However, his explanations provide sufficient evidence to determine its content and to relate that concept to socioeconomic discourse.[2] Economics

---

[1] The liberation theology of the "Salvadoran School" maintains the eschatological proviso, but without abandoning historical reality.

[2] Reference to and quotations from Ellacuría's concept of civilization of poverty throughout this section refer to the English translation of "Utopía y profetismo desde América Latina: un ensayo concreto de soteriología histórica," *Revista Latinoamericana de Teología* 17 (1989): 141–84, by James Brockman, J. Matthew Ashley, and Kevin Burke, provided as "Utopia and Propheticism from Latin America: A Concrete Essay in Historical Soteriology," in chapter 2 of this volume.

works with indicators that allow it to assess the scope of a process in light of its ultimate goal. In this sense the civilization of poverty could be interesting for those who do not share its "religious grammar," but only if its content is made explicit and some indicators are established. This task can be accomplished without having to reinvent the wheel; one can simply turn, for example, to the capabilities approach of Martha C. Nussbaum.[3]

Nussbaum presents a list of capabilities to which all human beings should have access.[4] In exploring what the most important of these capabilities are, such that, without them life would not be truly human, Nussbaum identifies ten. We can assume that Ellacuría would have agreed with the central aspects of this list and that he would have recognized his idea of "real freedom" in Amartya Sen's and Nussbaum's concept of "substantial freedom."

However, Ellacuría's concept of civilization of poverty goes far beyond the capabilities approach. First, Ellacuría starts from some "profound values" that have a metaphysical background and from a particular worldview. In contrast, Nussbaum defends a neutral worldview, renouncing the pursuit of one particular set of values—or a specific conception of the human. Second, Nussbaum defines capabilities as a minimum standard, albeit a very ambitious one.[5] Guaranteeing this minimum standard (no small task) would not give rise to problems or objections that come from a broad diversity of social postures. However, while Ellacuría does not fight for social equality only on the basis of a just starting point, neither is he satisfied with broad equality of opportunities alone. Despite these differences regarding the historical

---

[3] Nussbaum is a representative of political liberalism. Since the 1970s different concepts of political liberalism have been intensively discussed, by John Rawls, among others. Liberation theology could have made some allies with some of the currents of political liberalism. For Nussbaum's work on the issues treated here, see "Aristotelian Social Democracy," in *Liberalism and the Good*, ed. R. Douglass, Gerald M. Mara, and Henry S. Richardson, 203–52 (New York: Routledge, 1990); "Human Functioning and Social Justice: In Defense of Aristotelian Essentialism," *Political Theory* 20, no. 2 (1992): 202–46; "The Good as Discipline, the Good as Freedom," in *Ethics of Consumption: The Good Life, Justice, and Global Stewardship*, ed. David Crocker and Toby Linden, 312–41 (Lanham, MD: Rowman and Littlefield, 1998); *Women and Human Development: The Capabilities Approach* (Cambridge: Cambridge University Press, 2000); "Capabilities as Fundamental Entitlements: Sen and Social Justice," in *Feminist Economics* 9, no. 2–3 (2003): 33–59; *Frontiers of Justice: Disability, Nationality, Species Membership* (Cambridge, MA: Harvard University Press, 2006).

[4] "Aristotelian Social Democracy," 219–25; "Human Functioning and Social Justice," 216–22; "The Good as Discipline, the Good as Freedom," 318–20; *Women and Human Development*, 78–80; "Capabilities as Fundamental Entitlements," 41–42; *Frontiers of Justice*, 76–78.

[5] In the field of political liberalism in contemporary political philosophy, the true defender of the option for the poor is Nussbaum, not the famed J. Rawls.

mediations in general, it would be interesting to establish a dialogue between Ellacuría's thought, on the one hand, and Sen's and Nussbaum's, on the other.

Although for some this might seem audacious, what I do here is to systematize the civilization of poverty socioeconomically in terms of two complementary rules: maximization of social equality (R_{max}) and minimization of external costs (R_{min}). The first expresses a strong normative valorization, while the second includes an intergenerational context and the issue of economic effectiveness.

The maximization of social equality is derived from Ellacuría's concept of "the new human being." He attributes the "Cainite rupture of humanity" and the "formation of an exploitative, repressive, and violent human being" to "rapid and unequal enrichment."[6] Consequently, the new human being will "not come into existence until there is an entirely new relationship to deal with the phenomenon of wealth and the problem of unequal accumulation." Ellacuría does not understand social equality as "mechanical equalities" or "obligatory equality." However, "excessive and conflict-producing inequalities are to disappear in the real area of the social," and "the processes leading to attention-getting and conflict-provoking inequalities should be avoided."

Minimizing external costs starts from the premise that such costs are always bad for the common good. An external cost is anything that has to be paid by third parties not involved in the process that generated it. In this sense future generations may be among these third parties. Take, for example, the ecological costs of agribusiness that are not reflected in the actual price: global warming caused by carbon dioxide emissions and the loss of biodiversity caused by conventional agriculture. Exporting agricultural surplus from the European Union to African countries also brings about external costs. These products, which are heavily subsidized, flood the local market. There, due to their low price, they do not have any competition and, thereby, destroy the value-added chain and deprive poor farmers of their means of subsistence.

Similarly, the wages reflected in the labor market can cause external costs, as when they fall below the minimum needed to live with dignity. These external costs are paid by family networks or by governmental safety nets. In the first case, the family members are the third party that covers the external costs. In the second case, the costs are covered by taxpayers.

The minimization of the external costs avoids complicated discussions about economic growth, because in these discussions which economic sector ought to grow or not to grow has to be made clear. For example, when it

---

[6] Ellacuría's reference to the "Cainite rupture of humanity" is an allusion to the biblical story in which Cain murders his brother, Abel (Gn 4:1–16).—*Eds.*

comes to renewable energy, there is no reason to be in favor of technological innovation and growth.

Although it is true that Ellacuría does not refer explicitly to the minimization of external costs when speaking of economic growth, neither would he reject it, since he is aware of the scarcity of resources. For this reason he claims that it is impossible to universalize the lifestyle of the rich countries, although neither is it advisable to "reproduce" and "enlarge the present historical order significantly." Certainly, he does not mention the emissions that expanding the production of many goods would put into the atmosphere. But it should be recalled that this phenomenon becomes part of public discourse as a consequence of the prohibition of CFCs (chlorofluorocarbons) and the debates about global warming in the late twentieth century.

Chart of the Socioeconomic Mediations of the Civilization of Poverty

In this section I distinguish the micro and macro levels and use the two rules mentioned above. In the first level I analyze nation-state structures and transnational agreements,[7] while in the second I discuss four non-centralist initiatives that have in fact begun to transform the "civilization of capital and wealth" and have opened avenues to get closer to the construction of the civilization of poverty.

The Macro Level: The Arrangement of the Common Goods

Economic thought is not within the competence of liberation theology, or of any other theology, as Ellacuría himself made clear. To be sure, philosophers and theologians can indicate the *goal* (the range of normative goals, one of which, for the civilization of poverty, is social equality) of an economic configuration, but they do not spend a lot of time describing how to treat this configuration from an economic perspective. The economic mediation requires the participation and competence of economists who identify themselves with the utopia and the range of their normative goals.[8]

---

[7] It is obvious that in this process, organizations from civil society play a key role exerting pressure. However, the resolution of this matter is the responsibility of the political institutions with the relevant jurisdiction to intervene.

[8] Ignacio Ellacuría, "Liberation Theology and Socio-historical Change in Latin America," in *Toward a Society That Serves Its People: The Intellectual Contribution of El Salvador's Murdered Jesuits,* ed. J Hassett and H. Lacey (Washington, DC: Georgetown University Press, 1991), 29–30; idem, "On liberation," in *Ignacio Ellacuría: Essays on History, Liberation, and Salvation,* ed. Michael E. Lee (Maryknoll, NY: Orbis Books, 2013), 54–55.

Nonetheless, Ellacuría not only points out the *whither* (the goals that the configuration ought to achieve) but also indicates the *how* (how economic systems should be configured).

In "Utopia and Propheticism from Latin America," Chapter 2 above, Ellacuría refers in very strong terms to private appropriation of common goods:

> The private appropriation of common property is not needed in order to care for it and enjoy it. When the church's social doctrine, following Saint Thomas, holds that private appropriation of goods is the best practical manner for their primordial common destiny to be fulfilled in an orderly way, it is making a concession to "the hardness of their hearts," but "in the beginning it was not so." Only because of the greed and selfishness, connatural to original sin, can it be said that private ownership of property is the best guarantee of productive advancement and social order. But if "where sin abounded, grace abounded more" is to have historical verification, it is necessary to proclaim utopianly that a new earth with new human beings must be shaped with principles of greater altruism and solidarity. The great benefits of nature (the air, the seas and beaches, the mountains and forests, the rivers and lakes, in general all the natural resources for production, use, and enjoyment) need not be privately appropriated by an individual person, group, or nation, and in fact they are the grand medium of communication and common living. (42–43)

Many public goods (by definition, goods characterized by low levels of rivalry and difficulty in excluding their use) became scarcer over time, subject to rivalry, and in danger of overexploitation. They came thus to be considered common or community property. During the decades of growth characterized by high levels of fossil-fuel use and abundant emissions, the atmosphere was considered a public good that simply could not be overexploited. Indeed, the atmosphere was considered a "free dumpster for carbon dioxide, a by-product."[9] So now we face the following problem:

> To achieve a goal of 2 degrees [maximal global atmospheric temperature increase] with a median probability, we should deposit in the atmosphere only ~750 billion tons of carbon dioxide. A less ambitious goal only permits an additional 100 billion tons. Given the 33 billion tons of CO_2 global emissions in 2010—with an uptrend—it

---

[9] Ottmar Edenhofer, Christian Flachsland, and Bernard Lorentz, "Die Atmosphäre als globales Gemeingut," in *Commons: für eine neue Politik jenseits von Markt und Staat*, ed. Silke Helfrich and Heinrich-Böll-Stiftung (Bielefeld transcript 2012), 475.

is not difficult to calculate that the dumpster will be filled in a few decades. So then, the use of fossil energy should be limited globally.[10]

This is why economists invented the cap-and-trade approach for controlling emissions. Emissions permits, in the form of certificates, are purchased by governments and companies wishing to enter the market. Due to their scarcity—for example, when governments, other actors, or new companies are buying certificates—their value increases, which encourages companies to reduce their emissions. Thus the business with the emissions permits strengthens the same process of scarcity that has in the past turned public goods into common goods. From an ideal perspective, the cap-and-trade process conforms to the two basic rules mentioned above. On the one hand, it maximizes social equality, compensating areas with low emissions. In this way their non-emissions become an economic value. On the other hand, it means a firm step toward the internalization of the external costs that accompany production processes. These are external costs in the face of which, as a general rule, the poorest (those who generate less) are the most defenseless and vulnerable.

Another example that harmonizes with these two rules is the deal that Rafael Correa, president of Ecuador, offered the global community. Protecting Yasuni National Park meant not pumping anything more from the oil field that had been there before the park was created (around 850 million barrels). In exchange for this, the world community would make compensatory financial transfers. Since the park is useful for everyone, everyone—the entire global community—must pay a price. The money would be administered by a trust fund overseen by the United Nations Program for Development. The fund's board would include, among others, representatives of the government of Ecuador and of Ecuadorian civil society. Industrialized countries and private donors would pay Ecuador to preserve the rainforest and not to extract oil, and, thus, to protect the atmosphere and biodiversity. The deal would help Ecuador to finance its own development without resorting to methods with high levels of pollution and emissions. It was an opportunity for modernization, financed with transfers. In 2010, the Ecuadorian government began to define the use of the income:

> The funds would have to be used for the transformation of the Ecuadorian energy sector through the development of alternative energy sources, for nature restoration and reforestation in the Amazon, for improving living conditions (sustainable social development),

---

[10] Ibid., 475.

especially of the Amazonian people, and for investments in research for new technologies.[11]

The government estimated that the contributions of the governments and private donors would end up representing half of the money that oil extraction would produce. Thus, the Yasuní-ITT Initiative was conditional on the fund's ability to reach more than 350 million dollars.[12]

The growth of Latin American nations' and societies' negotiating power can be confirmed at various levels, above all in negotiations over natural resources. Many countries of the South can make use of natural resources—water, forest, and so on—to produce benefits. Also, the distribution of capital could be possible through the use of the appropriate political devices and the *multi-scale approach* in such a way that the sustainable use of global commons will be ensured.[13] In fact, the countries of the southern hemisphere already have a valuable basis for negotiation.

The Micro Level: Commercial and Noncommercial Approaches

At the micro level amazing steps have been accomplished in order to get closer to the maximization of social equality (R_{max}) and minimalization of external costs (R_{min}). These initiatives should be evaluated with control variables that specify both R_{max} and the R_{min}. Thus, profit maximization, altruism, and the promotion of equality are control variables for R_{max}, while minimizing costs, price tolerance, and resource consumption do the same for R_{min}. The first control variable refers to those who offer (O); the second, to those who demand (D); and the third, to society in general (SG). The assessment of altruism and price tolerance variables is based on strong normative values. On one hand, a high degree of altruism is considered less stable than a low level. As a consequence, the variable is scored negatively. On the other hand, high price tolerance seems to be positive.

These assessments should be understood as tendencies. In what follows I briefly describe the control variables and explain some of their particular features. Maximizing social equality is to some degree opposed to maximizing profits for the sellers. This contradiction becomes a problem when certain elements of the production process do not adequately participate in the profits; that is, profits are generated at the expense of others. Obviously, this

---

[11] Alberto Acosta, "Die komplexe Konstruktion der Utopie. Ein Blick auf die Initiative Yasuní-ITT," in Helfrich and Heinrich-Böll-Stiftung, *Commons,* 497.

[12] Ibid., 498.

[13] Elinor Ostrom, "A Multi-Scale Approach to Coping with Climate Change and Other Collective Action Problems," *Solutions* 1, no. 2 (March-April 2010): 27–36.

	Commercial approaches		Non-commercial approaches	
	Car-sharing (Carro del barrio)	Fair trade (Gepa-The Fair Trade Company)	Barter Exchange (Labor-hour for labor-hour)	Free Software (Linux)
R_{max}				
1 Maximizing the profit-O	**Yes**	Yes	N/A	N/A
2 Altruism-D	Low	**High**	*Depends*	Low
3 Promoting equality-SG	*Depends*	Yes	Yes	Yes
R_{min}				
1 Minimizing costs-O	**Yes**	No	N/A	N/A
2 Price tolerance-D	*Depends*	High	N/A	N/A
3 Resource consumption-SG	Decreasing	*Equal*	*Equal*	*Equal*

Favors the maximization of social equality or the minimization of external costs.

Indecision regarding the effects, the maximization of social equality, or the minimization of external costs.

Disfavors the maximization of social equality or the minimization of external costs.

Figure 1: Commercial and noncommercial approaches at the micro level: list of the control of effects regarding R_{max} and R_{min}

is directly related to R_{min}. In contrast with car-sharing, the fair-trade model is based on profit maximization for the benefit of the primary producers. The desire to maximize profit not only enriches one sector of the company. In the noncommercial approaches, profit maximization plays no relevant role.

Commercial and noncommercial approaches run contrary to altruistic values. In many cases the overwhelming maximization of individual utility is the factor that determines the decision to participate in car-sharing. In contrast, consumption of fair-trade products is heavily influenced by altruism, even more when they are not ecologically produced goods. The consumer of fair-trade products knows that the conditions of bananas or blouses meet certain standards of social business and that the plantation workers in Guatemala or the sewing-machine operators in Bangladesh do not risk their health and do receive just wages. However, in a barter exchange, altruism does not appear clearly; rather, it depends on the skills being offered. So, someone who offers a certain expertise that generally has a high monetary value in the labor market (for example, legal advice) is offering a skill either for altruistic reasons or because he or she likes the notion of solidarity maintained by the barter exchange. Someone with little income, because his or her skill does not have an adequate monetary equivalent in the market, might participate in the exchange for selfish reasons. In other words, he or she demands a service that, under market conditions, could not be financed. Usually, the demand for free software, for example, responds to a very selfish attitude because it has a dual purpose: to obtain a product for free and to obtain a product of high quality. Furthermore, when the source code is open and it is possible to program and even improve the program in order to accommodate one's own particular needs, we have a third kind of utility.

The *noncommercial approaches* (for example, the barter exchange and the free software) and the *commercial approach* to fair trade generally promote social equality. Fair trade redistributes income, because the primary producers in the production chain receive a more just and higher wage than they would get in the market, and consumers of these products are willing to pay a little more for bananas and other goods. Fair trade ensures that local primary producers are not exploited and can live with dignity from their work. Consumers are not only willing to pay a little more than the market price, but also to accept lower quality, as in the case of Nicaragua's *café solidario,* which cannot compete with the quality of the conventional coffee producers and roasters. The barter exchanges as well as free software exchanges promote social equality as well. In the first case, diplomas and titles do not matter, because what matters is the labor hour; that is, one hour of legal advice is as good as one hour of cleaning services. In the case of free software, there are no fees for the license to use it, which makes it easier to reduce the digital divide between rich and poor nations.

The minimization of the business' costs to the company corresponds to the maximization of profit. If the company minimizes its costs because, for example, the profit margin and the price flexibility are limited, the likelihood of externalizing costs is higher than in the opposite case. The price flexibility of fair trade is much higher than in the field of car-sharing. Those offering fair-trade products do not seek to minimize costs, which has a negative impact on the situation of the other members of the process of production of goods. In contrast, those selling car-sharing want to keep the cost of the entire fleet of cars to a minimum. In noncommercial approaches, the minimization of the costs for those selling the products or services is not relevant.

Neither does the control variable of price tolerance play an important role in noncommercial approaches. Conversely, the price tolerance of buyers in the car-sharing sector depends on the frequency of use and the price of the providers and on the conventional market for renting and selling cars. Car-sharing users are willing to pay a higher price for certain trips than they would pay if they had their own cars, since the cost of insurance and maintenance are nonexistent in car-sharing. Nonetheless, the price should not exceed a certain limit, because if it did the incentive would increase to acquire and maintain one's own vehicle. On the other hand, tolerance for fair-trade prices tends to be very flexible. To the extent that the high price of a product is justified by the benefits to the local primary producers, the consumer is willing to pay.

Of these four approaches, only car-sharing reduces resource consumption. In Germany and other European countries the car is no longer a status symbol for the younger generations, because they use a car to the extent that it satisfies their individual transportation needs, even if they have to share it with others. In a metropolis with a well-established infrastructure of public transportation, car-sharing saturates the market faster. Accordingly, the demand for cars stops and becomes regressive, above all when providers content themselves with renewing the vehicle fleet every four or five years. This business model combines the individual displacement with the social dimension.

   To sum up, all the approaches from the micro level are opposed to state control and paradigmatically favor private, complex, but flexible ways of organizing the community. From the perspective of the two rules, the maximization of social equality and minimization of external costs (R_{max} and R_{min}), the model of car-sharing has the disadvantage of maximizing profits and minimizing costs. In any case, the particular feature and strength of this approach is that it decreases consumption of limited resources. In contrast, fair trade is successful if the altruism of potential consumers is high. But if this altruism decreases or comes into conflict with egoism, as would happen if purchasing power decreased, a conflict of objectives would arise that would threaten this approach. Noncommercial approaches are the ones that do the best job of adjusting the two rules, even if they do not reduce consumption of resources. Of these approaches, free software, which is part of an open-access-commons and allows general and unlimited use, is a solution compatible with both rules. So then, three of the above-mentioned approaches—car-sharing, the barter exchanges, and free software—break the logic and the dynamics of possessive individualism.

Concluding Observations

In "Utopia and Propheticism from Latin America," Chapter 2 above, Ellacuría stresses that

> without propheticism there is no possibility of making a Christian concretion of utopia and, consequently, a historical realization of the reign of God. Without an intense and genuine exercise of Christian propheticism, the concretion of Christian utopia cannot be arrived at theoretically, much less practically. Here, too, the law cannot replace grace, the institution cannot replace life, and established tradition cannot replace the radical newness of the Spirit. (11)

Thus, Ellacuría raises propheticism to the status of a method for the historical mediations of the reign of God, meaning by prophecy "critical contrasting of the proclamation of the fullness of the reign of God with a specific historical situation" (11). Such propheticism, Ellacuría writes, requires "a radical transformation" (29).

In Latin America, where there are no longer revolutionary movements in the strict sense, and where many countries have introduced political democracy and the rule of law, mere criticism on its own does not lead anywhere. The differences and complexities of modern economies and societies do not admit of simple answers. However, one should not underestimate the need for propheticism. Still, the question of how an intervention is a scandal and a hindrance today remains an open one. *On the one hand*, some people committed to social movements prophetically raise their voices and oppose corporate and government projects. *On the other hand*, some people, who are wrapped up in the work of everyday life, expose the hidden negotiations between employers and legislators or ministers, unveil actions contrary to the common good on the part of political institutions, study social and environmental impacts, work out more just tax laws, and propose modifications to banking laws and regulations. All of them think and act in a way that is more institutional than prophetic. The two groups are necessary. Moreover, in many cases there is a coincidence on the personal level.

It is certainly true that in the second half of the twentieth century propheticism and liberation theology prompted major changes in Latin America. However, in retrospect, by distancing itself from the institutional and legislative thinkers, sometimes pejoratively called sectorial pragmatists, this theology did not do its cause a favor, much less the historical mediations it was seeking. The prophet does not think of the real possibilities but denounces what is wrong. But strong denunciation, insofar as it does not leave room for negotiation, runs the risk of failing because it places the goal too far off or reduces the complexity of reality, trapping itself in "social romanticism," so that little or nothing comes of it. The institutional type, seeking pragmatic modification of what is possible, runs the risk of getting lost in compromises and giving up in the face of the complexity of the problems, losing sight of the utopian horizon. Therefore, both activities, the prophetic and the institutional (linked to utopia), should understand themselves as complementary. In the same way that there is no possibility of rendering utopia concrete without propheticism, there is no possibility of rendering it concrete without a pragmatic and realistic approach either. This apparent dualism must be overcome. Utopia requires the unity of both approaches.[14]

---

[14] Ellacuría did a lot to overcome the historical-salvific dualism: on the one hand, the "earth," on the other, "heaven"; on one hand, "secular history," on the other, "sacred history." Overcoming these has had a longstanding influence on Latin American theology. In Ellacuría's insistence in the dialectics of poverty and wealth, socialism and capitalism, the prophetic and the pragmatic, a dualism appears that is in a peculiar contradiction to overcoming dualisms in the theological field.

Given current conditions, a propheticism without the pragmatic-realist contribution is like a blunt sword. What we are talking about here is making the pragmatic useful to utopian ends. From the perspective of the economic mediation of the 1970s (land reform) and the political mediations of the 1980s (negotiations to end the war), Ellacuría is himself a good example of such complementarity.

Perhaps the same argument used to demand structural changes in the church is also valid for the socioeconomic mediations that would make the civilization of poverty possible. Changes only occur from within. In the Germany of 1920s both the Christian and socialist unions justified their choice for an option within the capitalist model, while adopting a critical stance against it, arguing that "it is better to have the head and the finger stuck in the middle of the economy than to be out of it with one's fist raised."[15]

I fully identify myself with Ellacuría's utopia, but I think it is necessary to answer the question of how to approach utopia, how to transform the "no place" into a *topos* that can be historically experienced. This is only possible if ideologized positions are abandoned and if there is openness to the full plurality of possibilities. This is what I have tried to outline in these pages from the socioeconomic perspective. Twenty-five years after the assassination of Ellacuría, new communications media have created new possibilities for overcoming national borders and for inventing new forms of participation and creating an economy. The hope is to move forward with their assistance toward the maximization of social equality and the minimization of external costs.

—TRANSLATED BY J. MATTHEW ASHLEY AND RAÚL ZEGARRA

---

[15] Quoted in Horst Thum, *Wirtschaftsdemokratie und Mitbestimmung: von den Anfängen 1916 bis zum Mitbestimmungsgesetz 1976* (Köln: Bund-Verlag, 1991), 122. Interestingly, the liberation theologians seem to have chosen Marx and the epigones of Marxism, ignoring the developments of Marx's work by social-democratic theorists (for example, Rudolf Hilferding), who considered themselves deeply socialist but concluded that "the structure of capitalism itself is transformable and that rather than breaking it, capitalism can be bent" (Fritz Naphtali, *Wirtschaftsdemokratie: ihr Wesen, Weg und Ziel* [Berlin: Verlagsgesellschaft des Allgemeinen Deutschen Gewerkschaftsbundes, 1928], 12).

15

The Civilization of Poverty and Today's Global Challenges

MARTIN MAIER, SJ

It belongs to the prophets to sense fundamental phenomena indicative of crisis and of historical change before others do. Ignacio Ellacuría was one of these prophets. He was assassinated just a few days after the fall of the Berlin Wall. Yet even before this he had sensed that we stand before an epochal change. He was also aware of the crisis of the regnant model for civilization and of the need for another model, which he named programmatically a civilization of poverty. Jon Sobrino has followed up on this with a "civilization of shared austerity,"[1] which means, on the one hand, that it is necessary to share resources and wealth more equitably, and, on the other, that this will inevitably demand of those in wealthy countries some limitations on their lifestyle.

Not to recognize that we are living in a profound crisis of civilization is to close our eyes to reality: financial crisis, economic crisis, environmental crisis, climate crisis, a crisis of hunger, a demographic crisis, and an energy crisis. A radical change is inevitable. It is enough to look at some recently published German books. Sociologists Harald Welzer and Claus Leggewie have given their analysis of the current crisis in *The End of the World as We Once Knew It* (2009). Environmental economist Niko Paech sketches out the road to a "post-growth economy" with *Liberation from Excess* (2012). According to Paech, our model of well-being cannot be salvaged because it has a chronic dependence on growth. Ralf Fücks accents things differently in his book *Intelligent Growth* (2013), by relating economic growth to the project of a "green revolution." In *No Bread for the World* (2009), Wilfried Bommert takes up not only the question of food but also the question of

---

[1] Jon Sobrino, *Cartas a Ellacuría* (San Salvado: UCA Editores, 2004), 34.

the future capacity of our planet and of a new global order in general. In *The Land Grabbers* (2012) Fred Pearce describes the global battle over land. Philosopher Thomas Pogge insists on the categorical moral imperative to eradicate extreme poverty in *World Poverty and Human Rights* (2008).[2]

The common denominator to all these analyses is the identification of a crisis of systemic unsustainability. At the beginning of the 1930s Walter Benjamin said that "the catastrophe is that things keep going on this way." In a paradoxical formulation of the issue Erich Fried wrote, "Whoever wants the world to continue on the way it is does not want it to continue on." Similarly, Nicholas Stern, former economist of the World Bank, maintains that "in the coming years we have to change the indicators we use to assess future development of the global climate, but also of the economy, of our standard of life, and our energy sources."

In this chapter I relate the Ellacurian model of a civilization of poverty to the global challenges we face today. First I give an overview of this concept with the help of several of Ellacuría's writings. Then I outline the theological bases of a civilization of poverty. Its principle and foundation lie in human rights in their fullest sense—civil, political, economic, social, and cultural—and in the idea of the world's common goods as part of a new model for human civilization. I conclude with a reflection on utopia and hope.

The Concept of a Civilization of Poverty

Ignacio Ellacuría developed his concept of a civilization of poverty in a variety of different articles. By civilization he meant a global order for living together. He used the concept of poverty in various senses, just as the bishops did at Medellín (1968) and as the theology of liberation does. Fundamentally, it has three meanings. The first is poverty in its negative sense as an absence or privation of that which is necessary to live with dignity—poverty that must be eradicated and overcome. The second sense is positive: poverty as spiritual openness to God and as one of the evangelical

---

[2] Harald Welzer and Claus Leggewie, *The End of the World as We Once Knew It: The Climate, the Future, and the Prospects for Democracy* (Frankfurt am Main: S. Fischer Verlag, 2009); Niko Paech, *Liberation from Excess: The Road to a Post-Growth Economy* (Munich: Oekom Verlag, 2012); Ralf Fücks, *Intelligent wachsen: Die grüne Revolution* (Munich: Hanser Verlag, 2013); Wilfried Bommert, *Kein Brot für die Welt: Die Zukunft der Ernährung* (Munich: Riemann, 2009); Fred Pearce, *The Land Grabbers: The New Fight over Who Owns the Earth* (New York: Random House, 2012); Thomas Pogge, *World Poverty and Human Rights*, 2nd ed. (Cambridge, UK: Polity Press, 2008). See also Thomas Pogge, *Poverty, Human Rights, and the Global Order: Framing the Post-2015 Agenda* (Yale University, Global Justice Program, April 26, 2012), available online.—Eds.

counsels of perfection. The third is positive as well: poverty as solidarity with the poor and as a participation in their struggle for justice.

The civilization of poverty bears a certain resemblance to the civilization of love proclaimed from the very outset of his papacy by Pope John Paul II. In his first encyclical, *Redemptor hominis* (1979), the pope recalled that "man cannot live without love" (no. 10), that "Christ the Redeemer 'fully reveals man to himself'" (no. 10), and that "for the Church all ways lead to man" (no. 14), which is precisely why these ways lead the church to build a new humanity. Monsignor Oscar Romero discussed this favorite idea of the Polish pope in his homily of April 12, 1979:

> This civilization of love is no sentimental notion; it is justice and truth . . . A civilization of love that did not demand justice would not be a true civilization; it would not lay down the true relationships between men and women. This is why it is a caricature of love when we want to deal with things with alms that demand justice; when we want to get along with the appearance of beneficence when what is really lacking is social justice.[3]

Ignacio Ellacuría was clearly aware of these nuances of Monseñor Romero when he developed his vision of a civilization of poverty. In my opinion the concept appears for the first time in the article "The Kingdom of God and Unemployment in the Third World," published in 1982 in *Concilium*.[4] In this essay Ellacuría describes a new global order in these words:

> Here we are concerned more profoundly with the creation not only of a new world economic order in which relations of exchange are more just, but of a new civilization which is no longer built on the pillars of hegemony and domination, accumulation and difference, consumption and false well-being, but upon more human and more Christian foundations.[5]

He goes on to give a very broad explanation of this civilization of poverty:

---

[3] *Monsenor Oscar A. Romero: Su Pensamiento,* vol. 6 (San Salvador: Publicaciones del Arzobispado, 2000), 286.

[4] Ignacio Ellacuría, "The Kingdom of God and Unemployment in the Third World," in *Unemployment and the Right to Work,* ed. Jacques Pohier and Dietmar Mieth, English ed. Marcus Lefébure, *Concilium* 1982, no. 10 (New York: Seabury Press, 1982), 91–96. Spanish original in *Escritos Teológicos,* vol. 2 (San Salvador: UCA Editores, 2002), 295–305.

[5] Ellacuría, "The Kingdom of God and Unemployment in the Third World," 94–95.

[The civilization of poverty is one] in which poverty would not be the deprivation of necessary and fundamental needs, a deprivation caused by the historical action of social groups or classes and nations or alliances of nations. Poverty would be a universal state of things, in which the satisfaction of fundamental needs was guaranteed, and also the freedom of personal choice and an atmosphere of personal and communal creativity, which would allow for the appearance of new forms of life and culture, new relations with nature, other people, ourselves, and God.[6]

"The Mission of the Society of Jesus Today," which Ellacuría drew up together with a group of Central American Jesuits to prepare for the 33rd General Congregation of the Society of Jesus in 1983, sets up a connection between Christian salvation and the civilization of poverty. "Seen positively, the message of salvation ought to support putting in motion a civilization more akin to Christian faith, to the reality that human beings experience and to the relationship 'global resources–universal well-being.'"[7] Ellacuría here understands poverty in its positive dimension as an evangelical counsel of perfection: "This poverty is what really gives space to the Spirit, which will never be smothered by the longing to have more than others, by the concupiscent longing of having every kind of superfluity when the greater part of humanity is lacking what is most necessary."[8]

It is in a civilization of poverty that the basic values of the gospel and of the kingdom of God are realized. As he characterizes it in the following, Ellacuría almost anticipates Jon Sobrino's concept of a civilization of shared austerity. "We would thus be dealing with a civilization of poverty that is completely consistent with Jesus' preaching, a civilization of austerity, of sharing, of the communication of goods and of lives, of human creativity as the blossoming of an inward grace."[9]

In a 1987 lecture that he gave in Madrid, Ellacuría identifies the civilization of poverty with the "Jesus' project."[10] It is a question of substituting a system that corresponds to the option for the poor for one that makes its goal the accumulation of capital and of wealth. It is a question of a third way, one that goes beyond the current forms of capitalism and socialism. Capitalism does not know any internal bounds to growth. It is financed by debt and is fed by the boundless exploitation of natural resources.

---

[6] Ibid., 95.

[7] Ellacuría, *Escritos Teológicos*, vol. 4 (San Salvador: UCA Editores, 2002), 240.

[8] Ibid., 4:241.

[9] Ibid.

[10] Ellacuría, *Escritos Teológicos,* vol. 1 (San Salvador: UCA Editores, 2000), 27.

In 1989 Ellacuría took up the model of a civilization of poverty once again in his last major article, "Utopía y profetismo desde América Latina: un ensayo concreto de soteriología histórica."[11] There he relates the eschatological utopia of a new earth to a new economic order, a new social order, a new political order, and a new cultural order, and insists on the dialectical dimension of the contraposition of poverty and wealth:

> The civilization of poverty is so named in contrast to the civilization of wealth, and not because it proposes universal pauperization as an ideal of life. . . . What is here meant to be emphasized is the dialectical relationship between wealth and poverty, and not poverty in itself. In a world sinfully shaped by the dynamism of capital and wealth, it is necessary to stir up a different dynamism that will overcome it salvifically.

The dominant civilization in our world is constructed on the need to accumulate, to grow, and to have more and more. The civilization of poverty means an active negation that supersedes this model, which at the end of the day destroys lives and the environment.

Ellacuría does not, however, paint in black and white; rather, he recognizes that not everything in the current global order is negative. The civilization of wealth has also brought good things, but only to a minority, and in sum, there are more bad things than good. His sad affirmation is still valid: "Never have there been so many people who have lived so poorly." This is why it is not enough to correct the system; rather, its destructive course needs to be reversed.

Taking a more sociological perspective, and inspired by the social encyclicals of John Paul II, Ellacuría, in "Utopia and Propheticism from Latin America" advocates a civilization of work in place of a civilization of capital, and a materialist humanism in place of a materialist economism.

> The civilization of poverty, on the other hand, founded on a materialist humanism transformed by Christian light and inspiration, rejects the accumulation of capital as the engine of history and the possession and enjoyment of wealth as the principle of humanization. It makes the universal satisfaction of basic needs the principle of development and the growth of shared solidarity the foundation of humanization.

---

[11] *Revista Latinoamericana de Teología* 17 (1989): 141–84. References to and quotations from this essay in this chapter refer to the translation by James Brockman, J. Matthew Ashley, and Kevin Burke, "Utopia and Propheticism from Latin America: A Concrete Essay in Historical Soteriology," provided as Chapter 2 of this volume.

Ellacuría makes his own Kant's categorical imperative in order to justify a civilization of poverty over and against the current global order. According to Kant the categorical imperative can be expressed in three forms: (1) "Only act in such a way that you could desire that the maxim of your action would become a universal law;" (2) "Act in such a way that you make use of humanity, both in your own person and in that of any other person, always as an end and never solely as a means;" and (3) "Act as if by means of your maxims you were always a legislator for a universal kingdom of ends."[12] In his critique of the predominant system Ellacuría uses the argument from universality in particular. "But what is most serious is that the offer of humanization and of freedom that the rich nations make to the poor nations is not universalizable, and consequently is not human even for those who offer it." It is not universalizable "since there are not enough material resources on earth today to let all countries achieve the same level of production and consumption." Such a universalization is not possible; it is not even desirable. It does not humanize. It does not fulfill people or make them happy, as is shown, among other indices, by growing levels of drug consumption in the wealthy nations of the world.

In a lecture given in January of 1989 titled "The Latin American Quincentenary: Discovery or Cover-up?" Ellacuría took up the argument of universality from another angle in asserting that the United States is much poorer than Latin America: "Because the United States has a solution; but, in my opinion, it is a bad solution, both for them and for the world in general. In Latin America, on the other hand, there are no solutions, only problems; but as painful as they are, it is better to have problems than to have a bad solution for the future of history."[13] Ellacuría concludes from this that a solution that is not universalizable for the whole world is not a human solution.

In summary, and bringing the concept of the civilization of poverty up to date given the global challenges we face today, we can say that its decisive criteria have to be universality, justice, and sustainability. The economies of the rich nations of the north are not universalizable because of reasons having to do with the environment and because of limits of natural resources. Whatever is not universalizable cannot be defended ethically either, according to Kant's categorical imperative. On a global scale, justice means that all

---

[12] Immanuel Kant, *Groundwork of the Metaphysics of Morals,* ed. Mary Gregor, Cambridge Texts in the History of Philosophy (Cambridge: Cambridge University Press, 1997), 31, 38, 42.

[13] Ignacio Ellacuría, "The Latin American Quincentenary: Discovery or Cover-up?" in *Ignacio Ellacuría: Essays on History, Liberation, and Salvation,* ed. Michael E. Lee, 27–38 (Maryknoll, NY: Orbis Books, 2013), 34. For the original, see Ignacio Ellacuría, "Quinto centenario de America Latina ¿descubrimiento o encutrimiento?" in *Escritos Teológicos,* 2:533.

human beings have the same right to natural resources and to energy and that ecological consequences are distributed equitably or at least in a more or less similar way. Sustainability means administering resources in such a way that the foundations of action are not destroyed and that the rights and interests of future generations are borne in mind.

Theological Bases of the Civilization of Poverty

The theological bases for Ellacuría's concept of the civilization of poverty are his theology of history, his theologal and christological foundations for the option for the poor, and his historical soteriology, at the center of which is the crucified people as the most important sign of the times and as the historical bearer of salvation.

The most important systematic elaboration of his theology of history is found in "The Historicity of Christian Salvation," written in 1984.[14] Its fundamental thesis is that there are not two histories, one a history of God and the other a history of human beings, one a sacred history and the other a profane history. Rather, there is a single history of salvation. This insistence finds its root in the fact that the Word became history.

In this context Ellacuría critiques the false concept of transcendence that understands it as if it were something outside of or beyond that which we apprehend immediately as real. Over against this conception of transcendence he sets it out "as something that transcends *in* and not as something that transcends *away from*; as something that physically impels to *more* but not by taking *out of*; something that pushes forward, but at the same time retains."[15] It follows that "this transcendence . . . presents itself as historical, and history presents itself as transcendent, despite the great difficulty of finding adequate concepts to maintain that indivisible unity without confusion."[16] At the end of this passage we catch sight of the key for thinking about this differentiated unity between transcendence and history: the christological dogma of Chalcedon.

So Ellacuría denies the duality of history, in the sense of a profane history that is taken to be purely natural and another sacred history that is taken to be purely supernatural. "There is only one history, which arises from the loving and salvific will of the only true God, of the Trinitarian God as true God, so that one should do away with the real separation between a profane

---

[14] See Ignacio Ellacuría, "The Historicity of Christian Salvation," trans. Margaret D. Wilde, in Lee, *Ignacio Ellacuría*, 137–68. For the original, see Ignacio Ellacuría, "Historicidad de la salvación cristiana," *Revista Latinoamericana* 1 (1984): 5–45.

[15] Ellacuría, "The Historicity of Christian Salvation," 142.

[16] Ibid., 143.

history and a history of salvation, in spite of the many distinctions that must be made within the history of revelation and of salvation."[17] History is simultaneously the place in which human beings are realized and where the revelation of the absolute is realized. "It is in history that the pole of the divine and the pole of the human converge, where the encounter between human beings and God happens."[18]

But it is not a question of simply identifying God and history, but rather of an elevation of history to God. This is how history becomes the history of salvation without requiring that God intervene from the outside. Between a monist conception of history and a dualist one, Ellacuría understands history as a structural unity "in which the qualitative diversity of its elements is absorbed into the structural unity of its deepest reality. The structural concept preserves the unity of history and the diversity of its different elements without separation."[19] At the heart of the theology of liberation is the God of life, who opposes the idols of death. Jesus is the incarnation of the God of life. It follows from this for the civilization of poverty that "the fundamental principle on which the new order is based continues to be the principle 'that all might have life and have it more abundantly' (Jn 10:10)."[20] The preferential option for the poor is intimately linked with faith in the God of life, insofar as God defends the poor. Because of this, the option for the poor is the "fundamental way to combat the priority of wealth in the shaping of human beings."[21] Overcoming poverty happens by taking the combative road of solidarity that, ultimately, includes giving one's life for others.

Jon Sobrino has stressed that Ellacuría also worked out of the Ignatian tradition of the two standards. This meditation in Ignatius of Loyola's *Spiritual Exercises* affirms that there are two roads that decide between life and salvation and damnation. The three steps on the road to damnation are "riches, honors of the world, and surging pride."[22] What we find, then, is a dialectical counterpoising of three pairs: "poverty in opposition to riches; the second, reproaches or contempt in opposition to honor from the world;

---

[17] Ignacio Ellacuría, "Salvation History," trans. Margaret Wilde, in Lee, *Ignacio Ellacuría*, 169–94, here 189. For the original, see Ignacio Ellacuría, "História de la salvación," *Revista Latinoamericana de Teología* 28 (1993): 3–25.

[18] Ellacuría, "Tesis Sobre Posibilidad, Necesidad y Sentido de una Teología Latinoamericana," in *Escritos Teológicos* 1:288.

[19] Ellacuría, "Salvation History," 189.

[20] Ellacuría, "Utopia and Propheticism from Latin America."

[21] Ibid.

[22] Ignatius of Loyola, *The Spiritual Exercises of Saint Ignatius: A Translation and Commentary*, trans. and ed. George E. Ganss, SJ (St. Louis: Institute of Jesuit Sources, 1992), 66 (no. 142).

and the third, humility in opposition to pride"[23] Ellacuría's counterpoising the civilization of riches and the civilization of poverty corresponds to these pairs.

Human Rights and Global Common Goods

The principle and foundation of a new civilization of poverty or of shared austerity ought to be human rights, not only the civil and political rights defined in the 1948 Universal Declaration of Human Rights, but also economic, social, and cultural rights defined in the 1966 International Covenant on Economic, Social, and Cultural Rights. It is worthwhile recalling Article 1 of the Universal Declaration: "All human beings are born free and equal in dignity and rights. They are endowed with reason and conscience and should act towards one another in a spirit of brotherhood."

From the International Covenant we cite, by way of example, Article 7:

The States Parties to the present Covenant recognize the right of everyone to the enjoyment of just and favourable conditions of work which ensure, in particular: (a) Remuneration which provides all workers, as a minimum, with: (i) Fair wages and equal remuneration for work of equal value without distinction of any kind, in particular women being guaranteed conditions of work not inferior to those enjoyed by men, with equal pay for equal work; (ii) A decent living for themselves and their families in accordance with the provisions of the present Covenant; (b) Safe and healthy working conditions; (c) Equal opportunity for everyone to be promoted in his employment to an appropriate higher level, subject to no considerations other than those of seniority and competence; (d) Rest, leisure and reasonable limitation of working hours and periodic holidays with pay, as well as remuneration for public holidays.

Ellacuría is not advocating universal impoverishment as an ideal for life or for ordering our economies. The civilization of poverty is immediately and directly based on and directed toward the satisfaction of the basic necessities of life for all. These basic needs are appropriate nourishment, a minimal standard of housing, basic healthcare, primary education, sufficient job opportunities, and so on. In this way he takes up the essential elements of economic, social, and cultural rights given in the International Covenant of 1966. In this context Ellacuría speaks of "a fundamental right of every

---

[23] Ibid., 67 (no. 146).

person" and of human dignity. Another fundamental feature of the civilization of poverty is shared solidarity, as opposed to a closed, competitive individualism found in the civilization of wealth.[24]

With his concept of a civilization of poverty Ellacuría also anticipates the idea of global common goods, which has become very important in contemporary debates over development.[25] Global common goods include, among other things, water, earth, forests, the sea, and the atmosphere. Thomas Aquinas already championed the idea that the goods of the earth, as God's creation, belong to all human beings. Ellacuría puts it this way: "The great benefits of nature—the air, the seas and beaches, the mountains and forests, the rivers and lakes, in general all the natural resources for production, use and enjoyment—need not be privately appropriated by any individual person, group, or nation, and in fact they are the grand medium of communication and common living."

Environmental economist Ottmar Edenhofer updates this idea with his proposal for a new politics of climate.[26] We have 12,000 giga-tons of carbon in the ground, in the form of coal, oil, and gas. If we want to keep from increasing the temperature more than two degrees Centigrade, then we cannot put more than 230 giga-tons into the atmosphere. The challenge, then, is not a scarcity of fossil fuels, but the limits to the atmosphere's capacity to absorb carbon dioxide. It follows from this that a major part of the reserves of coal, oil, and gas must stay in the ground. This will mean a drop in profit and wealth for those who own these resources, which, of course, they will probably reject. But it could be justified on the following grounds.

If "created" natural goods ought to be at the common service of humanity, the institution of private ownership of natural resources can be justified only insofar as it serves the common good better than common ownership of natural resources. Private property is, thus, subject to social responsibility. A determination of the rights to use the atmosphere serves the common good if it can be shown that it avoids a dangerous climate change. Thus, a reduction in value of the rights to coal, oil, and gas can be justified in terms of the social responsibility incumbent on private property. Following Catholic social teaching, the universal destination of common goods and the social responsibility of private property have to serve the poor first and foremost.

---

[24] See Ellacuría, "Utopia and Propheticism from Latin America."

[25] See Silke Helfrich und Henrich-Böll-Stiftung, eds., *Commons: für eine neue Politik jenseits von Markt und Staat* (Bielefeld transcript, 2012), the contribution by Edenhofer, Flachsland, and Lorentz in particular (473–78).

[26] See Ottmar Edenhofer, Ch. Flachsland, and K. Lessmann, "Wem gehört die Atmosphäre? Nach dem Klimagipfel in Cancún," *Stimmen der Zeit* (February 2011): 75–88.

Utopia and Hope

One might object to Ellacuría's concept of a civilization of poverty with the argument that, in the first place, it is too general, and, in the second, that it is utopian. There is some warrant for these objections. Nonetheless, on the first point one could respond that Ellacuría's intent is not to propose a technical model for a new world order. But he certainly does want to open up a horizon for hope and perspectives for action. Teilhard de Chardin, SJ, said that "the world belongs to that which offers the greatest hope." Antoine de Saint-Exupéry recommended that "if you want to build a boat, don't start by looking for wood, cutting the boards or sharing out the work; rather, the first thing you have to do is evoke in men and women a longing for the open sea." I am convinced that, in this sense, what we need is a vision to build a new civilization of poverty and of shared austerity.

Moreover, concrete proposals on how to shape a new world order do exist. I want to name only a few of them: (1) opening up markets in the rich nations to exports from poor nations; (2) abolishing agricultural subsidies and aid in the rich nations; (3) a tax on financial transactions along the lines of the Tobin Tax; (4) a tax on the use of global common goods; and (5) the creation of an international humanitarian foundation to combat extreme poverty.

This notwithstanding, scientific knowledge and technical proposals are not by themselves sufficient to generate fundamental changes. Revolutions begin in the mind, in thinking differently. What is needed is a fundamental change of conscience and values, related to a new way of understanding quality of life and the environment, and the integration of ecological factors into the idea of well-being and progress. We can learn from the poor that a more austere standard of life need not mean less happiness. Happiness, after all, cannot be measured by gross domestic product—or individual product, for that matter! Moral philosopher Martha Nussbaum calls for *world citizens*, citizens who have the capacity to understand themselves as part a human family that extends beyond local and regional borders.[27] "It is better to live well than to have a lot" was the motto used by Misereor some years ago for its fasting campaign.[28]

To the second objection one might respond that Ellacuría was consciously utopian by virtue of his faith. He was convinced that the civilization of poverty needed a new person, inspired by the values of the gospel,

---

[27] See Martha C. Nussbaum, *Cultivating Humanity: A Classical Defense of Reform in Liberal Education* (Cambridge, MA: Harvard University Press, 1997).—*Eds.*

[28] Founded in 1958, *Misereor* is the Organization for Development Cooperation of the German Catholic Bishops Conference.—*Eds.*

and in "Utopia and Propheticism from Latin America" he insists that "the new human being . . . will not come into existence until there is an entirely new relationship to deal with the phenomenon of wealth and the problem of unequal accumulation." In Ellacuría's view, the utopia of a new human being includes a new relationship with nature as well. This comes from the cosmic vision of the ancestral peoples of Latin America: "Nature cannot be seen merely as raw material or a place to invest but as a manifestation and gift of God that is to be enjoyed with veneration and not ill-treated with contempt and exploitation." It is possible here to make interesting links with the concept of "living well"—the *sumak kawsay* of the indigenous cultures in central South America.

Realizing a culture of poverty or of shared austerity is a massive challenge. It requires a new social contract among the economy, science, and politics. The complex interpenetration of problems demands an interdisciplinary effort. Environmental damage knows neither national nor confessional borders. In view of its global scope the ecological question has to occupy a primary place in interreligious dialogue. This is what Hans Küng is after with his project of a global ethics and common ethical norms for all of humanity. His motto is "There will not be world peace without peace among the religions; there will not be peace among the religions without dialogue among the religions."[29]

Movements for renewal in the church have almost always been connected with gospel poverty and a living contact with the poor. I am convinced that today as well the path for the renewal of the church has to pass through the poor of the world, and that this is how it will continue to be. Those who put themselves on the side of the poor with any frequency have the happy experience of being given more than they can give. To be precise, among the poor we find human qualities such as hospitality, gratitude, and affection, which have, at the least, been drowned out in societies characterized by abundance. In this vein Jon Sobrino sketches an alternative kind of globalization:

> While a trivialized figure of faith and of life is being globalized today, while consumerism and egoism are being globalized, but also contempt and exclusion for hundreds of millions of people, if not billions of people, it is extremely important to call attention to another kind of globalization: the globalization of truth, of commitment, of love and of tenderness.

---

[29] See Hans Küng, *Global Responsibility: In Search of a New World Ethic* (New York: Crossroad, 1991); see also the website of the Global Ethic Foundation, www.wellethos.org.—*Eds.*

Are there any possible ways to bring this about? Ethologist Konrad Lorenz claims that humanity only learns from medium-scale catastrophes. Ignacio Ellacuría was increasingly optimistic and utopian. Thus in "Utopia and Propheticism from Latin America," which many take to be his final testament, he said:

This new human being is defined in part by active protest and permanent struggle. This new human being seeks to overcome the dominant structural injustice which is considered an evil and a sin because it keeps most of the human population in conditions of inhumane living. This unjust situation is negative, but its negativity propels escape from it as from a catapult. The positive aspect is the dynamic of overcoming. In that overcoming the Spirit breathes in multiple ways, of which the supreme way of all is readiness to give one's life for the rest, whether in tireless daily commitment or in sacrifice unto death violently suffered.

—Translated by J. Matthew Ashley

16

The Crucified People
as a Historical Subject?

Contemporary Relevance of Two Concepts
of Ignacio Ellacuría's Philosophy and Theology

SEBASTIAN PITTL

On the tomb of the six Jesuit martyrs, in the chapel of the UCA in San Salvador, one can read some sentences that express the profound meaning of their life and death with great force: "What does it mean to be a Jesuit today? It means to commit oneself, under the banner of the cross, to the decisive struggle of our time: the struggle for faith, which includes the struggle for justice."[1]

Radical commitment to justice was something that the six Jesuits had in common. But each had his own way of facing this struggle, with his own talents and creativity. Ellacuría assumed it by putting the issue of justice in the center of his theological, philosophical, and political reflections. In his writings he approached the subject from diverse perspectives, with different methods and approaches, but always with the fundamental orientation of contributing to an effective liberating praxis that could eradicate structural injustice and improve the situation of the poor popular majorities.

This essay explores one of the many aspects of the complex theme of justice in Ellacuría's thought, an aspect that, given our current intellectual milieu, so skeptical of any grand narrative and any form of utopian thinking,

---

[1] For the official English translation of this text from the 32nd General Congregation, see *Documents of the 31st and 32nd General Congregations of the Society of Jesus* (St. Louis: The Institute of Jesuit Sources, 1977), 401. Upon the adoption of the famous decree 4, "Our Mission Today," from which these words are taken, the general of the Society of Jesus, Pedro Arrupe, is reported to have said, "We will not commit ourselves to the promotion of justice without paying a price for it."—*Eds.*

I consider to be of great importance: the question of whether there is, after all, a subject capable of promoting and attaining justice in history, and if the answer is yes, the question of the identity of such a subject.

The relevance of the question is obvious for at least two reasons. The first is that if the hope for a more just world cannot account for the identity of the subject in a position to do this justice, such hope is in danger of becoming impotent and even an alienating illusion.[2] The second reason is that to be effective, the struggle for justice must critically analyze who can change the course of an unjust history and how.

From a theological point of view the question also refers to the debated topic of grace. The Protestant tradition has insisted in a particular way on the fact that, in the end, only God justifies and realizes justice. However, unless it wants to become a cynical flight from our historical responsibility this statement, which rightly defends the transcendence of Christian hope, cannot refuse the difficult task of determining which are the subjects and historical processes through which the justice of God is realized or hindered.

In the following pages I offer some clues for answering these questions, starting from two key concepts of Ellacuría's thought: the historical subject and the crucified people. I interpret these concepts and their relationship, asking for their relevance for a liberating Christian praxis in an age that takes for granted the end of history and the end of the grand narratives.[3]

My essay has four parts. In the first I outline some of the problems that every philosophy (and theology) of history with pretensions of universality faces today. In the second part I discuss some of the central aspects of the historical subject in Ellacuría. The third part is devoted to his reflections on the crucified people, and the fourth part summarizes the central question of this study, namely, whether or not (and in what sense) the crucified people can be considered as the liberating subject of history. I conclude with some reflections on the contributions that Ellacuría's ideas on the crucified people might offer to the current philosophical and theological discussions focused on the relevance of religious traditions in today's world.

---

[2] Karl Marx, "Contribution to the Critique of Hegel's Philosophy of Right: Introduction," in *The Marx-Engels Reader*, 2nd ed., ed. Robert Tucker (New York: Norton, 1978), 11–13.

[3] On the end of history, see Francis Fukuyama, *The End of History and the Last Man* (New York: Free Press, 1992); on the critique of metanarratives, see Jean-François Lyotard, *The Postmodern Condition: A Report on Knowledge* (Minneapolis: University of Minnesota Press, 1984).

The Possibility, Necessity, and Meaning of the Question About History and Its Subject

All contemporary philosophy of history encounters the following dilemma: Is it still possible today to speak of *one* history? Is it necessary to speak of *one* history? Given that this universal perspective (which according to Ellacuría does not exclude but rather requires the careful contextualization of all thought) is a fundamental feature of Ellacuría's writings, these questions are critical to any attempt to update his thought in the current intellectual environment.

To speak of *one* history and *one* subject of history today is undoubtedly highly suspicious. A paradigmatic example of the criticisms that in recent decades any project of one philosophy of history has received is the standpoint of the French philosopher Jean-François Lyotard.[4] An exposition of his reservations regarding "grand narratives" will help us to appreciate more clearly the possibilities of a new philosophy of history like the one of Ellacuría.

Lyotard's critique starts from the analysis of the situation of knowledge in post-industrial societies. Lyotard confirms the end of the credibility of the grand narratives, and not just those of Christianity and Marxism, but also of liberalism and the Enlightenment, which until recently pretended, and to some extent succeeded in that effort, to unify the plurality of science and knowledge in a central narrative that guided everything else. But the catastrophic experiences of the twentieth century (Auschwitz, the workers insurrections in Berlin in 1953, Budapest in 1956, the Czech Republic in 1968, and Poland in 1980, the pollution of the environment, the economic crises of 1911 and 1929, and so on) have demolished the credibility of those grand narratives and have exposed their violent and totalitarian face. Lyotard shows how all the grand narratives tend to exclude and oppress anything that does not fit into their logic. In order to ensure their own coherence, they necessarily have to nullify the pluralism of systems of value, beliefs, and the convictions of people with their lifestyles. It is interesting

---

[4] Other major critics of the project of the traditional philosophy of history are Theodor Adorno and Max Horkheimer, *Dialectic of Enlightenment* (New York: Herder and Herder, 1972); Hans Jonas, *The Imperative of Responsibility: Foundations of an Ethics for the Technological Age* (Chicago: University of Chicago Press, 1984); Odo Marquard, *Schwierigkeiten mit der Geschichtsphilosophie: Aufsätze* (Frankfurt am Main: Suhrkamp, 1973); and Karl R. Popper, *The Open Society and Its Enemies* (New York: Harper and Row, 1963).

to note that the continued misery of the people of the nations of the South, according to Lyotard, "[is] perhaps the central point of modernity's failure."[5]

Despite the fundamental critique by Lyotard and others, however, the grand narratives remain, although they are no longer defended by philosophy. Globally, the most influential and effective grand narrative is, without any doubt, the one of capitalist neoliberalism. It is a narrative that, despite the fact that its credibility no longer seems to be as strong as in the 1990s and 2000s, due to the global crisis, still seems to have enough strength to configure world history from China to Chile. Despite its simplicity—free markets themselves guarantee the greatest happiness of humanity and the freer they are the happier humanity will be—it is significant that this narrative has survived the criticism of the grand narratives and has become the only narrative that, in practice, has global discipleship even today.

Apparently, the deterioration of the philosophy of history left a propitious gap for the flourishing of these kinds of pseudo-utopias and universalisms. Most of today's philosophical currents are unable to confront the challenges of an increasingly globalized world—climate change, environmental pollution, scarcity of resources, multinational companies, and so on—and fail to propose alternative models to organize the coexistence of diverse peoples. Either they do not achieve a universal perspective, or they become lost in abstract formalisms. Because of this, perhaps the universal horizon of the classical philosophy of history should be recovered, thus providing interpretations of history that transcend the almost exclusively economic perspective that is currently predominant.

Therefore, is it possible to develop a new philosophy of history without falling into the dangers that Lyotard reproached? I think this is possible if at least two parameters are respected: the plurality of perspectives and the location in the "dark side" of history.

Central to building a philosophy of history that would not be from the very outset a totalitarian and irrational project is the inclusion of a plurality of perspectives. Almost all traditional philosophies of history have been European and therefore have considered history from an exclusively European perspective. Other perspectives, already existing from the times of the conquest and colonization of other continents by European armies, were excluded or ignored, many times on the pretext that they did not represent a mature and universal form of philosophical thought.[6] A new philosophy of

---

[5] Jean-François Lyotard, "Note on the Meaning of 'Post-'" in *The Postmodern Explained: Correspondence, 1982-1985* (Minneapolis: University of Minnesota Press, 1992), 75-80, here 79.

[6] See, for example, Ibn Khaldun, *The Muqaddimah: An Introduction to History* (Princeton, NJ: Princeton University Press, 1974); Felipe Guamán Poma de Ayala, *The First New Chronicle and Good Government: On the History of the World and the Incas*

history with a claim of universality cannot be made just from the perspective of only one place; rather, ideally, it should be a project that is developed in dialogue with all cultures and that includes all perspectives.

The second main point that I consider central is that the new philosophy of history must critically place itself within the "dark side" of history, that is, in the most marginalized contexts. These contexts are those that are more easily forgotten or ignored, but in their silent reality they also indicate what current history excludes and oppresses. This is their hermeneutical value. Every philosophy or theology is born in a particular place, which inevitably shapes its questions, its content, its ways of thinking, and its fundamental orientation. Placing itself in marginalized contexts would help critical reflection free itself from prejudices and the apparent evidence of a privileged context. This will also help it to see history from another perspective and to make it sensitive to the victims produced by every political or economic system.

Ignacio Ellacuría's philosophy of history represents a philosophy that meets these two conditions in an extraordinary manner. His philosophy of history self-consciously places itself in a context that is not only non-European, but also is a clearly disadvantaged one. It is characterized by a fundamental option for the liberation of the exploited and marginalized of this context—the Salvadoran society of the 1960s, 1970s, and 1980s—an option to which all of his intellectual work is subordinated. "What is essential is to dedicate oneself, philosophically, to the most integral and prosperous liberation of our people and our persons; the constitution of philosophy then will follow."[7]

It would be interesting to explore in more detail the relevance of the hermeneutical locus of a philosophy or theology of history in relation to its ideological character. Would not the totalitarian and exclusionary character that Lyotard alleges the philosophy of history of having depend very much on the hermeneutical locus that is chosen for looking at it? For now, I will leave aside this question in order to analyze Ellacuría's ideas on the subject of history.

---

up to 1615, trans. Roland Hamilton (Austin: University of Texas Press, 2009); José Vasconcelos, *La Raza Cósmica: Misión de la raza latinoamericana* (Mexico City: Editorial Porrúa, 2010); Youwei Kang, *Da tong shu: The One-World Philosophy of K`ang Yu-wei* (London: Allen and Unwin, 1958); Jawaharlal Nehru, *Glimpses of World History: Being Further Letters to His Daughter, Written in Prison, and Containing a Rambling Account of History for Young People* (Oxford: Oxford University Press, 1985).

[7] Ignacio Ellacuría, "The Liberating Function of Philosophy," in *Ignacio Ellacuría: Essays on History, Liberation, and Salvation,* ed. Michael E. Lee, 93–119 (Maryknoll, NY: Orbis Books, 2013), 118. Originally published as "Función liberadora de la filosofía," in *Escritos políticos,* vol. 1, 93–121 (San Salvador: UCA Editores, 1991).

The Question of the Subject of History

In the preface to Ellacuría's *Filosofía de la realidad histórica*, the editor, Antonio González, characterizes the text as "an attempt to lay down the foundations of the theoretical concept of *historical praxis* starting from the structural analysis of the elements that compose it, from matter to the person, from the individual to society."[8] In the same sense, *Filosofía de la realidad histórica* may also be taken to be an attempt to lay down the foundations of the theoretical concept of the subject of that praxis, especially considering that Ellacuría wanted to include in his book a chapter devoted to this topic.

It seems clear that the question of the subject of history for Ellacuría involves a detailed study of the elements of historical praxis, because the subject of this praxis cannot be less complex than the praxis itself. Thus, the answer to the question of the character of the subject of historical praxis requires a study of all the moments of the philosophy of historical reality. One is only prepared to indicate to what extent the praxis of this subject is something natural, social or historical, and what these terms mean, when they are applied to such a subject. However, demonstrating in detail how materiality, sociality, personality, historicity, and so on, condition the reality of the subject of historical praxis exceeds the scope of this essay. Therefore, I limit myself to making some brief indications, based on "The Object of Philosophy," an essay that Ellacuría considered a good introduction to his philosophy of historical reality.[9]

In this text Ellacuría details what historical reality means in five theses that present historical reality as a physical, structural, dynamic, differentiated, and ascending unity in a process of permanent realization, a unity that is supremely manifested in historical praxis. I outline briefly what each of these aspects means for comprehending the subject of historical praxis in Ellacuría's thought, relating them to what has been discussed so far.

The emphasis that Ellacuría puts on the unity of historical reality is alien to a totalitarian theoretical project, which aims to nullify all the differences and make the world a uniform reality. Unlike Lyotard, Ellacuría does not think that conceptualizing everything leads to the cancellation of differences; rather, it presupposes them. The totality of reality is not for him something closed; rather, it is open both to the new things that occur in the historical process, as well as to what transcends reality, as intramundane reality. Thus, the true antithesis of the accentuation of the physical

---

[8] Antonio González, "Prólogo," in Ignacio Ellacuría, *Filosofía de la realidad histórica* (San Salvador: UCA Editores, 1990), 10.

[9] Ibid., 11.

unity of historical reality would not be the defense of the plurality and diversity of reality, but rather the atomistic conception of it. According to Ellacuría, this atomistic conception not only fails to acknowledge the true reality of things, but also has serious practical consequences. Only starting from the unity of reality can philosophy achieve an approach that does not consider the elements of reality—nature, individuals, society, culture, history, and so forth—separately and, consequently, abstractly, but realizes their rich interdependence. The tendency of some postmodern thinkers to fragment the world in order to rescue differences has the subsequent danger of ignoring these interdependencies and thus loses view of things in their ultimate realization.

The second aspect of reality is rooted in its physical character. Without going into details, we can say that Ellacuría, like his philosophical teacher, Zubiri, assumes some motifs of historical materialism, although without falling into a naive and reductionist materialism. The materiality of things is for him the beginning of its presence-character [*presencialidad*] in the world. No reality can have presence without somehow becoming material. For this reason, Ellacuría states that it would be a mistake to reduce the reality of history to a pure history of ideas or an alleged spirit and ignore the concrete corporeality of humans. Praxis, too, an element that we are interested in, is drastically reduced if not linked to a material change of reality. Ellacuría insightfully warns that limiting oneself simply to change the interpretation of reality can easily become an elusive praxis that changes interpretations in order to avoid having to change reality.[10]

Besides being a physical reality, historical reality is also a dynamic reality. Its dynamic character is appropriate for historical reality of its very nature. Therefore, the classical metaphysical question about the cause of the movement is false. The fundamental dynamism of reality consists in a giving of itself [*dar-de-sí*], in which strictly new forms of reality arise. The dynamicity of reality is for Ellacuría as transcendental as reality itself, so any static conception of it "is not just an escape from reality, but a reaction against it, a true counter-realization." A liberating praxis must take this very much into account. It is not the transformation of a static reality, but the transformation of the complex fabric of real dynamisms: "Praxis will

---

[10] "To believe that by changing one's interpretations of things, one has changed the things themselves or at least one's depth of consciousness of his or her embeddedness in the world, represents a grave epistemological error and a profound ethical breakdown. Interpretive changes of meaning and even the purely objective analyses of a reality in its social-historical features do not constitute real changes. They are not even real changes of their proper meaning but most of the time changes in their formulations." See "Laying the Philosophical Foundations of Latin American Theological Method," 64–91, in Lee, *Ignacio Ellacuría*, 81.

have to be understood from this essential connection not only of reality, but of real dynamisms."[11]

Basically, the dynamism of historical reality can be understood as a process of realization in which reality itself is realized, giving of itself new forms of reality that transcend and surpass the ones that already exist. This process is constitutively open in such a way that, according to Ellacuría, we will not know what reality is until it has given all it can give of itself. In order to understand this process correctly, it is necessary to analyze in more detail how new forms of reality arise from existing ones. We have already mentioned that in the process of realization something new in the strictest sense is given, which should not be ignored or reduced to a mere variation of what already exists. But this does not mean that the forms of existing reality are nullified by the new forms. Quite the contrary. A careful analysis shows that new forms can only arise from the lower forms, and that these, in turn, are present in the new ones. History, for example, can only arise on the basis of nature. Natural elements are present in the historical process, although history is not reduced to them but transforms them in multiple ways. The highest reality, where the process of realization reaches its peak, is what Ellacuría calls historical reality. In it, all other dynamisms of reality are present, from those of nature to those of society, which are oriented to and, at the same time, surpassed by historical praxis. Thus, historical praxis has, in Ellacuría's thought, a very special metaphysical density. It is the place of maximum openness of reality, the place of maximum novelty, and the place where the whole of reality gets its maximum concretion. From the epistemological perspective it is also "the place that gives truth."[12]

Given what has been explained, it is clear that historical practice is a highly complex reality that entails natural, personal, social, and historical elements, and it is at the same time an objective and subjective reality. It is, in the end, the dynamism of all reality. Therefore, the question of whether there is a subject of this praxis and the question of in what sense we can speak of it are not easy to answer.

In Ellacuría's class notes and diagrams there is one on the subject of history in which Ellacuría distinguishes between being the subject *of* history and being the subject confronting history.[13] There he criticizes the attempt to identify *one* subject of history. He admits that there are historical times in which certain peoples or groups of people come to have such influence

---

[11] Ellacuría, *La Filosofía de la realidad historica*, 594.

[12] See Victor Flores García, *El lugar que da verdad: La filosofía de la realidad histórica de Ignacio Ellacuría* (México City: Universidad Iberoamericana, 1997).

[13] See Ignacio Ellacuría, "El sujeto de la historia," in *Cursos Universitarios* (San Salvador: UCA Editores, 2009), 281–326.

over a particular people that it seems legitimate to speak of them, in some way, as subjects of the history of a particular people or country. But he adds that, for the moment, "there is no verifiable empirical subject to which can be attributed the character of being the subject of all these histories,"[14] and, therefore, of History (written with a capital letter).

Nevertheless, this corroboration does not mean necessarily abandoning the universal perspective. This is because, although the existence of one subject of history as a whole cannot be verified, Ellacuría thinks that it is possible to be a "subject confronting history from out of a particular history." This means that one can rationally deal with the whole of reality and try to "introduce into the historical process dynamisms that are not pure mechanical reflection . . . of the given stimuli."[15] The fact that for the time being no human subject or group can claim to be the subject of history does not mean that it is not possible to exert some influence over history.

This is not to deny either the possibility that someday something like a subject of History might appear. Ellacuría cautions that this does not lead necessarily to a denial of the subjectivity of individuals. It is at least conceivable that one day humanity as a whole will become a subject that rationally rules the course of its own history. Ellacuría does not give specific clues about this, but we can imagine that this rational scheme of history would resemble a democratic world government with power to curb abuses and excesses of the current neoliberal globalization, a government that, within a legal framework, allows people to regain their ability for self-determination, an idea that already appears in Kant.[16]

The Crucified People

After this journey, certainly very fragmentary, through some of Ellacuría's ideas about the philosophy of historical reality and his thoughts on the subject of history, I turn now to another major theme of this essay: the crucified people.

Before discussing the relationships that might exist between the concept of subject of history in Ellacuría and his theological reflections on the crucified people, I summarize briefly how he understands the crucified people. I will focus on the article "The Crucified People: An Essay in Historical

---

[14] Ibid., 324.

[15] Ibid., 325.

[16] See Immanuel Kant, "To Perpetual Peace: A Philosophical Sketch," in *Perpetual Peace, and Other Essays on Politics, History and Moral Practice*, trans. Ted Humphrey (Indianapolis: Hackett Publishing Company, 1983), 107–43.

Soteriology," the most important of Ellacuría's texts on this theme.[17] So now we enter the realm of Ellacuría's theology.

The text begins by noting that the people of God is not, primarily, a theoretical concept but the expression of a reality, namely, "the existence of a vast portion of humankind, which is literally and historically crucified by natural oppressions and especially by historical and personal oppressions."[18] It is certainly true that describing much of humanity as "crucified" is not a neutral description, something impossible, according to the theory of intelligence of Zubiri and Ellacuría, but rather something born from Ellacuría's Christian perspective. It is the experience of the popular majorities and Christians engaged in the struggle for liberation, trying to interpret the reality of a suffering people from their faith.

But faith not only helps to interpret the reality of the suffering people, but it also sheds new light on the texts of scripture in a way that rediscovers in them aspects that were obscured for centuries by an individualistic and overly pious reading. In the same way that interpreting the reality of the suffering people starting from the accounts of Jesus' passion can sensitize us to perceive the hidden presence of the saving reality of Jesus in this people, a reading of the passion narratives starting from the reality of the people can help to discover their social and political dimension, as well as the scandal that their proclamation of a condemned and crucified savior must have inspired in the first Christians' contemporaries.

Ellacuría uses the suffering servant songs to explain the intimate connection of the fate of the suffering peoples of the Third World to the fate of Jesus of Nazareth, manifest in the religious experience of the Latin American Christian people. The first Christians used these songs to interpret and understand what happened to Jesus. Ellacuría highlights with awe how they also apply to the reality of the suffering people. The most characteristic features are these: (1) the servant is chosen by God to bring right and justice to the nations. His mission has a universal character, given that it extends as far as the "islands"; (2) the mission of bringing justice is concretized as the liberation of the oppressed and imprisoned; it points to historical realities but is not limited to a political mission; (3) the mission of the servant of Yahweh is linked to the building of a new earth and a new people—the people will come out of their poverty, oppression, and obscurity into a new state of abundance, freedom, and light; (4) God chooses in the servant a figure whose current situation differs drastically from the importance and

---

[17]   Ignacio Ellacuría, "The Crucified People: An Essay in Historical Soteriology," in Lee, *Ignacio Ellacuría*, 195–224. Originally published as Ignacio Ellacuría, "El pueblo crucificado: Ensayo de soteriología histórica," in *Escritos Teológicos*, vol. 2 (San Salvador: UCA Editores, 2000), 137–70.

[18]   Ibid., 196.

greatness of his mission. People are frightened of him because he is a broken figure, a man of sorrows, who seems to have been condemned by God and is seen as a sinner; (5) despite appearances, the servant is innocent, loaded with sins he did not commit, and thus he justifies many; (6) the servant freely accepts his role and sacrifices himself to save others; (7) God accepts this sacrifice and even loads on the servant the crimes of others. Thus God attributes a salvific value to an act of "absolute historical injustice";[19] (8) the servant dies but eventually triumphs. He will see his offspring, he shall prolong his years, and he will see the light and be satisfied with knowledge.

It is much easier to see the parallel between the fate of the servant of Yahweh and the reality of the suffering people when it comes to the suffering, the contempt of the powerful, and their having to bear the consequences of the sins of others, than to accept that this people, apparently totally powerless, has as its mission saving and liberating all of humanity. However, as Ellacuría recalls, the early Christian proclamation of a crucified Messiah was also a scandal for both Jews and Greeks of that time. To retrieve this fundamental scandal of Christian proclamation and to interpret it in the light of the story of the last judgment in Matthew 25, in which the Son of man is explicitly identified with the hungry, the thirsty, the imprisoned, the naked, the sick, and the strangers, raises the question of whether, ultimately, and despite all appearances, the crucified people, in whom Christ's saving work continues today, is not, in some way, the subject through which the history of salvation is realized today.

The Crucified People as the Subject of History?

Now, if it seems that, at least in a certain sense, the crucified people are the subject of the history of salvation, it should be asked whether the crucified people can also be considered as the subject of history. In the end, this is a question for the relationship between salvation history and profane history. What is the relationship between them? Are they two completely parallel histories that in the best of the cases occasionally cross each other? Or is there an intrinsic relationship between them, so that they cannot be separated?

The relationship between salvation history and profane history is, for Ellacuría, the fundamental question of liberation theology. In "The Historicity of Christian Salvation" he points out that history has to be radically considered as only one history.[20] The real opposition is not between the

---

[19] Ibid., 218.

[20] See Ignacio Ellacuría, "The Historicity of Christian Salvation," in Lee, *Ignacio Ellacuría*, 137–68.

history of salvation, on the one hand, and profane history, on the other, but between the history of good (the history of grace) and the history of evil (the history of sin). Christian transcendence, therefore, must be interpreted as something that "transcends *in* and not as something that transcends *away from*; as something that physically impels to *more* but not by taking *out of*; as something that pushes forward but at the same time retains."[21] It is a transcendence that needs to be historicized without being reduced to what is purely historical.

This conception of the historicity and transcendence of Christian salvation has serious consequences for the question of the how Ellacuría's theological reflection on the crucified people relates to his philosophical reflection on the subject of history.

Given the necessary historicity of the contents of Christianity, the crucified people also needs be embodied in some way in history. We have already seen that it is easy to find in the suffering peoples some features of the servant of Yahweh, such as suffering, contempt, and so on. Nonetheless, if the proclamation of the crucified people not only as suffering but also as savior of the world intends to be more than a purely eschatological statement, then its role as savior of humanity must be historicized in some way; if the crucified people is to be considered as a truly salvific reality, then it has to take on in some way the reality of being the historical subject of liberation.

How is this possible, without the crucified people losing its transcendent character and without falling into the trap of a fundamentalist theologization of politics? Ellacuría is aware of this twofold danger and tries to avoid it. To do this he establishes the criteria to be met by anyone who claims to be the historical continuation of the servant of Yahweh, and he distinguishes the aspect by which the crucified people brings salvation to the world from the aspect by which it realizes that salvation historically and politically. He takes the criteria from the servant songs:

> Any present-day approximation of the Servant will have to be crucified for the sins of the world; it will have to become what the worldly have cast out, and its appearance will not be human precisely because it has been dehumanized. It will have to have a high degree of universality, since it will have to be a figure that redeems the whole world. It will have to suffer this utter dehumanization, not for its sins, but because it bears the sins of others. It will have to be cast out and despised precisely as savior of the world, in such a way that this world does not accept it as its savior but, on the contrary, judges it as the most

---

[21]   Ibid., 142.

complete expression of what must be avoided and even condemned. Finally, there must be a connection between its passion and the working out of the Reign of God.[22]

The criteria are, on the one hand, too broad to identify definitively a person or human group with the servant of Yahweh; the "suffering servant of Yahweh is [rather] anyone unjustly crucified for the sins of human beings, because all crucified people form a single unity." But the criteria, on the other hand, are sufficiently specific as to claim that the so-called Third World, the oppressed classes, and those struggling for justice are more in this line than the First World and the rich and oppressing classes.[23]

In addition to establishing criteria, Ellacuría warns that the historical figure of the servant of Yahweh should not be identified with any particular organization of the crucified people, whose purpose is political power. Obviously, the salvation that the servant of Yahweh brings must be historicized in order to have historical objectivity, but we must distinguish carefully between these objectifications and that aspect by which the crucified people is the historical continuation of Jesus Christ. The reality of the crucified people, according to Ellacuría, ultimately transcends every historical concretion that may take place of itself, and thus remains in a certain indeterminacy. The crucified people cannot be identified with a particular historical group, class, nation, or with the church. What is appropriate to the crucified people, in this sense, is an especially critical function vis-à-vis every philosophy or theology of history that identifies in advance a real subject of the historical process.

By Way of Summary:
The Contribution of Ellacuría's Philosophy
and Theology of History

A few years back in Germany philosopher and sociologist Jürgen Habermas questioned the capacity of practical reason to "waken and keep awake in the profane souls awareness of a wounded solidarity throughout the world, the awareness of what is missing, of what is crying to heaven."[24] Because of this practical reason cannot ignore the moral potential preserved by religious traditions, although it would have to be translated into a secular language.

---

[22] Ellacuría, "The Crucified People," 221–22.

[23] Ibid. 222.

[24] Jürgen Habermas, "An Awareness of What Is Missing," in Jürgen Habermas et al., *An Awareness of What Is Missing: Faith and Reason in a Post-Secular Age*, 15–23 (Malden, MA: Polity Press, 2010), 19.

I will not go into the question of whether Habermas adequately describes the role of religious traditions in "post-secular" societies. Rather, I want to emphasize, as a conclusion, that Ellacuría's concept of the crucified people can be considered to be a very interesting example of what religious traditions can contribute to the globalized world. It is a striking example of how a religious worldview can awaken, develop, and maintain the "awareness of a wounded solidarity throughout the world," an awareness about which Habermas is so worried. Ellacuría's texts on the crucified people represent an efficacious effort to give voice to the millions of people worldwide deprived of their dignity and of the possibility of a humane life, and to promote a praxis that fully liberates such persons and peoples, regardless of their nationality, ethnicity, gender, or religious denominations.

However, when the question of the contribution of religious traditions to a liberating praxis arises, we must keep in mind that the political dimension of religion has always been ambiguous. It is enough to recall the political consequences of the different kinds of fundamentalism. The reflections of Ellacuría avoid this danger because, without falling into ahistorical escapism, they affirm the transcendence of the crucified people, which refuses any definitive identification. Ellacuría pays close attention to the possible ideologizations of Christian faith and carefully distinguishes it from any politics of power. Thus, his reflections on the crucified people can be of great value to determine what a Christian contribution can be to a world that sometimes seems no longer able to know what resources it can use to build a better future for all.

—Translated by Raúl Zegarra and J. Matthew Ashley

Conclusion

Ignacio Ellacuría

Spirituality, Discernment, and Good News

J. Matthew Ashley

In one of the few essays on spirituality published during his lifetime, Ignacio Ellacuría led off with a list of elements or dimensions of the human, enumerated in pairs, that need to be kept in play in giving an adequate account of spirituality:

> Thus, the spiritual and the material; the individual and the social; the personal and the structural; the transcendent and the immanent; the Christian and the human; the supernatural and the natural; conversion and transformation; contemplation and action; work and prayer; faith and justice, etc.: none of these are identified one with the other in such a way that by cultivating one of the extremes the other is ipso facto cultivated, such that it is nothing but a reflection or accidental supplement. But neither are they separated one from the other in such a way that they could be cultivated without an intrinsic, essential, and efficacious mutual determination. Whatever separations it might be possible to make in the abstract, in concrete historical reality, just as God has effected it, these dimensions present themselves in unity and in mutual dependence.
>
> This differentiated unity is not easy to maintain. It is not easy to maintain in the relative and requisite autonomy of the different dimensions or in their proportionate and appropriate connection.[1]

---

[1] Ignacio Ellacuría, "Christian Spirituality," in *Ignacio Ellacuría: Essays on History, Liberation, and Salvation,* ed. Michael E. Lee, 275–84 (Maryknoll, NY: Orbis Books, 2013), 276.

The essays in this book amply demonstrate how seriously Ellacuría took the challenge raised in this passage. He endeavored to describe the human being, constituted in and constitutive of historical reality, with all the complexity this entailed, and to keep this in view, particularly in its social and historical dimension, in all that he did. In this he grappled with the complex task of keeping these different dualities (and others) in creative relationship, striving to avoid both sterile juxtaposition and destructive counterposition. He took the tools he learned from thinkers such as Karl Rahner and Xavier Zubiri to provide a philosophical-theological frame that would facilitate and structure this task, and patiently teased out the implications of one or another side of each pairing, without losing sight of the other, and without losing sight of the other pairs. This is evident in his treatments of the church, of the university, of economic structures, and, finally, of Christian spirituality.

I conclude with a consideration of spirituality, chastened by Ellacuría's warnings, but not because I take it to be one of the most common themes taken up in Ellacuría's writing. It is not, although it appears frequently albeit briefly. Nor do I contend that it provides the most direct and immediately comprehensive access to the whole that is his work. The other essays in this book provide avenues that are at least equally useful, and perhaps more so. I do, however, take it to be an indispensable avenue, and this for a reason that Gustavo Gutiérrez has persuasively argued, drawing on one of his favorite theologians, Marie-Dominique Chenu, whom he quotes in his own book on Christian spirituality:

> The fact is that in the final analysis theological systems are simply the expressions of spirituality. It is this that that gives them their interest and grandeur. . . . The grandeur and truth of Bonaventuran and Scotist Augustinianism is entirely derived from the spiritual experience of St. Francis, which inspired his sons; the grandeur and truth of Molinism derives from the spiritual experience of the *Exercises* of St. Ignatius. One does not get to the heart of a system via the logical coherence of its structure or the plausibility of its conclusions. One gets to that heart by grasping it in its origins via that fundamental intuition that serves to guide a spiritual life and provides the intellectual regimen proper to that life.[2]

---

[2] Gustavo Gutiérrez, *We Drink from Our Own Wells* (Maryknoll, NY: Orbis Books, 1984), 147n2. The quoted passage is from Chenu's small, but at the time controversial, book on the proper study of Thomas Aquinas: Marie-Dominique Chenu, *Le Saulchoir: Une école de théologie* (Etiolles, France: Le Saulchoir, 1937).

As Jon Sobrino reminds us in Chapter 3, "It is not easy—in the end, it is not possible—to penetrate adequately into this ultimate dimension of another person." How can we find at least an initial access? First by remembering that, as Sobrino has often insisted, and as Rodolfo Cardenal points out in Chapter 9, Ellacuría's theology does not *start* from books, however much it subsequently grapples with books. It starts with his experience of people; his is a theology "that springs from life itself." Ellacuría himself contends that the two great sources for an incarnate spirituality are scripture and "the word of God in the living reality of history and in the life of men and women filled with the spirit."[3] As Jon Sobrino suggests, paramount in this theology and spirituality that spring from life were encounters with other persons, such as Karl Rahner, Pedro Arrupe, and most of all, Monseñor Romero.[4] His relationships with them, how he thought about them, remembered, and celebrated their lives provide clues for our search. But he also himself experienced, lived, and reflected Ignatian spirituality. He wrote about it, lectured on it, and as Robert Lassalle-Klein has documented, utilized it to structure the deliberations of the Central American Jesuits concerning how to configure or reconfigure their institutions to correspond to the call of Medellín.[5] So we have some texts as well that can help us come a little closer to this "fundamental intuition" that served to guide his spiritual life and provided "the intellectual regimen proper to that life."

Space prohibits the fuller task of taking us any great distance along this path. Instead I hope to shed a little light on Ellacuría's understanding and practice of Ignatian spirituality—as a scholar, a public intellectual, an academic, an administrator, and so on—drawing on the thought of two other theologians who have reflected on the importance of spirituality for understanding both the challenges and the opportunities confronting modern Christian theology and practice: Karl Rahner and Jon Sobrino. Of course, in using them to shed light on Ellacuría's thought on this topic, the light will be reflected back to give us a more profound access to these interlocutors and to a richer account of Christian spirituality.

---

[3] Ellacuría, "Christian Spirituality," 282.

[4] See also Kevin Burke, *The Ground Beneath the Cross: The Theology of Ignacio Ellacuría* (Washington, DC: Georgetown University Press, 2000), 15–32.

[5] For Ellacuría's lecture notes on the *Spiritual Exercises*, see "A Latin American Reading of the Spiritual Exercises of Saint Ignatius," trans. J. Matthew Ashley, *Spiritus: A Journal of Christian Spirituality*, 10, no. 2 (Fall 2010): 205–42. For his presentations to the Jesuits of Central America, grounded in the spirituality of the *Exercises*, see Robert Lassalle-Klein, *Blood and Ink: Ignacio Ellacuría, Jon Sobrino, and the Jesuit Martyrs of Central America* (Maryknoll, NY: Orbis Books, 2014), 32–52.

Karl Rahner, the "More" of History, and Contemplation in Action for Justice

Toward the end of his life Karl Rahner wrote a short essay entitled "Plea for a Nameless Virtue."[6] This virtue maps out an alternative to a skeptical relativism that, aware of the impossibility of giving an exhaustive theoretical justification in advance for making a decisive choice in the midst of the host of complex and pressing problems facing us today, takes refuge in a resigned withdrawal from any choice or makes it "arbitrarily, according to whim, origin, and so on."[7] On the other hand, it seeks to avoid an ideological fanaticism on the part of those who act "as though the justification for their own standpoint were completely clear and only ignorance and ill will could prevent people from recognizing this."[8] In between is the response facilitated by the nameless virtue, one that engages with all seriousness in the most rigorous analysis and reflection before making a decision, but

> nonetheless does not demand more of the reflection than it can provide, which honestly admits its problematic nature and despite this does not stand in the way of the courage for a serene and brave decision, [and is a decision that] is the hallmark of the proper self-understanding of a person who is neither the god of an absolute and universal certainty and clarity nor the creature of a sterile arbitrariness which views everything as equally right and equally wrong, a person who has human qualities that command respect even if these qualities do not have the effulgence of the divine or the transparence of the obvious.[9]

He concludes by averring that it is in part our inability adequately to grasp and authentically to live the complex unity-in-difference of theory and praxis that makes us unable to name precisely or value appropriately this

---

[6] Karl Rahner, *Theological Investigations*, vol. 23 (New York: Crossroad, 1992), 33–37. The title of the original essay is telling: "Die Spannung austragen zwischen Leben und Denken" [dealing with the tension between life and thought], in *Mut zur Tugend: Von der Fähigkeit menschlicher zu leben,* ed. Karl Rahner and Bernard Welte (Freiburg: Herder, 1980), 11–18.

[7] Rahner, "Plea for a Nameless Virtue," 35.

[8] Ibid.

[9] Ibid., 36–37. One thinks here of Rahner himself, who, at the time of this writing, wrote about "faith in a wintry season," or Ellacuría's point that "Rahner carried his doubts about his faith elegantly," a point that Sobrino turns to describe Ellacuría as well.

"nameless virtue." Nonetheless, "it ought to be practiced. Today, especially, when one could get the impression that the majority of humankind is divided into weary relativists and obstinate fanatics."[10]

As it happens, Rahner had already broached this problem in an earlier essay and provided a solution: not a conceptual one, but one that relied on the resources of Ignatian spirituality.[11] Reflecting on the Ignatian motto *Ad maiorem Dei gloriam*, Rahner argues that it responds to a uniquely modern (that is, post-Enlightenment) paradox that, on the one hand, we experience ourselves as masters of our world in an unprecedented way, by virtue of scientific and technological advances, but we are also, on the other, deeply aware of the degree to which contingent and uncontrollable factors influence the future that we are trying control, which do not become less unmanageable with the intervention of our own technological power.[12] We can make decisions (and must make them, to the extent that not to decide is itself a decision) that will have future consequences for us and for our children that we cannot fully understand, and we make these decisions against an almost infinite horizon of possibilities that we could make a reality, given sufficient will and the application of our scientific and technological power. This is, according to Rahner, a uniquely modern situation. He thus arrives, by a different route, and twenty-one years earlier, at the dilemma for which skeptical relativism and ideological fanaticism proffer (false) alternatives. Yet, on Rahner's reading, Ignatius provides an innovative and very "modern" response to this dilemma:

> For Ignatius there really is something like an existential and ethical attitude on man's part, which precisely implies an openness to that which lies beyond the data which can be calculated and deduced on the rational, abstract and essentialist plane. And this existential and

---

[10] Ibid., 37.

[11] Karl Rahner, "Being Open to God as Ever Greater," *Theological Investigations,* vol. 7 (London: Darton, Longman and Todd, 1971), 25–46. This essay originated in a talk that Rahner gave at a meeting of Jesuits at Rottmannshöhe during Holy Week of 1959. While I am not aware that Ellacuría was there, it is true that he had begun studies in Innsbruck (where Rahner was on the faculty) in 1958, and that he named Rahner as the only Innsbruck theologian who had a lasting impact on him. Whether or not he was at this specific lecture, it is at least plausible to assume that Ellacuría's thinking about the *Exercises* was influenced by Rahner, since the latter often presented on the *Exercises*, in Innsbruck and elsewhere, due to the many symposia and collections that commemorated the recent (1956) four-hundredth anniversary of Ignatius's death.

[12] One need think only of the threat posed by global climate change, outlined by Martin Maier above, to confirm this, and to confirm the prevalence of skeptical relativists and ideological fanatics in this and other debates over our global common good.

ethical attitude finds expression both in his *Exercises* and in the saying "ad majorem Dei gloriam."[13]

The key lies in understanding the crucial mediating term: the God who both "disposes of us" by placing us in a particular historical situation, with all of its imponderables, calls us both to accept, indeed to embrace that situation (thus the importance of Ignatian indifference), *and* to "dispose of" it, to transform it by planning and working for a future that gives greater glory to God, a future that is thereby the one in which we find our deepest fulfillment. But this is not a call and a disposition to be understood, but to be experienced and practiced—which is precisely the point of the *Spiritual Exercises*, as Rahner interprets it. For Rahner, the *Exercises* accept—indeed, *presume*—a future characterized by a disorienting openness, incalculability, and uncontrollability, which is, nonetheless, a future in and about which we are called to make a binding and decisive commitment.

> In other words in the concept of 'major Dei gloria' the explicit, reflexive conscious planning of life really is included, even though man is, and necessarily must be, the one who submits to being disposed of, who accepts, and in a certain sense, who is not capable of planning. It is in this explicit, conscious and constant awareness of man's own further openness to the possibility of having conditions imposed upon him either by God or by man himself that what is definitive in the [most crucial] element involved in the 'major Dei gloria' really consists. In this saying we must realize what it means when it says 'ad majorem Dei gloriam.' The 'major Dei gloria' is not so much that which is actually done, but rather that towards which our acts are orientated in order, as it were, that they may attain to it as their ultimate goal.[14]

With this orientation point, other elements of Ignatian spirituality fall into place. Indifference is central because it keeps one free of a disordered attachment to any one particular good in the present, for the sake of finding in that present (and not outside of it) precisely the dynamism that leads toward this greater glory and so orient our actions toward "their ultimate goal." Discernment becomes that process that, not rejecting or ignoring rational analysis and prudential planning, allows them to nourish

---

[13] Karl Rahner, "Being Open to God as Ever Greater," 43.

[14] Ibid., 37–38. This can be read as a Rahnerian "translation" of the point made at the outset of the *Exercises* in its "Principle and Foundation." See *The Spiritual Exercises of Saint Ignatius: A Translation and Commentary*, trans. and ed. George Ganss, SJ (St. Louis: Institute of Jesuit Sources, 1992), no. 23, p. 32.

a decision that cannot proceed on grounds that they provide alone (and hence serves and completes the "nameless virtue" of which Rahner wrote later). One finds God in all things because, while no one of those things is in itself God, any one of them can be the occasion for one to bring about a greater glory of God that is not one's own work separate from God, but a work in which one is caught up in, and in some sense experiences, the very creative-redemptive-sanctificatory work and presence of God that is the deepest foundation of all things. That is, one is simultaneously contemplative (profoundly united with God) and active (at work in the world).

Ellacuría understood this insight with great clarity. For him, the Ignatian contemplative in action is one for whom "contemplation of God *in* all things" is always and necessarily giving way to "contemplation in acting among and with all things," in which, simultaneously and in the same action, "God becomes present to the person acting, and the person makes God present [for others] and becomes present [himself or herself] to a God acting."[15] For Ellacuría, too, all of this is oriented toward action *ad majorem Dei Gloriam*, but it is a glory discerned and realized in history. This is not itself a step outside of Rahner's approach, although it does press it forward by bringing Rahner's approach to Ignatian spirituality, just sketched, together with his thesis on the unity of profane and salvation history. Indeed, Rahner is typically adduced as one who introduced or reinforced in Ellacuría the conviction that there are not two histories, profane and sacred, humanity, *simpliciter*, and the history of God saving humanity.[16] The corollary of this, as many authors of this book note, is that we can only speak of God by also speaking of history—that is, of the reigning of God in history. This is, perhaps, the feature of an adequate philosophical and theological system on which Ellacuría insists most frequently, insistently and pervasively, as can be seen from virtually every essay in this book.

To pull these points together, then, the greater glory of God, which is the expansive, indeed unlimited, horizon that orients our actions, is a glory of God *in* history. The "greater" of God's glory is discerned only by catching sight of a "greater" in history. This greater glory can only be, as Romero famously remarked, the poor person fully alive, and thus contemplation in

---

[15] Ellacuría, "A Latin American Reading of the Spiritual Exercises of Saint Ignatius," 239. See also his reflections on the ideal of "contemplation in action" in *Fe y Justicia* (Bilbao: Desclée, 1999), 207–16.

[16] See Gustavo Gutiérrez, "The Cost of Discipleship," chap. 4 in this volume. For further reflection on Rahner's impact on Ellacuría, see Martin Maier, SJ, "Karl Rahner: Ignacio Ellacuría's Teacher," in *Love That Produces Hope: The Thought of Ignacio Ellacuría*, ed. Kevin F. Burke and Robert Lassalle-Klein, 128–43 (Collegeville, MN: Liturgical Press, 2006).

action can only be contemplation in action for justice, which seeks precisely this "more" in history.

Ignacio Ellacuría was certainly someone who planned and analyzed before acting, as is clear from the scope and depth of his writings. He demanded of others that they do the same and committed himself to the university as a social instrument for doing just that. His rigor and passion in this regard explain his continuing capacity to provoke reflection on economics, politics, the modern university, as well as on the philosophical framework that will make those reflections most fruitful, evident in the essays of this book. Yet it was all oriented by "an openness to that which lies beyond the data which can be calculated and deduced on the rational, abstract and essentialist plane." If it lies beyond the data, however, it does not lie beyond history, except in the sense that it is that of which we only "catch a glimpse": the God who liberates and saves in history, beyond the histories that follow one upon the other.[17] It is, finally, a "catching glimpse of" that orients us toward the future but only occurs in discerning and responding to the signs of the times now.

Jon Sobrino, Discernment, and
Allowing Ourselves to be Affected by Christ

There are many obvious ways to use the writings of Jon Sobrino to shed light on the fundamental intuition guiding Ellacuría's spiritual life and providing a glimpse of the heart of his thought. Sobrino's own writings on spirituality come easily to mind: his insistence that spirituality is always a following of Jesus that is not an imitation but a following *(seguir)* that carries forward *(pro-seguir)* Jesus's mission;[18] that it involves a fundamental, "theologal" dimension according to which "living with Spirit" always arises out of and returns to our embeddedness in our historical reality;[19] that it has a necessary

---

[17] See Sobrino, "Monseñor Romero's Impact on Ignacio Ellacuría," chap. 3 in this volume.

[18] See Michael E. Lee, "Toward a New, Historical Evanglization," chap. 12 in this volume; Jon Sobrino, "Spirituality and the Following of Jesus," in *Mysterium Liberationis: Fundamental Concepts of Liberation,* ed. Jon Sobrino and Ignacio Ellacuría, 677–701 (Maryknoll, NY: Orbis Books, 1993), 686–87. This focus on discipleship as the core of Christian spirituality is shared by many, of course, including, for example, Gustavo Gutiérrez, who defines spirituality as "a concrete way, inspired by the Spirit, of living the Gospel . . . of living 'before the Lord' in solidarity with all human beings." Gustavo Gutiérrez, *Spiritual Writings,* intro. Daniel G. Groody (Maryknoll, NY: Orbis Books, 2011), 47, cf. 197–98.

[19] Sobrino, "Spirituality and the Following of Jesus," 680–85. Sobrino's use and expansion of Ellacuría's concepts and arguments are clear; see, for example, Ignacio Ellacuría,

ecclesial dimension, but one in which the following of Jesus configures the ecclesial character of the spirituality, and not the reverse.

Rather than follow these ways I follow one that begins with a reflection on Sobrino's Christology, as he is commenting on the christological titles in the New Testament. In addition to ones more traditionally treated—Messiah, High Priest, Lord, Son of man, Word of God, etc.—he considers one that is not so typically taken up: Jesus as *Eu-Aggelion*, "Good News."[20] Christological titles intend to make Jesus intelligible and relevant to a given situation, and, Sobrino maintains, what our situation today most needs is the sense that it might be possible for there to be good news.

> We live in a world in which the news is not generally good, and in which goodness is not news. What is worse, while expectation of salvation—the coming of the kingdom of freedom, of the classless society, or whatever—was, in principle, constitutive of modernity, postmodernity, neo-liberalism, and globalization are setting limits to, if not annulling expectation as such. The greatest hurdle facing evangelization is the lack of conviction that good news is possible.[21]

In such a situation Jesus can and must be presented not only as Lord or Savior or Liberator, but as *Eu-Aggelion*, as Good News, highlighting not just what he proclaimed and what he did, but the *way* in which he did it: being honest to and with the real; being merciful and faithful; being joyful and ready to celebrate; attending to the smallest of needs while maintaining the greatest breadth of aspiration; combining tenderness and mercy with prophetic denunciation, confidence in God, and loneliness before God.[22] "Jesus is not only *good* at mediating the Kingdom, effective in his theory and practice, but a *good* mediator, welcoming, compassionate, trustworthy for the poor and afflicted, the recipients of the Kingdom."[23] If we do not understand that and how he is a good mediator, we will not fully understand what it was he mediated and be able to "continue forward" *(proseguir)* the good news that he mediated.

This may sound trivial, obvious, or easy, but it is so far from being so for Sobrino that he adds a third characteristic of an authentic faith to the

---

"Laying the Philosophical Foundations of Latin American Theological Method," in *Ignacio Ellacuría: Essay on History, Liberation the Theology*, 80.

[20] See Jon Sobrino, *Christ the Liberator: A View from the Victims,* trans. Paul Burns (Maryknoll, NY: Orbis Books, 2001), 209–18.

[21] Ibid., 215, translation slightly emended; cf. Jon Sobrino, *La fe en Jesucristo: Ensayo desde las Víctimas* (Madrid: Trotta, 1999), 309.

[22] Sobrino, *Christ the Liberator,* 215–16.

[23] Ibid., 216.

traditional pairing of (unfortunately, too, sometimes opposing of) *orthodoxy* and *orthopraxis*: *orthopathy*. Examining the "good news" dimension of Jesus, Sobrino claims, "means that in our relationship to him we have to add what, for lack of a better word, we might call *orthopathy* to *orthodoxy* and *orthopraxis*. By *orthopathy* I mean the correct way of letting ourselves be affected by the reality of Christ."[24] This third cannot be reduced to the other two or replaced by them. This is because, ultimately,

> faith is not just an acceptance of an *interpretation*, nor is the act of faith in its deepest sense acceptance of a witness. When all is said and done it is the confrontation with and acceptance—in trust and in a willingness to make oneself available to it—of a historical reality that leads beyond itself, and that then can certainly be interpreted transcendentally and be an object of faith. The good news of Jesus in the New Testament is not only a belief—that the pasch brings salvation—but also an experience of a reality—that Jesus' mercy, honesty, loyalty and fidelity are good things for the human race.[25]

Appropriating this into theology is no easy thing, and, indeed it involves "the most basic way of relating Christology [and with it, thus, theology] and spirituality."[26] This is the clue that I follow now to shed further light on Ellacuría's spirituality and theology.

In elaborating what he means by orthopathy, Sobrino considers Leonardo Boff, Karl Rahner, and Ellacuría. On Ellacuría he quotes a recollection of a student in Ellacuría's classroom:

> In a theology lecture Fr. Ellacuría was analyzing Jesus' life, and suddenly reasoning departed and his heart took over. And he said: "The fact is that Jesus had the justice to go to the depths and at the same time he had the eyes and the bowels of mercy to understand human beings." Ellacu was silent for a while and then finished by saying of Jesus: "He was a great man."[27]

Reason did not, perhaps, so much depart as show its foundation in a deep and prior intuition, a spiritual one, and one essential for understanding what reason can and should produce. Let us explore a bit further. We can find in Ellacuría's theology a similar allusion to a need not just to understand Jesus

---

[24] Ibid., 210.

[25] Ibid., 212; translation emended. See also Sobrino, *La Fe en Jesucristo,* 305.

[26] Sobrino, *Christ the Liberator,* 213.

[27] Ibid., 214.

and follow Jesus, but to be affected correctly by him. In his own reflection on the need for a new kind of Christology, Ellacuría wrote:

> This new Christology ought to accord full revelatory status to the flesh of Jesus, that is, to his history. Today nothing would be more ridiculous than to try to construct a Christology in which the historical realization of Jesus' life did not have decisive significance. *What has heretofore been dealt with—and much less so today—under the rubric of "the mysteries of the life of Jesus," as something peripheral and ascetical, must now regain its full meaning.* Of course, this presupposes an historical-exegetical reading of what the life of Jesus really was. What is necessary is a transition to an historical logos, without which every other logos is merely speculative and idealist. This historical logos would have to start with the fact, incontrovertible to the eyes of faith, that the historical life of Jesus is the fullest revelation of the Christian God, and it would have to be practiced as a logos of history that subsumes and transcends the logos of nature (emphasis added).[28]

Much will sound familiar here to those who have worked through this book, particularly the exigency of shifting to a "historical logos" (a historical framing of meaning and action) that is different from a logos of nature, and that alone allows one to do justice to the historical life of Jesus (and thereby of the God revealed in Jesus). What I want to draw attention to is his remark that one must retrieve into theology "the mysteries of the life of Jesus." This is the traditional naming of presentations of Jesus, stories from his life in particular, insofar as they are taken as subjects for Christian prayer.[29] More specifically, the "mysteries of Jesus' life" are the subject matter for the "Second Week" of Ignatius of Loyola's *Spiritual Exercises* and are named such by Ignatius.[30] In the "Second Week" one takes up gospel stories about Jesus, not just intellectually-exegetically, but imaginatively and with the eyes of one's heart open, in order to inhabit them with reason and with heart, to gain an "interior knowledge" by which to "love him more intensely and follow him more closely."[31] This method of praying is Ignatius's way of

---

[28] Ignacio Ellacuría, *Freedom Made Flesh: The Mission of Christ and His Church*, trans. John Drury (Maryknoll, NY: Orbis Books, 1973), 26, translation emended; cf. Ignacio Ellacuría, *Teología Política* (San Salvador: Ediciones del Secretariado Social Interdiocesano, 1973), 13.

[29] Such usage is still current in talk of the "mysteries" of the Rosary, which include, of course, presentations of Mary's life in a similar way.

[30] Ignatius of Loyola, *Spiritual Exercises*, no. 261, in Ganss, *The Spiritual Exercises of Saint Ignatius*, 101. See Ganss's brief but helpful commentary on the term: 187–88n136.

[31] Ibid., no. 104 (p. 56).

following Jesus' own strategy, of "attracting us" to follow his way of framing the logic and meaning of life, as Ignatius imagines it in the "Meditation on the Two Standards."[32]

Much could be said of what it means to retrieve these mysteries—which is to say spirituality—into Christology, and into theology as a whole. For our purposes I make do here with two comments. First, Ellacuría saw the "Second Week," where the "mysteries" are located, as the most original and innovative part of the *Spiritual Exercises*. "The totality made up by Ignatius's *Exercises* has its interpretive key in the disposition of the 'Second Week' itself, and in the theology of its fundamental meditations."[33] According to him, "they contain those texts that are most original to Saint Ignatius," and "open up the way of life" that the *Spiritual Exercises* represent, including all those aspects conveyed by the well-known Ignatian maxims, "contemplation in action" and *ad maiorem Dei gloriam*. They operate according to the principle that God is necessarily revealed not ultimately in the things of nature, and not ultimately in words, not even the words of scripture, but in "a human presence and an historical action."[34] This is why a following that starts from a "personal adherence" (attraction) to Jesus, "a fellowship with him, in his own being and life," is not only the response to Jesus that we ought to make, but forms a life that is already in itself the most effective form of evangelization, of presenting him as good news, to others.[35] Hence, it follows that if one does not receive Jesus' life as good news (that is, if one does not "allow oneself to be correctly affected by Christ"), then one cannot present his or her life to others as such. It is in this sense that orthodoxy and orthopraxis are ultimately ineffective unless joined by orthopathy.

Second, a remark on discernment: Ignatius's understanding of discernment, and his framing of "rules" for discernment, are justly praised as one of his most important innovations and contributions to Christian spirituality. It

---

[32] Ibid., no. 146 (p. 66). Whereas Jesus is in a low and humble place and urges his disciples to persuade by "attracting," the enemy has an "aspect horrible and terrifying" (no. 140) and urges the strategy of "setting up snares and chains"—that is, deception (no. 142).

[33] Ellacuría, "A Reading of the Spiritual Exercises," 219.

[34] Ibid. To be sure, this puts things too starkly, because it contrasts "nature" and "history" in an unwarranted way, as Ellacuría's made clear in his philosophy. Nature is a constitutive element of historical reality, and reveals God as such. See, among others, Sebastian Pittl, chap. 16 in this volume.

[35] Ellacuría, "A Reading of the Spiritual Exercises." "A life defined in this way as following Jesus is a life that follows because in some way it has already been internalized and is *a life that shows in its own being the faith that it has*" (ibid., emphasis added). For the ramifications of this insight for the "new evangelization," both when it comes to individual Christians and to the church as a whole, see Lee, "Toward a New, Historical Evangelization," Chapter 12 in this volume.

is certainly true that discernment, both individual and corporate, is a crucial element of Ellacuría's thought, as his pervasive emphasis on the need to discern "the signs of the times" makes clear. Many others emphasize this signal achievement of Ignatius. What is sometimes overlooked is that, for Ignatius, discernment and the "election" or choice in which it issues do not take place in the abstract as the application of a set of rules that only analyzes the options at hand and decides between them using the spirituality and psychology laid out in the "Rules for the Discernment of Spirits." Discernment and election take place during the "Second Week," during which the majority of time is not spent in "discernment" per se, but rather in contemplations on the mysteries of Christ's life in the manner just described.[36] That is, there is no successful discernment, on Ignatius's view of things, without "allowing oneself to be correctly affected by Christ." In so doing, one's imagination and hope is transformed by the possibilities presented by Jesus, so that one can imagine, hope, and choose differently when it comes to the choice that one faces now. But this process will not take root unless one is "attracted" to the vision and the life that the "mysteries" of Jesus' life present, precisely because one discovers it to be, deeply, stirringly, "good news." Thus, "he was a great man" is more than an expression of admiration or a parenthetic comment within an intellectual discourse on Ellacuría's part; it is an expression of the root of that discourse's meaning and effectiveness.

Conclusion: Theology as a Source of Consolation

Much more could be said.[37] Perhaps the foregoing shows why, as Sobrino and Cardenal have emphasized, it is probably more important to attend to the *people* who had an impact on Ellacuría than the many texts that he read and analyzed (even the text of the *Spiritual Exercises*). Monseñor Romero was a theological source for Ellacuría, not necessarily because of Romero's philosophical and theological insights, but precisely because through him Ellacuría was able to be affected correctly by Jesus—which is the furthest thing possible from a pious claim, however much on the surface it seems

---

[36] Ignatius does not, in fact, actually prescribe that *any* of the prayer periods be explicitly devoted to discerning the choice that one has come to the *Exercises* for assistance in making, although he does have some other exercises beyond meditations on the mysteries of Jesus's life—the "Meditation on the Two Standards," for instance.

[37] I have ignored, for example, what is probably the most striking homology between Ellacuría's reading of the *Spiritual Exercises* and his philosophical, theological, political, and economic realities, which is between the "Meditation on the Two Standards" and his notion of the civilization of poverty (opposed dialectically to the civilization of wealth), for which one should consult all the essays in Part IV of this book, in concert with Ellacuría, "A Latin American Reading of the *Spiritual Exercises*," 223–27.

to verge on hagiography in the pejorative sense. The same might be said of Pedro Arrupe, with whom Ellacuría had many, many arguments, and others as well.[38] Ultimately, as Sobrino, Gutiérrez, and Cardenal point out, it was the poor of El Salvador that drove Ellacuría's work, and this for the same reason: in and through them he was affected by and attracted to Jesus.

It is this being affected deeply by Jesus that opened Ellacuría to the "more" of and in history. It informed his rigorous analysis of the historical reality in which he lived, not to come to an absolute certainty about what is to be done, impossible even for someone with as formidable an intellect as his, but to exercise that "nameless virtue" of which Rahner spoke: to discern the signs of the times and a way forward, always tentative, but never tentatively exercised, always aiming at that more of history that only becomes visible when one is "catching sight of" the God who loves us and enters history to liberate us from all that threatens us. In this, his life became and remains "good news" in a world desperately in need of it.

---

[38] See Ellacuría, "Pedro Arrupe: Renovador de la vida religiosa," in *Escritos Teológicos*, vol. 4 (San Salvador: UCA Editores, 2002), 263–87.

Contributors

J. Matthew Ashley is associate professor of systematic theology and department chair in the Department of Theology at the University of Notre Dame. His teaching and research interests include theology and science, liberation and political theology, and Ignatian spirituality. He is author of *Interruptions: Mysticism, Politics and Theology in the Work of Johann Baptist Metz* (1998), and editor and translator of several books, including J. B. Metz, *Faith in History and Society: Studies for a Practical Fundamental Theology*, 2nd English edition, translated and edited by J. Matthew Ashley (2007); and Joseph Ratzinger, Johann Baptist Metz, Jürgen Moltmann, and Eveline Goodman-Thau, *The End of Time? The Provocation of Talking about God*, translated and edited by J. Matthew Ashley (2004).

Kevin F. Burke is associate professor of systematic theology, director of doctoral studies, and former dean of the Jesuit School of Theology in Berkeley. His areas of teaching and research expertise include Christology, fundamental theology, Ignatian spirituality, theology and aesthetics, and liberation theology. He is author of one book, *The Ground Beneath the Cross: The Theology of Ignacio Ellacuría* (2000), and editor or co-editor of three others: *Pedro Arrupe: Essential Writings* (2004); with Robert Lassalle-Klein, *Love That Produces Hope: The Thought of Ignacio Ellacuría* (2006); with Eileen Burke-Sullivan, *The Ignatian Tradition* (2009).

Rodolfo Cardenal, SJ, was born in Managua, Nicaragua, and is one of the survivors of the community of martyrs of the UCA. His areas of expertise include liberation theology, church history, and the history of Central America. A professor of Latin American history and Latin American church history at the University of Central America "José Simeón Cañas" (UCA), he has also served there as editor of the journal *Estudios Centroamericanos* and as academic vice-rector and vice-rector for social projection. His books include *Manual de Historia de Centroamérica* (1996), *El poder eclesiástico en El Salvador, 1871-1931* (1980), and *Historia de una esperanza: vida de Rutilio Grande* (1985).

Ignacio Ellacuría was born in Portugalete in the Basque country in 1930. He entered the Society of Jesus (Jesuits) in 1947 and the following year traveled to El Salvador to join the Central American mission. He did his graduate studies in theology in Innsbruck and in philosophy in Madrid, working with Xavier Zubiri. In 1967 he joined the faculty and administration of the University of Central America "José Simeón Cañas" (UCA). He assumed the responsibilities of the rector (president) of the UCA in 1979, a position he held until his martyrdom in 1989. Along with his major work in philosophy, *Filosofía de la realidad histórica* (1990), and *Freedom Made Flesh: The Mission of Christ and His Church* (1976), Ellacuría wrote nearly 250 published theological, philosophical, and political essays. These, along with numerous other posthumously published writings, can be found in the following critical editions from UCA Editores, San Salvador: *Veinte años de historia en El Salvador (1969–1989)*; *Escritos políticos* (3 volumes, 1991); *Escritos filosóficos* (3 volumes, 1996, 1999, 2001); *Escritos universitarios* (1999); *Escritos teológicos* (4 volumes, 2000, 2002); *Cursos universitarios* (2009). A recent English collection is *Ignacio Ellacuría: Essays on History, Liberation, and Salvation*, edited by Michael Lee (2013).

Thomas Fornet-Ponse is Laurentius-Klein-Chair for Biblical and Ecumenical Theology and dean of studies of the German Academic Programme for Theology in Jerusalem. His research interests include liberation theology and philosophy (especially that of Ignacio Ellacuría), intercultural theology and philosophy, and ecumenics and interreligious dialogue. His published books include *Ökumene in drei Dimensionen. Jüdische Anstöße für die innerchristliche Ökumene* (2011) and *Freiheit und Befreiung. Untersuchungen zur Kontextualität und Universalität des Philosophierens* (2013).

David Ignatius Gandolfo earned the PhD in philosophy from Loyola University of Chicago and is currently on the faculty at Furman University as associate professor of philosophy. He is also chair of the Poverty Studies program at Furman. His teaching interests include the ethics of globalization, poverty studies, Latin American philosophy and Africana philosophy. His research interests include economic ethics, liberation philosophy, international justice, and the responsibility of a university in the realm of social justice. Gandolfo is married to theologian Dr. Elizabeth O'Donnell Gandolfo. They have four young children.

Gustavo Gutiérrez is John Cardinal O'Hara Professor of Theology at the University of Notre Dame and a member of the Peruvian Academy of Language. After studies in medicine and literature in Peru, he studied psychology and philosophy at Louvain, and eventually took at doctorate at the Institut Catholique in Lyons. His books, which have been translated from Spanish into multiple languages, include *A Theology of Liberation: History,*

Politics, Salvation (1988); *We Drink from Our Own Wells: The Spiritual Journey of a People* (1984); *The Density of the Present: Selected Writings* (1999); *On Job: God-Talk and the Suffering of the Innocent* (1987); and *Las Casas: In Search of the Poor of Jesus Christ* (1993). He is currently working on a book exploring the historical background and continuing theological relevance of the preferential option for the poor.

Jonas Hagedorn, born in 1981, has done advanced studies of theology and the social sciences in Münster (Germany), Innsbruck (Austria), and San Salvador (El Salvador). He earned the scholarship of the Cusanuswerk for outstanding doctoral students and research assistants at the Institute of Social Ethics and Theology at the University of Darmstadt. His research topics include Catholic social teachings, social policy, corporatism, and the theory of the German welfare state.

Francisco de Aquino Júnior, a Brazilian, holds a licentiate in philosophy from the Universidade Estadual do Ceará and a doctorate in theology from the Westfälische Wilhelms-Universität of Münster in Germany. He is professor of theology on the Catholic faculty of Fortaleza and a priest of the diocese of Limoeiro do Norte, and he works with Caritas and with pastoral and social movements in the diocese. His publications include *A teologia como intelección do reinado de Deus: o método da teologia da libertação segundo Ignacio Ellacuría* (2010); *A dimensão sócioestrutural do reinado de Deus: escritos de teologia social"* (2011); *Teoria teológica—práxis teologal: sobre o método da teologia da libertação* (2012); and *Viver segundo o espírito de Jesus Cristo. Espiritualidade como seguimento* (2014).

Robert Lassalle-Klein is currently professor of religious studies and philosophy at Holy Names University (Oakland, California). Twenty-seven years ago he co-founded the Oakland Catholic Worker serving immigrant families and still serves on its board. Recent publications include *Blood and Ink: Ignacio Ellacuría, Jon Sobrino, and the Jesuit Martyrs of the University of Central America* (2014), "Ignacio Ellacuría's Rahnerian Fundamental Theology for a Global Church" (2013), and two edited volumes: *Jesus of Galilee: Contextual Christology for the Twenty-first Century* (2011), and *Theological Studies,* Special Issue on the Galilean Jesus (Spring 2009). His current projects include *The Spiritual Writings of Jon Sobrino* (Orbis Books) and research for a book on *Jesus the Immigrant.*

Michael E. Lee is associate professor of systematic theology and on the faculty of the Latin American and Latino Studies Institute at Fordham University. He has served on the board, and most recently, as president of the

Academy of Catholic Hispanic Theologians of the United States (ACHTUS). He has published *Bearing the Weight of Salvation: The Soteriology of Ignacio Ellacuría* (2010) and edited *Ignacio Ellacuría: Essays on History, Liberation, and Salvation* (2013). He is currently completing a book about Archbishop Óscar Romero of El Salvador.

Martin Maier, SJ, was born in 1960 in Messkirch, Germany, and has done advanced studies in philosophy and theology (in Innsbruck and San Salvador) and music (Paris). From 1995 to 2009 he was editor-in-chief of the German journal *Stimmen der Zeit,* and since then he has served as the rector of the Berchmanskolleg in Munich, also serving regularly as a visiting professor at the University of Central America "José Simeón Cañas" and at the Centre Sèvres in Paris. Among his books are *Pedro Arrupe—Zeuge und Prophet* (2007); with Gianni La Bella (eds.): *Pedro Arrupe—Generaloberer der Gesellschaft Jesu. Neue biographische Perspektiven* (2008); *Oscar Romero—Kämpfer für Glaube und Gerechtigkeit* (2009); *Der Mensch ist gut, nur die Leute sind schlecht. Mit Karl Valentin Sinn und Wahnsinn des Lebens entschlüsseln* (2012).

Sebastian Pittl studied theology, philosophy, and psychology in Vienna and Madrid. He currently works as a university assistant in the Department of Systematic Theology at the University of Vienna. His research interests include Latin American liberation theology, intercultural and interreligious dialogue, and theology of history. His most recent publication is *La Realidad Histórica del Pueblo Crucificado como Lugar de la Teología: Reflexiones Sobre el Lugar Hermenéutico de la Teología en el Pensamiento de Ignacio Ellacuría* (2013).

Andrew Prevot earned the PhD in systematic theology at the University of Notre Dame and currently holds the position of assistant professor of theology at Boston College. He researches and teaches in the areas of spiritual, philosophical, and political theology. Recent publications include "The Aporia of Race and Identity: J. Kameron Carter and the Future of Black Liberation Theology," in *Religion, Economics, and Culture in Conflict and Conversation,* edited by Laurie Cassidy and Maureen O'Connell (2011); and "Reversed Thunder: The Significance of Prayer for Political Theology," in *The Other Journal* 21 (2012).

Héctor Samour earned his doctorate in Iberoamerican philosophy from the University of Central America "José Simeón Cañas" in El Salvador. Since 1975 he has been a research professor in that university's Department of Philosophy, where he has also taught courses on various topics, including cosmology, history of philosophy, metaphysics, epistemology, political philosophy, philosophy of law, and Latin American philosophy. Among his books are *Crítica y liberación. Ellacuría y la realidad histórica contemporánea* (2012), *Voluntad de Liberación. El pensamiento filosófico de Ignacio Ellacuría* (2003), *Filosofía del Derecho* (1999), and *Visión existencialista del ser humano* (1988).

Jon Sobrino, SJ, was born in Barcelona in 1938 but has lived in El Salvador since 1957 and was one of the members of the community of martyrs at the UCA who survived the events of November 16, 1989. With degrees in philosophy and engineering from St. Louis University, he took his doctorate in theology from the University of Frankfurt. He is currently professor of theology and director of the Monseñor Romero Center at the University of Central America "José Simeón Cañas" (UCA) in San Salvador. One of the major figures in Latin American liberation theology, among his many books are *Spirituality of Liberation: Toward Political Holiness* (1988), *Jesus the Liberator: A Historical-Theological Reading of Jesus of Nazareth* (1994), *The Principle of Mercy: Taking the Crucified People from the Cross* (1994), *Christ the Liberator: A View from the Victims* (2001), *Witnesses to the Kingdom: The Martyrs of El Salvador and the Crucified Peoples* (2003), and *No Salvation Outside the Poor* (2008).

José Sols Lucia is the chair of Ethics and Christian Thought at IQS, University Ramon Llull, Barcelona, Spain. He is the coordinator of Group of Christian Social Thought in UNIJES (the Jesuit Universities of Spain), and the coordinator of the research group LACS—Laboratorio de Análisis y Crítica Social. He has published *Pensamiento social cristiano abierto al siglo XXI* (2014), *Cinco lecciones de pensamiento social cristiano* (2013), *Atrapados en la violencia* (2008), *One Hundred Years of Violence* (2003), and *The Legacy of Ignacio Ellacuría* (1998).

Index